OCCASIONAL PAPER No. 31

LOCAL AUTHORITY HOUSING POLICY AND PRACTICE—

A Case Study Approach

PAT NINER

CENTRE FOR URBAN AND REGIONAL STUDIES
THE UNIVERSITY OF BIRMINGHAM
1975

Printed in Great Britain by Suttons (Printers) Limited, Birmingham

Contents

List of Tables

Preface and Acknowledgements

In 1970, the Centre for Urban and Regional Studies received a grant from the Social Science Research Council to undertake a programme of research examining the housing system. The underlying assumption of the programme is that the housing system consists of a complex of housing sectors, sub-systems or sub-markets, with different locations, physical and social characteristics, tenures and costs. Attempts are being made to describe and understand this complex. Three main areas of concern have been defined as requiring particular research attention. These are:

(a) Classification of the housing system—how can households and houses best be described and grouped?

(b) Housing dynamics—which factors are important in determining residential mobility and immobility?

(c) Institutional controls—what influence do the institutions (that is central and local government, building societies, estate agents, builders and developers), have on determining access to, and choice within the housing system?

The present research, which is reported here, has been designed to answer some of the questions raised under the third heading, with the focus of attention falling on local authority policy and performance in various housing fields. This project has been completely financed from SSRC funds as an integral part of the Housing Systems Programme.

I am particularly grateful to my colleagues at the Centre for Urban and Regional Studies for providing comments and advice during the research work, and to Mrs. K. Williams and David Smith who helped me with data collection in the local authorities.

Above all, I must thank the various local authority officers who spared the time to talk to me about housing, explaining so patiently the particular policies and procedures followed by their Councils, and the Councils themselves, who by allowing me access to records and files made this research possible. Responsibility for the conclusions and the opinions expressed, is, of course, my own.

PART 1

1. Introduction

Background to the Study

Local authorities have, and exercise, a wide variety of powers to influence the housing situation within their boundaries. These powers reflect the pattern of public involvement in housing matters which has developed over the years; central government provides a legislative framework and may provide finance, advice, guidance and exhortation; implementation of 'national housing policy' is in the hands of local authorities, builders, building societies, landlords, housing associations or individual property owners. Local authorities can be regarded as chief actors in this field, and, for example, are responsible for building, letting and managing council houses, dealing directly or indirectly with the older, sub-standard housing stock, and may influence developments in the private sector.

Any examination of the housing legislation through which local authorities act reveals wide areas of apparent local discretions. Many powers are given by a statement that a local authority 'may' rather than that a local authority 'shall'. Discretion can take two forms—sometimes relating to *how* a policy should be operated, and sometimes to *whether* or to *what extent* it should be operated. The allocation of council houses is an example of the first, and the sale of council houses an example of the second.[1]

However, limits on a local authority's freedom of action are very apparent in practice. Conversation with any councillor or local government officer is more likely to emphasize constraints than choices. Central government is most likely to be seen as the chief limiting factor, and since action usually involves expenditure, and central government has control over so much local spending, the influence is undeniable. But it is by no means the only constraint. The general economic situation, and, for example, the supply of funds for building societies profoundly affect the demands made on a local authority for rehousing or mortgages. The inherited housing situation, in terms of the size and composition of the council stock and the general physical condition of dwellings, constrains the present possibilities for action. Ultimately, the local political situation and what will be acceptable to voters and ratepayers provides the background for all policies.

Bearing all this in mind, just what scope remains for individual interpretation of policies by different councils? Do policies differ, and if they do, how far are such differences reflected in performance?

The influence of local authorities on the housing system is of particular significance because they directly or indirectly affect access to housing, and the range of choice in housing available to individual households. This is obviously true when it comes to determining who shall be offered the tenancy of a vacant council house, but it is no less true if the availability of a council mortgage

[1] C. J. Watson, 'The Housing Question' in *Urban Planning Problems* (ed.) G. E. Cherry, Leonard Hill Books 1974.

allows someone to buy a house for which finance would not otherwise be available, or if the possibility of an improvement grant offers the only opportunity for an improvement of living conditions.

Are any particular groups of households being helped by local authority housing policies? Equally important, are any groups of households being 'discriminated' against, or overlooked by the operation of local policies?

The research reported here was designed to give some answers to the two sets of question posed. To summarize, the 'terms of reference' can be defined as concerning the following:

(a) How far do housing policies adopted by one local authority differ from those adopted by another?

(b) To what extent do apparently different policies produce different end results, or apparently similar policies produce similar end results?

(c) Which types of households are helped to gain access to housing or to better housing by local authority policies, and which are excluded?

Method of Enquiry

It would be impossible to cover the whole field of local authority housing policies, which can extend from the grant of planning permission for a large private estate to the decoration and repair of an individual council house, running through clearance, improvement, council house building and allocation on the way. The first step, therefore, was to decide which policy areas should be examined.

The aims of the study provide the main criteria for selection. First there must be scope in the legislation for the exercise of local discretion, and preferably some variation between councils in the use of powers. Secondly, there must be some way of defining and measuring local performance, and information available (or potentially available) for this. Lastly, the policy must influence access to housing or to better housing, and the households being helped must be identifiable. These criteria exclude some policy areas. For example, the setting of rent and rebate levels was largely removed from the sphere of local discretion by the Housing Finance Act 1972, and many welfare and management policies on council estates do not affect access to, or choice in, housing. A variety of possibilities remain, however, and the final choice owed as much to familiarity with the topic as to more objective arguments.

The main themes selected for study are as follows:

(a) *Council house allocation policies and practice.* These have direct impact on determining access to the council stock, and represent perhaps the widest area of local discretion. The requirements of section 113 of the Housing

Act 1957 are broadly defined, and many reports[1] make it clear that wide variations occur between policies adopted by local councils.

(b) *Improvement grant policies and practice.* Except when considering applications for standard grants, a local authority again has considerable scope for individual interpretation of allowable works and costs (as the very name 'discretionary' improvement grant implies). Improvement policies in general vary between councils.[2] The availability of improvement grants increases the possibility of getting a better house without movement.

(c) *Council mortgage lending policies and practice.* Very little is known about the operation of local authority lending schemes. Councils have a choice of legislation (Small Dwellings Acquisition Acts 1899 to 1923 or Housing (Financial Provisions) Act 1958), and while guidance is given in DoE Circular 22/71 on the categories of applicant to be favoured for lending purposes,[3] the list is not necessarily exhaustive. Variations in rules and regulations certainly exist.[4] Access to particular sections of the housing stock may be greatly influenced by council lending policies.

(d) *Council house sales policy and practice.* This has become a strongly debated issue in party political terms. In recent years local authority discretion *not* to sell has been exercised in the face of considerable central government pressure to allow sales. Despite this, local policies vary.[5] If sales are allowed, access to a different tenure sector is possible without residential mobility.

[1] For example:

Selection of Tenants and Transfers and Exchanges. Third Report of the Housing Management Sub-Committee of the Central Housing Advisory Committee. H.M.S.O. 1949.
Residential Qualifications. Fifth Report of the Housing Management Sub-Committee of the Central Housing Advisory Committee. H.M.S.O. 1955.
Allocating Council Houses. Report of the Sub-Committee of the Scottish Housing Advisory Committee. H.M.S.O. 1967.
Council Housing—Purposes, Procedures and Priorities. Ninth Report of the Housing Management Sub-Committee of the Central Housing Advisory Committee. H.M.S.O. 1969.

[2] For example:

T. L. C. Duncan, *Housing Improvement Policies in England and Wales,* Research Memorandum No. 28. Centre for Urban and Regional Studies, University of Birmingham, January 1974. Expenditure Committee, Tenth Report, *House Improvement Grants,* House of Commons Paper 349-1, July 1973.

[3] See Chapter 2 (page 35) of this report for details of the categories.

[4] For example:

Shelter, *Mortgages in London,* S.H.A.C. Pamphlet No. 2. Shelter Housing Aid Centre, London, 1973.
Statistics of Advances for House Purchase 1964-5. Institute of Municipal Treasurers and Accountants, April 1967.

[5] A. S. Murie, *The Sale of Council Houses: a study in social policy* (forthcoming).

To examine these areas of housing policy a technique already developed by the Centre for Urban and Regional Studies in Dudley County Borough[1] has been used. The approach involves interviews with local authority officers working on housing matters, and in the course of these interviews council policies and procedures are discussed. This is followed by a detailed analysis of records kept by the local authority to see what has actually been happening under the policy provisions. Such analyses can serve as a basis for comparing performance between authorities, and as a means of identifying and describing the households helped in different ways. Since collection of information at this level is a fairly lengthy process, only a limited number of authorities can be covered.

In following this approach the obvious alternative of a widely distributed postal questionnaire has been rejected. Questionnaires have been used before,[2,3] and have undoubtedly yielded valuable results. The possibility of wide geographical coverage, and the fact that local authorities themselves do most of the data collection stand as clear advantages. However, a questionnaire to cover all the items of interest here would be immensely long, especially as previous experience suggests the questions would have to be very detailed to avoid any ambiguity of response. Again, performance measures are unlikely to be complete, and even more unlikely to be comparable between authorities, since the statistics produced for annual reports and other documents vary widely. The arrival of such a questionnaire on the desk of an official harassed with the prospects of 'reorganisation' would hardly be propitious. The probability of a high non-response rate alone argued forcibly against this method of approach. Most important of all, though, a questionnaire survey would inevitably be superficial, and could not show in detail what actually happens as a result of policies and procedures, nor how far policies affect local residents seen as a series of individual households in the housing system. It could not fulfil the stated aims of the research.

So an approach was chosen which demanded a high degree of co-operation on the part of the selected local authorities—a willingness on the part of officers to spend time talking about housing, and the consent of the council to allow access to files kept on council house, improvement grant and mortgage applicants.

A standard introductory letter was sent to 15 local housing authorities in the north western sector of the West Midlands Region, addressed to the Town Clerk or Chief Executive Officer in each case. The survey was restricted to a single geographical area both to reduce travelling problems, and to avoid the extremes of housing conditions which exist at a national scale, and which may owe more to regional development issues than to the policies of any local authority. Within the area, authorities were selected to include a cross-section of conditions from conurbation centre to rural district. This also, of course, implies a variety of

[1] C. J. Watson, Pat Niner, Gillian R. Vale with Barbara M. D. Smith, *Estimating Local Housing Needs—A case study and discussion of methods*. Occasional Paper No. 24 C.U.R.S. University of Birmingham, 1973.

[2] *Council Housing—Purposes, Procedures and Priorities*—op. cit.

[3] T. L. C. Duncan, *Housing Improvement Policies in England and Wales*—op. cit.

authority size and status. Where possible adjoining areas which would be amalgamated by the local government reorganization of April, 1974, were contacted.

Two authorities replied and expressed themselves unwilling to co-operate because of shortage of staff and time to help in the survey. Five authorities simply failed to reply, and no further effort was made to contact them as a large enough sample volunteered as a result of the initial letter. Two authorities, though replying, did not, in fact, allow the work to be fully completed. The remaining six authorities proved extremely helpful, and it is information gathered from these areas which provides the basis of this report. The full list of authorities surveyed is West Bromwich CB, Warley CB, Wolverhampton CB. Halesowen MB, Stafford MB and Ludlow RD.

The usual pattern of working was as follows:

(a) Initial letter explaining project and requesting meeting.

(b) Response, and general meeting with group of officers concerned with housing matters.

(c) Detailed meeting with officers dealing with council house allocation, improvement grants and council lending policies. At this meeting policies and procedures were discussed. Also at this stage, details of the records kept and forms used were taken.

(d) Preparation for data collection. Discussions on the samples to be used, and design of sheets for recording the different pieces of information. (See Appendices I and II).

(e) Collection of information from the local authority files, including samples of waiting list applicants, transfer applicants (both at survey date), council house allocations made during the year April 1st 1972 to March 31st 1973, improvement grants approved from January 1972 to survey date, recent mortgage advances for the purchase of a private house, and recent mortgage advances for the purchase of a council house.

(f) Analysis of the survey information.

(g) Production of Information Papers for each contributing local authority, including factual information on the policies and performance of that single authority. Information Papers of this type had been promised in the initial contact letter as an incentive for local authorities to co-operate, and as a part of the attempt to make the research as useful as possible to all concerned.

(h) Final analyses and report writing.

In addition to working with the local authorities, estate agents and building societies operating in the surveyed areas were contacted. Council policies can only be fully seen and assessed against a background of the housing situation in general. Information from agencies involved with private housing, and with owner-occupation in particular, was intended to provide such a background. Local building society managers proved very helpful in giving details of policies being operated (though these tended to change rapidly during the survey period!)

and general information about the area. Statistics, where available, usually related to the region rather than local areas.

Estate agents proved rather less helpful—less than half replying to an initial letter requesting a meeting. Again their information tended to be very general, being based on impressions and hunches rather than hard facts. In the end, statistical information on houses for sale in the area was collected from the details available to potential purchasers on request from estate agents. While not altogether satisfactory, this, together with the building society details, does serve as a general guide to the owner-occupied housing sector within the survey area.

All the survey work was completed during the period March to October 1973. It is worth making two points concerning the timing. First of all, the survey almost immediately preceded local government reorganisation. Most of the authorities surveyed ceased to exist as geographical administrative units in April 1974. Wolverhampton, the only unit to remain unchanged geographically, now has changed powers and responsibilities. The survey, then, presents a picture of housing policies and performance immediately prior to an extensive reorganisation. As such it could provide a useful 'before' analysis if the effects of reorganisation were to be examined. It is also useful in checking the performance of small housing authorities before their disappearance.

It is also necessary to draw attention to the timing of the study since it is, by definition, a cross-sectional survey taken at a point in time. No attempt has been made to update any of the information on policies given by the local authorities to accord with changes taking place since the survey date. Equally, there is no guarantee that external conditions have not changed affecting authorities' housing performance. In this way the survey is guilty of all the faults of a static, time-based study. This does not, however, invalidate findings which attempt to describe and explain the situation discovered, nor does it prevent comparisons being made between authorities. It does suggest that, just as it would be unwise to presume that the relationships discovered in selected West Midland authorities could be directly applied in other regions of Britain, so it would be unwise to assume that the relationships will hold precisely constant over time.

The Vocabulary of Housing in Local Authorities

The general reader, who is not closely involved in local authority housing administration, may find it useful to have some of the terms which are used frequently in this report defined at the outset. As with all subjects of a technical nature, it is hard to avoid the use of jargon!

It may seem strange to start with the term *local authority*. *Local authority* throughout this report is used to mean a local housing authority as defined by the various Housing Acts; namely a County Borough Council or, in county areas, a Municipal Borough, Urban District or Rural District Council. While the Council has ultimate responsibility for housing matters, the functions described are most often administered by different Committees and Departments within the local authority (Housing, Public Health, Clerk's and Treasurer's Departments were all involved in the authorities surveyed). Local authority as used here is intended to include all these administrative divisions.

The allocation and management of council houses makes use of a specialized vocabulary. *Housing need* is, perhaps, the fundamental concept, yet it tends to have a different meaning in every authority as it is effectively defined by the policies which determine which 'needs' can be legitimately met by the Council. Chapters 2, 3 and 4 explain these definitions, and their limitations, more fully. It might be more accurate to write need in inverted commas throughout the report to indicate that the limited definition is being employed. This, however, seems rather pedantic—it is necessary only to remember that the term *is* limited.

Households applying for a council house may be referred to as *general needs applicants*, or, using a convenient shorthand, simply as *waiting list applicants*. In either case the implication is that the households have registered an application for a council house. In some of the larger authorities, a distinction is made between the *live* and the *dormant* waiting lists. All applicants on the *live list* have satisfied all necessary eligibility criteria, and their application can be expected to receive attention under the priority scheme in operation. Those registered on the *dormant list*, however, are not to be considered immediately for housing. In some cases the delay may be at the applicant's own request, but in others, the council has ruled that the applicant is not yet fully eligible for consideration (maybe the residential qualification is not satisfied, or the family is not considered to be sufficiently in 'need' of housing).

In the surveyed authorities, the two main types of scheme for determining allocation priorities between successfully registered waiting list applicants were *date order* and *points* schemes. Under a *date order scheme*, as the name suggests, priorities are determined simply on the basis of the date of application; early applicants receive priority over later. Registered applicants are normally grouped according to the type, size and location of property they require, and applications are considered in date order within these groupings. The aim of a *points scheme* is to achieve a more sophisticated and sensitive assessment of housing need, so that the rehousing of a recent applicant in extremely poor housing conditions will not be unduly delayed just because he *is* a recent applicant. Points are awarded for different elements of housing need (for example, overcrowding or lack of amenities) as well as for length of time on this list. The different elements of need are weighted against each other through the number of points available. The applicant with the greatest number of points receives priority, usually again within house type and location groupings.

Movement within the council stock is accommodated by *transfers* and *exchanges*. *Mutual exchanges* are usually arranged on the initiative of the tenants themselves. A tenant of a house on Estate A wants to live on Estate B. He must find a tenant on Estate B willing to change houses with him, and, provided that certain basic conditions are met, the Housing Department will allow the exchange to go ahead. *Transfers*, in contrast, are arranged by the Housing Department, and involve the letting of a vacant property to an existing council tenant, and, of course, result in another vacancy when the move has taken place.

The term *vacancy* itself may require some clarification. As used here, a *vacancy* is any council house becoming available for letting. Vacancies can be divided into *new dwellings*—either newly built council houses ready to be let for the first time, or newly acquired houses formerly in the private sector—and *relets*—existing council houses which become vacant as a result of death, movement from the council sector or transfer.

Most of the terms used in connection with improvement grants are introduced by the Housing Act 1969, the major empowering legislation. The most significant distinction is between works of *improvement* and *repair and replacement*—a necessary distinction since only one half of total approved costs can be made up of repair expenditure. In spite of guidance from central government (improvement is defined in Section 27 of the 1969 Act, and Circular 64/69 describes some of the kinds of work to be considered as repairs), there is still leeway for councils to make their own definitions. Broadly speaking, *improvements* may be thought of as works necessary to bring a property to the 12 point standard of fitness[1], and as including alteration and enlargement, while *repairs* are works either incidental to the improvement, or deemed necessary to make the improvement fully effective. Distinctions beyond this lie in the realm of individual local authority policy, and, as such, are discussed in Chapter 2.

The lending policies of local authorities share a vocabulary with the building societies and other institutions which provide finance for house purchase. Terms such as *valuation*, *advance*, *repayment period* and *interest rates* are all used in their commonly accepted meanings. Only the concept of *housing need* for mortgages, as implied by the categories of applicants to be favoured, which are listed in DoE Circular 22/71, is in any way unique to local authority procedures. Again these categories are described in Chapter 2.

Organization of the Report

The report has been organized in three parts. This Introduction constitutes the first Part. Part II has four chapters, which, in effect, present the general conclusions from the survey material. This is done within the framework of the research questions set out earlier. Chapter 2 examines policies, their variations and similarities between authorities. Chapter 3 is concerned with the practical aspects of housing activities—how the authorities actually function, and whether policy differences show in performance differences. Finally, Chapter 4 returns to the question of access to housing, and the influence local authorities exercise in this respect. Part III is made up of six chapters, each being a case study of one of the local authorities covered by the survey. In each the main feature of policies and survey findings are presented to give some idea of how different authorities perform, and how the different strands of policy interrelate at local level.

A general reader may wish to concentrate on Parts I and II, though the case study chapters are useful in providing more detailed information than is available in Part II. The case studies also give an indication of how an individual authority now tackles the several fields of housing policy, and how it sees its role overall. This is particularly valuable since one of the major conclusions of the report is a plea for a more comprehensive approach to housing matters as a whole.

[1] See Appendix IV.

PART II

2. Local Authority Housing Policies

INTRODUCTION

How far do housing policies adopted by one local authority differ from those adopted by another? This is one of the major research questions posed in Chapter I. Drawing on the information from the series of case studies (presented in Part III of this report) some answers can be given. Policies were selected for study specifically because they appeared to allow the local authority a degree of discretion, and because variability was thought to exist. Was this borne out by the survey evidence?

Council house allocation policies are considered first, then policies for improvement grants, council mortgages and council house sales.

COUNCIL HOUSE ALLOCATION POLICIES

Section 91 of the Housing Act 1957 states that 'it shall be the duty of every local authority to consider housing conditions in their district and the needs of the district with respect to the provision of further housing accommodation . . .' There is, then, a general requirement to consider the district's housing needs.

In two instances there are more precise requirements as well. Local authorities have a duty to consider 'the number of new houses required to abate overcrowding . . . unless they are satisfied that the required number of houses will be otherwise provided' (Section 76 of the 1957 Act). Before declaring a Clearance Area 'the authority shall satisfy themselves that, in so far as suitable accommodation available for the persons who will be displaced . . . does not already exist, the authority can provide, or secure the provisions of, such accommodation . . . ' (Section 42 of the 1957 Act). The Land Compensation Act 1973 extends the rehousing responsibility to persons displaced by any housing order, resolution or undertaking, or by compulsory purchase thus: 'where . . . suitable alternative residential accommodation on reasonable terms is not otherwise available . . . then . . . it shall be the duty of the relevant authority to secure that he will be provided with such other accommodation.' (s.39 Land Compensation Act 1973.)

So council housing is to be provided to meet the needs of the district, and particularly to relieve overcrowding and provide alternative accommodation for those displaced by public action. In the selection of their tenants, local authorities 'shall secure (that) a reasonable preference is given to persons who are occupying insanitary or over-crowded houses, have large families or are living under unsatisfactory housing conditions' (s.113 Housing Act 1957). In this statement only 'overcrowded' has a statutory definition. 'Insanitary', 'large families', 'unsatisfactory housing conditions' and above all 'reasonable preference' are all open to individual interpretation.

Further guidance on selection of tenants and allocation priorities and procedures has been given to local authorities from time to time by circular (the needs of those seeking exchanges and transfers, of midwives, ex-servicemen, the elderly and key workers have been mentioned among others), and through a series of reports by the Housing Management Sub-Committee of the Central Housing Advisory Committee. These last have been particularly concerned with the ways in which local authorities define legitimate housing need (eligibility for housing), and the methods of allocation adopted (ordering of priorities among those eligible). It is not appropriate here to go into details of findings and recommendations, since these are available within the reports themselves .[1,2] Rather broad statements from the Ninth Report, *Council Housing, Purposes, Procedures and Priorities* will be used as a framework for the discussion of policies found in the surveyed local authorities.

Eligibility for Council Housing

On general needs applicants, the CHAC Report states that: 'there should be no barrier to acceptance on a housing list, . . . We therefore recommend that there should be no residential qualification for admission to a housing list. Indeed, we go further and hold it to be fundamental that no one should be precluded from applying for, or being considered for, a council tenancy on any ground whatsoever'.[3]

On exchanges and transfers: 'The objectives of policy should be . . . to provide for the maximum freedom of choice and to facilitate mobility'.[4]

On rehousing obligations: 'obligations of local authorities should extend to *all* households and parts of households (irrespective of size or tenure), the rehousing obligations should operate from the date on which the relevant Order becomes operative.'[5]

Turning first to general needs applicants, examination of Table 2.1 shows that none of the case study local authorities completely satisfies the Sub-Committee's recommendation that no one should be precluded from applying for, or being considered for, a council tenancy. All require some form of residential qualification (or employment qualification), though in three cases this is no more than the stipulation that the applicant must live (or work) in the area at the time the application is made. In the remaining authorities a minimum period is specified either for inclusion on the list or for consideration for a tenancy.

The other criteria on which a potential applicant is judged are age and marital status, tenure, and housing need (a mixture of tenure, housing condition, occupancy and health).

Only Warley sets a significant age limit for single persons without dependants, though in West Bromwich all applications from single persons living alone and under pensionable age are considered individually by the Committee when their

[1] *Selection of Tenants and Transfers and Exchanges*. Third Report of the Housing Management Sub-Committee of the Central Housing Advisory Committee. H.M.S.O. 1949.

[2] *Council Housing—Purposes, Procedures and Priorities*. Ninth Report of the Housing Management Sub-Committee of the Central Housing Advisory Committee. H.M.S.O. 1969.

[3] *Council Housing—Purposes, Procedures and Priorities*—. cit., paragraph 468.

[4] *Ibid* paragraph 470.

[5] *Ibid* paragraphs 483 and 485.

Table 2.1. General Needs Applicants and Eligibility, all Authorities: 1973

Regulations:	West Bromwich	Warley	Wolverhampton	Halesowen	Stafford	Ludlow
Eligibility for inclusion on the list						
Residential qualification	None	Must live in CB, or have lived in town for 2 years and not lived outside for more than 5 years, or have worked in Warley for 10 years	Must live in Wolverhampton	Must have lived or worked in MB for all preceding 12 months, or have lived in Borough most of life (Restricted list less stringent—live or work in Halesowen, or born in town)	Must live or work within 10 miles of Stafford town centre	Must live or work in the Rural District
Other qualifications	None	Single person without dependants must be aged 25 or over	None	Over age 18, and have established a prima facie need for housing	None	None
Eligibility for consideration	Must have lived or worked in CB for past 12 months, or lived in town for 10 of the 15 years immediately prior to application	Applicant (or wife) must complete 2 years' residence in Warley	As above	As above	As above	As above
Other qualifications	Must be in housing need: —lodgers —overcrowded families —living in flat after 5 years —living in house without a bath after 5 years —ill health	Must not be, or have been in previous 3 years, an owner-occupier of self-contained accommodation. Must not be tenant of adequate sized, self-contained accommodation with all amenities and in good state of repair	If a private tenant of self-contained premises must establish specified evidence of housing need. If an owner-occupier must have evidence of severe ill health or social need	None; though an owner-occupier may have to accept a nominated tenant for his property as a condition of rehousing	None	None

turn for allocation is reached. Engaged couples are often allowed on the list, though consideration may be delayed until marriage takes place. In all authorities single persons with children are considered in the same way as 'normal' families.

Tenure is a more significant excluding factor. Generally, private tenants of self-contained accommodation have to establish some definite evidence of 'housing need' for consideration for a tenancy. Need may be defined as over-crowding, lack of amenities, living in a flat, having a tied tenancy arrangement, or suffering from ill health. Owner-occupiers may be actually barred from the normal waiting list procedures (Warley), have to prove severe ill health or social need (Wolverhampton), or be willing to sell their house to the council or let it to a nominated tenant, if so required. In West Bromwich all applications from owner-occupiers are considered by the Committee.

Housing need, by implication, is most usually defined in terms of tenure, occupancy, housing conditions and ill health. In Halesowen—the only authority where a prima facie need must be established for inclusion on the list—financial problems experienced by retired owner-occupiers will be accepted as evidence of need.

The above statements, and the points set out in Table 2.1 are generalizations only, relating to the main stream eligibility requirements for applicants. Exceptions are always possible. For example, the residential qualifications may be waived in Halesowen if the applicant can convince the Council that there are special reasons for this to be done. In this way elderly relations of Halesowen residents coming from outside the Borough may be eligible for inclusion on the list. Again, Wolverhampton will allow an elderly person who has previously lived in the town for 20 years, but has since moved away, to register. Even in authorities where this flexibility is not built into the waiting list system itself, there is always the possibility of considering otherwise ineligible persons as special cases. In Warley, for example, any applicant precluded from registering by the residential qualifications may be referred to the Committee where there are 'exceptional circumstances' and owner-occupiers may be considered for rehousing on medical grounds, or if they run into mortgage problems. Deserted wives, tenants facing eviction and the homeless (no information on definitions used) are commonly considered for tenancies as special cases, and are allocated a dwelling where the Committee consider it right and necessary.

Other types of 'special cases' are recognised as well. Among the authorities studied, all allocate service tenancies to caretakers, and may house incoming local authority employees. Key workers for private employers are housed only by Stafford, on a normal tenancy basis (as opposed to a tied tenancy).

The impressions given by this evidence may be summed up as follows:

(a) Eligibility rules are made by all authorities, though considerable flexibility is also allowed for dealing with those excluded.

(b) Eligibility rules are highly variable. No two authorities examined were identical in this respect.

(c) Very generally, the more restrictive eligibility requirements are set by authorities under housing pressure, and where local authority boundaries are meaningless in housing terms. Thus, as would be expected, the conurbation authorities are more restrictive. Wolverhampton proves to be an exception to this generalization.

There is a similar degree of variability evident when eligibility to transfer is considered. Usually there are three types of requirement to be met. First, the applicant must have been the tenant of the property he wishes to transfer from for some specified minimum period. In Warley, the period is two years (unless an increase in family size has occurred to cause overcrowding), and in West Bromwich and Wolverhampton is twelve months. Elsewhere this is not a requirement.

Secondly, some evidence of 'need' for a transfer is required. This applies in West Bromwich, Warley and Halesowen where 'need' must be established either for inclusion on the list (Warley and Halesowen) or for active consideration for a tenancy (West Bromwich). 'Need' in these terms is defined basically as overcrowding or underoccupation, or health requirements. West Bromwich and Halesowen allow transfers from flats to houses after a minimum of five years tenancy. The definition of 'need' in Warley includes the desire to be nearer work, school or relatives who need assistance, the requirement for a garage, the wish to change area or house after a bereavement, and the bona fide intention to adopt a child where this is being delayed or prevented for accommodation reasons. Transfers from flats to houses are not considered legitimate unless one or more of these reasons applies. In all authorities a mutual exchange system exists to enable tenants to move for 'non-recognized' reasons.

Finally, the local authority must be satisfied that the transfer applicant is a 'good' tenant. Inevitably the suggestion that 'deserving' cases will be rewarded by the transfer system arises. A clear rent record for some specified period prior to an offer being made, and a satisfactory report in terms of house and garden maintenance is required in most authorities. It may also be a condition of a transfer that the Council will not be involved in any additional expense because of the move.

Although housing pressure is not of direct relevance for transfers (since a vacancy is created as well as used), it is interesting that the authorities with greater restrictions on general needs eligibility are also those concerned to limit eligibility for transfers. In no case, however, do the restrictions, in themselves, seem to unduly limit freedom of choice or to inhibit mobility.

The authorities studied vary considerably in the size of their clearance programmes, and thus in the number of properties required each year for rehousing purposes. The most common pattern is to accept responsibility for all those resident in the affected dwelling at a specified date, but to try as far as possible to avoid giving 'two houses for one'. This means that accommodation will be provided of a size to allow tenants or owners to be rehoused together with any lodgers or sub-tenants who were living with them on the appointed day. Exceptions may be made where the lodger family has a housing application near allocation level, in which case separate accommodation will be offered (West

Bromwich and Warley). Single persons are most vulnerable. In Stafford, single persons from multi-occupied premises are unlikely to be rehoused, while in West Bromwich, the cases involving single lodgers are considered separately by Committee. Only in Halesowen was it specifically stated that everyone would be rehoused, even in the case of multi-occupied houses.

The date at which the rehousing commitment applies is as follows:

Date of representation to Committee—West Bromwich
Date of making the Order—Stafford and Warley
Date of confirmation of the Order—Wolverhampton and Halesowen.

Ludlow is not included here since the Council operate demolition and redevelopment by purchasing houses individually on a voluntary basis rather than through a widespread use of Orders. Rehousing thus takes place through the transfer system. Persons moving into an affected area after the appointed day usually constitute special cases. The comment was usually that the authority would accept the responsibility to rehouse if children were involved.

The authorities studied, then, do not *necessarily* satisfy all the rehousing recommendations of the CHAC Sub-Committee, though may do so in practice when individual cases are examined.

Priorities for Council Housing

There are two aspects of priority which are of interest here—priority between groups and priorities within groups (waiting list, transfers etc.).

Priorities between groups are shown in Table 2.2. It is clear that clearance rehousing enjoys priority in most authorities, though only in one is a fixed possible percentage of lettings set. Transfers (where the request is considered legitimate, or there are management advantages to the Housing Department) generally take precedence over general needs applicants. In Stafford, transfers have priority in certain instances because an aim of the transfer system is to use the stock as well as possible. Thus a transfer would have priority over a general needs applicant for a specific letting if the property so vacated were needed for some other urgent requirement. In Warley, the apparent equality of transfers and waiting list applicants is misleading, since a waiting list applicant registering since January 1st 1966 is eligible only for a flat or maisonette, unless there are approved medical, overcrowding or management grounds for an exception.

Of course, priority given to transfer applicants, whether implicit or explicit, does not reduce the chances of waiting list applicants being housed, since a vacancy will still exist to be offered to a 'new' tenant, regardless of the number of transfers made in the interim. By sensitive use of a transfer system, chains of movement can be built up in the public sector, with each link (or move) representing a housing gain to the household involved, and the whole sequence resulting in a more appropriate use of the dwelling stock. In these circumstances it is hardly surprising that priority is given to transfer applications, though it is important to remember that the decision to give such priority can affect the type and size of property available for offer to general needs applicants, and may affect the speed of rehousing for any individual applicant from the waiting list. These points are examined in much greater detail in the following Chapter.

Table 2.2.   Allocation Priorities between Groups, all Authorities: 1973

Priority:	West Bromwich	Warley	Wolverhampton	Halesowen	Stafford	Ludlow
First	Clearance	Clearance	Clearance and special cases	Strongly recommended medical	Clearance	No stated policy
Second	Improvement area	Medical 'A'	Transfers	Clearance	Medical	
Third	Transfers	Transfer and waiting list	General needs	Transfers for houses and bungalows	Over-crowding	
Fourth	General needs			Transfers and general for flats and maisonettes	Other	

The procedures for determining within-group priorities for transfer applicants can be dealt with rapidly. This is because formal priority systems do not exist in any authority but Warley. Transfer allocations are usually made at the discretion of the Housing Manager. Several criteria are mentioned as relevant—need (occupancy), medical priority, date of application, length of tenancy in the dwelling to be transferred from, financial reasons, and management reasons related to the best use of the housing stock and vacancies arising. It is never clear, however, how the various conflicting demands are weighed. The personal interests of the officers making the decisions, their local knowledge, and other such informal factors appear as important in determining the outcome as any more formal policies.

In Warley, a date order priority scheme is operated with applicants grouped according to the size of property they need and the area in which they want to live. Length of tenancy and medical priority are taken into account by an ingenious weighting system whereby applicants are given a bonus of so many months waiting time, and then considered within the overall scheme.

In contrast, priorities among general needs applicants are formalized and determined according to standardized procedures in each authority. The CHAC Sub-Committee says 'the highest priority for council housing should go to those households in bad conditions with which they are unable to cope and where the potential ability to improve the situation themselves is low'.[1] They add that 'no one system of selection is appropriate generally'.[2] It is as well that the last point is made, since, once again, variation is the pattern among the case study authorities.

[1] *Council Housing—Purposes, Procedures and Priorities*—op. cit., paragraph 464.

[2] *Ibid* paragraph 466

Warley and Halesowen operate date order schemes with applicants placed in queues according to the size and location of accommodation they require. In both cases housing need has previously been established by the eligibility requirements.

West Bromwich, Wolverhampton and Ludlow have points schemes (the latter operating separate schemes for family and old age pensioner applicants). Points are awarded for the items listed in Table 2.3. While the standard measures of overcrowding and sharing of accommodation are represented in each scheme, when the details are examined, considerable variations occur. For example, overcrowding in a three-bedroomed, one-living room house would be defined as over 5 person-units in Wolverhampton, over 4 person-units in West Bromwich and over $7\frac{1}{2}$ person-units in Ludlow. Only in Ludlow is the statutory definition of overcrowding (set by section 77 of the Housing Act 1957) adopted. The variation in measures of overcrowding is, in fact, even greater than appears at first sight, since the definitions of 'person-units' also vary; the age at which a child is treated as a full person-unit can either be 7 or 10 years. More fundamental variation in the items included can also be seen in Table 2.3; lack of amenities is not pointed in Wolverhampton and other features occur only in one of the schemes.

Table 2.3. Items included in Points Schemes, West Bromwich, Wolverhampton and Ludlow: 1973

Item:	West Bromwich	Wolverhampton	Ludlow
Date of application	★	★	
Bedroom deficiency in applicant's accommodation	★	★	★
Size of family	★		
Living in rooms as distinct from self-contained house or flat	★	★	
No separate living room	★	★	★
Bedsitting room only (with children)	★		
General overcrowding	★	★	★
Living apart because of accommodation	★	★	
Sex overcrowding in sleeping arrangements	★	★	
Ill health or disability	★	★	★
Lack of amenities	★		
Service tenants where employer terminates employment or tenancy, or tenant resigns his job		★	
Sharing a kitchen			★
Unsuitable accommodation (conditions, location, etc.)			★
Discretionary points awarded by Tenancy Committee			★
Age (over pensionable age)			★
Suitability of applicant (for O.P.D.)			★
Length of time in a flat			★

In Stafford, all allocation priorities are at the discretion of the Housing Manager. Procedures are, therefore, Housing Department rather than Council approved. Priorities are determined within three groups—lodgers, householders and old age pensioners. Lack of amenities; other needs including the relationship between income and rent paid; and application date are all taken into account, but the precise procedures are not formalized.

The variations in priorities as a result of the different schemes can be shown with an example. Imagine four identical families making an application to a local authority. In each case the household consists of a man, his wife and one child aged 6.

Family A are tenants of a two-bedroomed private house with no hot water system or fixed bath, and with the WC at some distance from the house. They registered on the waiting list in 1968.

Family B are living with in-laws (parents only) in a two-bedroomed house. They have use of one bedroom, but have no separate living room. They registered in 1970.

Family C are living with in-laws and the husband's three brothers aged 18, 15 and 13, in a three-bedroomed house. They have use of one bedroom, but have no separate living room. They registered in 1971.

Family D are living in a bedsitting room in a house let off in such rooms. There are six rooms in all and 10 other persons live in the house. The applicants share bathroom and kitchen with other tenants. They have lived in the house for three years and registered on the waiting list in 1972.

If the order of priority between these cases were to be assessed by the different authorities at the end of 1973, the different rankings shown in Table 2.4 would result. Stafford is excluded since the allocation system is not formalized sufficiently for the calculations to be made. The differences apparent stem mainly from the weight given to different types of overcrowding, and date of application; they are explicable, though it is doubtful if the logic could always be appreciated by applicants involved.

Table 2.4. Example of Priorities for Waiting List Allocations, all Authorities except Stafford: 1973

Priority:	West Bromwich	Warley	Wolverhampton	Halesowen	Ludlow
First	B	A	C	A	D
Second	C, D	B	B	B	B, C
Third		C	D	C	
Fourth	A	D	A	D	A
			(not eligible)		

Clearly, priorities vary, but the variation is one of detail and not of basic intent. In every case housing need is the relevant feature, and need is defined in terms of tenure, occupancy, house condition and ill health, with more or less attention paid to these different need items. These authorities are, in effect, taking account of only half the CHAC Sub-Committee's requirement for priorities quoted on page 25. They are defining households in bad conditions, but not assessing ability to cope with those conditions or potential ability to improve the situation. Only Stafford seeks and makes use of information on household income. Elsewhere, financial problems can be grounds for consideration as a special case, but have no influence over priorities within the normal allocation procedures. Ill health and physical disability are obvious indirect measures of ability to cope, and all authorities consider medical claims in their schemes. Age is considered only in Ludlow. These, however are specific exceptions—as a generalization it remains true that *social* need, expressed as an inability to better one's own housing circumstances, is not satisfactorily assessed by waiting list procedures. All authorities have the safety device of 'special cases' if extreme needs arise, but the very name 'special' implies that they are intended as minority procedures only.

In fact, it might even be argued that allocation policies conflict with this idea of social need in two ways. First, almost all the authorities operate some sort of grading system, based on a house visit, whereby prospective tenants are matched to the type of accommodation they will be offered. These grading systems are developed to different degrees in the different authorities, but they usually exist. Inability to cope with bad housing conditions is likely to manifest itself in poor housekeeping standards or rent arrears—not evidence that the applicant will be a 'good tenant'. While a poor house visit report may not harm the applicant's chance of being rehoused (only Warley specifies the right to refuse an offer to an 'unsuitable tenant'—the term is not defined—though Wolverhampton will not consider a former council tenant until any rent arrears outstanding have been paid) it certainly can influence the type and age of property offered. If properties of a specific grade are in short supply, grading can also influence the speed with which applicants are rehoused. Applicants with a poor visit record certainly do not enjoy any particular allocation priority.

The second point is this. The allocation schemes followed tend to inhibit such self-help as may exist among applicants. While remaining lodgers with their parents, applicants can earn priority points, particularly if considerable over-crowding is produced at the same time. But if they move into rented accommodation, they may render themselves ineligible for consideration, or by reducing crowding, lower their point score. Lack of basic amenities never carries equal weight with sharing accommodation, except in a date order scheme. If the applicant buys a house as a last desperate measure to help his family, but still wants a council tenancy, he will normally lose any chance of that tenancy. Again, couples who feel it is unfair to have children in a single room do not get the priority they would with a child and another baby expected. Date order schemes again avoid this problem provided the 'considerate' couples are eligible for consideration at all.

This should not be taken as a criticism of the concept of helping families in greatest need, but simply as a reminder of what can happen if the operational definition of need is inadequate. It becomes particularly serious if households in considerable social need, and those unable to help themselves, are forced to compete with households who *could* help themselves if the system did not discourage such action. A greater number of applicants competing for a given number of vacancies suggests that rehousing may be delayed for those who have no real alternative to a council tenancy for improving their housing situation.

Council House Allocations—General

The CHAC Sub-Committee has this to say, in general terms, of allocation systems: 'the first requirement of any public activity is publicity . . . It follows that selection schemes should be freely available . . . The selection of individual tenants for council houses should in general be undertaken by officers, not by elected members . . . Whatever scheme is used it must be published and be readily available. It should also be as simple as possible.'[1]

As in all other aspects, the local authorities vary in these respects. Publicity for the selection scheme ranges from West Bromwich and Wolverhampton where details of the points scheme are available to the applicants (actually as part of the application form in Wolverhampton), to Warley and Stafford where no details are available to the public; in Stafford, no details exist even for internal council purposes. Date order schemes are simple, but the prior eligibility requirements can make them as difficult to understand as a complex points scheme. Apart from special cases (and allocations to owner-occupiers and single persons in some instances) only Ludlow involves the elected members in the selection procedures. Here the actual waiting list priority is approved by the Committee, and the Housing Manager makes allocations in this order. With the use of discretionary points the Committee can actually influence the priority ranking to some extent (the total number of discretionary points which may be awarded is 10, and 10 points are also available for medical priority).

This discussion has so far only referred to general needs applications. When transfers and clearance rehousing are included the situation changes. In no cases are all the complexities of the total selection scheme published, and in no case is the process simple. In all cases the responsibility for transfer allocations is within the discretion of the Housing Manager. It must be concluded that none of the selection schemes examined satisfy all the requirements of the Sub-Committee in this respect.

But are all the CHAC recommendations in fact reasonable and attainable? The main policy areas in which the local authorities studied fall short of the recommendations are eligibility for council housing (limitations are set on those eligible to register on the waiting list or to be considered for a tenancy); definition of 'need' for a council house (partial definitions are used which ignore social aspects of need); and openness and simplicity of the allocation procedures (a lack of publicity exists, and schemes used are often extremely complex).

It would be relatively simple for each of the authorities to open the waiting list to all potential applicants, regardless of present residence or tenure. This

[1] *Council Housing—Purposes, Procedures and Priorities*—op. cit., paragraphs 454, 465 and 466.

would undoubtedly give a more accurate indication of the number of households who would like a council house in the area, and, as such, would provide a better basis for estimating future housing requirements and planning building programmes. Against such a course of action is the argument that allowing a person to register on the waiting list implies that there is a possibility that the authority will be able to offer a tenancy within a reasonable period of time. While applications exceed vacancies, and councils are forced to set priorities, this is clearly not true for all households; allowing everyone to register on the list may be seen as fostering false hopes. On balance, however, the benefits of a fully open list seem to outweigh the drawbacks. Any person should be allowed to register on a local authority waiting list.

The issues involved in suggesting that every person should have an equal opportunity of being considered for a tenancy are much more complex. In effect, this would mean that newcomers to an area would be treated equally with long-established residents, owner-occupiers with lodgers, and single people with families including children. No applicant would be ruled out of consideration simply because he belonged to some pre-determined group; each case would be considered according to its individual merits. At the same time, those merits would be assessed in relation to a wider definition of 'need' which includes social considerations as well as the present immediate housing situation. It is undeniable that, in an ideal world, this would be highly desirable, and would allow council housing to play a full part in general social and welfare policy. However, the present is not an ideal world. Rather than attempting to discuss this question exhaustively, four points can be made.

First, while council housing remains a local government function it is understandable that councils will feel a continuing responsibility for their own residents (voters and rate payers) in allocation policies. For this reason alone, residential qualifications are unlikely to be totally abandoned in areas of population pressure while housing demand from local residents exists.

Secondly, even leaving aside political arguments (which are not always considered legitimate in a discussion of social policy), there are profound technical problems in devising a priority system to the specifications outlined above. It is doubtful if any scheme in use with any authority fully recognizes the possible conflict between social need and orthodox housing need. How can concepts of 'ability to cope' and the potential for self-help be built into a workable system? Certainly, none of the CHAC recommendations make this clear.

The closest approach is found in the treatment of special cases where each applicant *is* considered individually, and the social needs, brought to crisis point by homelessness, threat of eviction, or marital breakdown, are all relevant. However, at this point the third problem appears. Housing Departments, as they are presently organized and staffed simply could not cope administratively if they had to consider every applicant as a special case. The present allocation systems work *because* applicants are grouped and dealt with according to pre-determined rules; numbers become manageable *because* some households are automatically excluded from consideration. The more factors there are to be taken into account, the more unweildly the administrative procedures become. It is hard to envisage a highly individualized system which would be manageable in a large authority where several hundred allocations must be made each week.

Finally, it is fair to point out an apparent contradiction within the recommendation of the CHAC Sub-Committee. On the one hand they suggest a wider definition of need and advocate considering the demands of all applicants, while on the other they recommend an open, fair and simple system for deciding priorities. Present open schemes tend to be those with clearly (and often narrowly) defined priorities. They have arisen because of a genuine desire to treat all applicants consistently and fairly, and an equal desire to be seen to be consistent and fair. Schemes which, like that operated at Stafford, attempt to take individual situations into account, and to weigh priorities on a more personal level, are, of necessity, vague and complex. It becomes increasingly difficult to explain to a disappointed applicant just why he has not been offered a house. The paradox is clear.

This discussion has certainly raised questions, rather than provided answers! Perhaps the major conclusion to emerge is the great difficulty encountered in making realistic recommendations for local authority allocation policies. While the report of the CHAC Sub-Committee is particularly valuable in drawing attention to issues often thought to lie outside the realm of 'orthodox' council housing purposes and policies, the means by which the concepts could be made operational are less fully treated. This is an obvious avenue for research in the future.

IMPROVEMENT GRANT POLICIES

The present code for improvement grants is set by the Housing Act 1969. 'A local authority shall approve an application for a standard grant if they are satisfied . . . that when the works . . . have been carried out

(a) the dwelling will be provided with all standard amenities for the exclusive use of its occupants; and

(b) the dwelling will be in good repair having regard to its age, character and locality, and disregarding internal decorative repair, and will in all respects be fit for human habitation;

and that the dwelling is likely to remain fit for human habitation and available for use as a dwelling for a period of not less than 15 years (section 9). Local authorities have some discretion in approving grants when the work has been started, where all the standard amenities are not provided, and where a shorter life than 15 years is estimated.

Discretion is greater in the case of Special Grants for the installations of standard amenities in shared accommodation, where a local authority may approve an application 'in such circumstances as they think fit' (section 14).

A local authority may also approve and pay an improvement grant (referred to throughout this report as a discretionary grant). The authority 'shall not approve an application . . . unless they are satisfied the dwelling . . . will provide satisfactory housing accommodation for such period and conform with such requirements with respect to construction and physical conditions and the provision of services and amenities as may . . . be specified . . . by the Minister' (section 3). The 'specified' period is normally 30 years and the standard the 12 point standard,[1] though there are possibilities for grants for shorter life properties and improvement to a lower standard. The authority has discretion to define the works which will be eligible for grant aid, and sets the level of approved expenses for the work, including the element for repair and replacement. This last cannot exceed half of the total approved expenses.

DoE Circular 64/69 gives guidance to the local authorities on the aims and uses of the new grant code: 'the scale and type of work done to improve or repair the existing stock of houses . . . (will be regarded) as an integral part of the authority's housing programme. Their efforts to bring about improvement and repair . . . will mainly consist of encouraging owners to make use of the grants offered and to maintain their property in a reasonable standard of repair having regard to its age, character and locality . . . The new grant code is designed to apply to a very wide range of housing conditions, and is therefore limited by a minimum of statutory requirements . . . Grant aided improvements have social and economic aspects . . . A keynote of the new legislation is greater flexibility. One feature of this is the wider discretion given to local authorities to adapt grants to meet individual needs'. Clearly the circular is more concerned to point out the scope of local authority discretion than to give precise guidance on how that discretion should be exercised.

It is relevant here to quote from an earlier circular (29/62), since this appears to have coloured local authority thinking in a manner which is still apparent. This circular says 'One aim (of grants) is to encourage owners to provide services and amenities in houses which are sound, but which were built to a lower standard than is generally acceptable nowadays. The other is to encourage the provision of additional satisfactory dwellings, either by converting an old building into one or more dwellings or by converting a large outmoded house from one dwelling to a number of flats . . . Where the owner of a house capable of improvement to the standard of a modern house seeks a standard grant, there is much to be said for the practice of those authorities who try to persuade him to carry out a more comprehensive scheme with the help of a discretionary grant. . . . The purpose of improvement grants is to encourage improvements and although a reasonable standard of repair must be insisted on . . ., the setting of too high a standard becomes self-defeating when, as a result, owners are deterred from carrying out the works at all.'

Policies for Discretionary Improvement Grants

How do the surveyed local authorities react to the elements of discretion in the grant system? In fact, it is not easy to compare improvement grant policies since formal statements of policy rarely exist. An attempt to compare the local authorities will, however, be made in terms of general attitudes expressed towards improvement grants, the types of work approved for grant purposes, and the

[1] See Appendix IV for definition.

life and standard of property aimed at when the work is complete.

Stafford gave the clearest account of the aims of its improvement grant activities. These were threefold—to save houses from clearance, to modernize otherwise sound houses, and to produce extra accommodation units. By implication the aims of the grant system in other authorities seem very similar. In West Bromwich, for example, the aim is to assist in the general upgrading of as much of the housing stock as possible.

Allowable works for grant purposes also seem very similar. In all authorities the installation of basic plumbing amenities and the conversion of dwellings to flats are allowed. In no authority was the provision of an additional bedroom allowed as the sole piece of improvement work. The same applies to the installation of central heating by itself. All authorities except Ludlow did, however, allow extension work to kitchens as an 'improvement', though the size allowed varied; for example, 'Parker Morris' in Stafford and '75 square feet' in Warley. Minor variations in classification of works to be defined as replacement or repair rather than improvement were beyond the scope of this study, so again the general impression is one of similarity between authorities, with the exception of Ludlow RD. This is particularly hard to judge since Wolverhampton is the only area where a publicly available leaflet outlining allowable works exists. Elsewhere reliance is placed on personal contact and negotiation between local authority officers and potential improvers over the works which will rank for grant aid.

Every authority claimed that discretionary grants were given to bring a dwelling to the 12 point standard, and to give it a 30 year life when the works were complete. All said they hoped to persuade an applicant to make use of a discretionary rather than a standard grant. Certain distinctions exist however in the qualifications made to the general statements. In Warley and Stafford such qualifications were most explicit. In Warley, applicants are encouraged to make use of discretionary grants and to achieve as high a standard as possible, 'but at the same time it is borne in mind that, if things are made too difficult for the applicant, no improvement at all may result'. Social arguments may temper the purely physical in Stafford, so that a reduced life (less than 30 years) may be acceptable.

Other slight variations exist in policies and procedures. West Bromwich may approve grants in any house which is over 25 years old. Elsewhere the 1961 date statutorily defined for standard grants is applied for all grants. Applications from private landlords of vacant property in Wolverhampton are referred to Committee for decision. In Ludlow, standard grants only will be given on property known to be a second home. There are no examples of limits being set by the properties' value, or the owners' financial capacities.

In terms of policies alone, it seems that there is broad similarity between the surveyed authorities, with differences in degree or emphasis rather than on any fundamental bases. Only Ludlow emerges as distinctive—a fact readily explained by the very different housing market situation which exists in an attractive rural area. How far performance varies despite policy likenesses will be seen in the following chapter.

MORTGAGE LENDING POLICIES

Local authorities are empowered to make advances for house purchase under three separate pieces of legislation, two relating to houses in the private sector, and one to council houses which are sold. The private sector regulations will be dealt with first. Under section 43 of the Housing (Financial Provisions) Act 1958, authorities can make advances to any person for acquiring, constructing, converting, altering, enlarging or improving houses. Under the Small Dwellings Acquisition Acts 1899–1923 (SDAA), advances can be made for house purchase. Both sets of legislation are enabling—there is no statutory duty placed upon local authorities to lend money for house purchase.

The two lending codes are slightly different, and in general the Housing Act powers are less restrictive in terms of the conditions to be met by property or purchaser. A detailed comparison of the statutory requirements is not appropriate here,[1] but the following selected differences exist:

(a) SDAA advances can only be made on property within the local authority area. There is no such limitation placed on loans made under the Housing Act.

(b) SDAA advances can only be made on leasehold property if there is a 60 year unexpired term of lease at the time the advance is made. The requirement for Housing Act advances is that at least 10 years unexpired lease should remain when repayments are complete.

(c) A maximum repayment period of 30 years is set by the Small Dwelling Acquisition Act. No maximum is set by the Housing Acts.

(d) Neither powers set a limit on the amount which may be advanced in terms of proportion of valuation.

(e) SDAA interest rates are to be set at $\frac{1}{4}\%$ above the current rate charged to local authorities by the Public Works Loan Board. No interest rate rulings are laid down in the Housing Acts.

DoE Circular 22/71 makes it quite clear that the objective of local authority lending is 'to supplement rather than replace the activities of the main mortgage institutions'. Accordingly a series of categories are defined to which local authorities should give preference in their lending policies. These are:

(a) Existing tenants of a local authority, people who are high on the authority's waiting list for housing, or people displaced by slum clearance or other public authority development whom the council would otherwise be obliged to rehouse.

(b) Applicants who are homeless or threatened with homelessness or living in conditions that are overcrowded or otherwise detrimental to health.

(c) Individual members of self-build groups when they are about to occupy the premises as individual mortgagors.

(d) Applicants who wish to buy older and smaller property unlikely to

---

[1] A comparison may be found in John P. Macey and Charles Vivian Baker, *Housing Management*, Estates Gazette Ltd., London, 1965, pages 148–151.

attract a commercial mortgage advance, and more particularly, persons who want to acquire a house with a view to subsequently improving it for their own occupation.

(e) Applicants who wish to buy larger property for only partial occupation by themselves, in areas where conditions of overcrowding seem liable to develop. The council is encouraged to give special consideration to applicants in this category who wish to buy large houses for conversion into self-contained flats.

(f) Applicants taking up residence in or around a Development or Intermediate Area, or overspill receiving area.

(g) Urgently needed staff, where the local authority is satisfied that they are needed in the interests of the efficiency of the public service, and that they are unlikely to obtain the requisite mortgage advance from another source.

Additional categories may be added, with the approval of the Department of the Environment where 'an authority thinks that in their area there is some distinct and special need not coming within these categories'. It is suggested in circular 22/71 that, by lending within the outlined categories, and by making 'responsible and judicious' use of their powers, the local authorities may 'relieve housing need and benefit the condition of the housing stock in a measure far out of scale with the capital advanced'. Clearly mortgage lending is seen as complementary both to the provision and allocation of council houses and to policies for dealing with the older housing stock.

When local authorities sell council houses, section 104 of the Housing Act 1957 gives them the powers to 'agree to the price . . . being paid by instalments or to a payment of part thereof being secured by a mortgage of the premises'. Circular 54/70 makes it clear that 'in the Minister's view it would not be appropriate in such cases to make advances under the Small Dwellings Acquisition Acts or under section 43 of the Housing (Financial Provisions) Act 1958' (though the reasons for this are not stated). No further statutory requirements are laid down for this alternative form of housing advance. Circular 54/70 also assumes that 'authorities will not dispose of houses on such terms that the interest rates they charge represent a loss to the authority or a concealed subsidy to the buyer or lessee'. Generally interest rates should 'bear a close relationship' with those charged in respect of loans made under section 43 of the Housing (Financial Provisions) Act 1958. No mention is made of a maximum limit or recommended repayment period for section 104 'payments by instalment'.

Lending for Private House Purchase

All the local authorities studied make advances for the purchase of houses in the private sector. Wolverhampton and Ludlow use Small Dwellings Acquisition Acts powers, while the other four councils make advances under the Housing (Financial Provisions) Act 1958. It is interesting that, while the lending schemes vary in detail, the fundamentals are very similar between authorities, regardless of legislation involved. In no case is the full freedom of Housing Act lending found to be usual practice.

Table 2.5. Some Regulations of Mortgage Lending, all Authorities: 1973

Regulations:	West Bromwich	Warley	Wolverhampton	Halesowen	Stafford	Ludlow
Amount of advance	Normal maximum 95% valuation. 100% in special cases. Maximum if estimated life under 20 years is 85% valuation. No advance if estimated life is 15 years or less	Normal maximum 95% valuation. 100% in special cases	Normal maximum 90% valuation. Percentage may be lower with age of property dependent on valuer's report	Normal maximum 95% valuation. 100% in special cases	Normal maximum 95% valuation. 100% in special cases	Normal loans 90–100% of valuation
Relationship of advance and income	Repayments must not exceed 20% of average income. Wife's earnings are not usually considered	Repayments plus rates, etc. must not exceed 25% gross average income. Wife's earnings up to age 40 not usually considered	Must be able to satisfy Council can meet repayments and find deposit. Full wife's earnings rarely taken into account	Monthly repayments shall not exceed gross weekly earnings. Basic income and overtime plus $\frac{1}{2}$ wife's earnings	5 yr. loan—$1\frac{1}{2}$ income 10 " —2 " 15 " —$2\frac{1}{4}$ " 20 " —$2\frac{1}{2}$ " 25 " " —$2\frac{3}{4}$ " Applicant's income excluding overtime and wife's earnings (under 40 years)	Limited to $2\frac{1}{2}$ times applicant's income. Wife's earnings rarely taken into account
Repayment period	Maximum 25 years. Repayments should be complete when borrower reaches 65 years	Maximum 30 years, limited to difference between age of house and 80 years. House exceeding 70 years old may have maximum 10-year loan. Repayments usually to be complete by retiring age	Normal maximum 25 years, 30 years as special case. Age and condition of property considered	Maximum 30 years. May be reduced to take account of age and condition of property	Maximum 25 years. May be reduced on valuer's report.	Maximum 30 years; 20 years advised. May be reduced on valuer's advice
Interest Rate	Variable pool rate. Usually in line with Building Societies	Fixed at $\frac{1}{4}$% above Council's external borrowing rate	Fixed at $\frac{1}{4}$% above PWLB rates	Fixed at $\frac{1}{4}$% above PWLB rates	Fixed at $\frac{1}{4}$% above PWLB rates	Fixed at $\frac{1}{4}$% above PWBL rates
Other	Houses within CB only. Value limit £12,000	Houses within CB only. Value limit £7,000	Houses within CB only. Value limit £5,000	Houses within MB only. Value limit £10,000	Houses within new DC area. No upper limit	Limited to houses within RD. Maximum £6,000 lent

This can be seen in Table 2.5 which shows some of the regulations adopted by the different authorities. In each case the aim of lending is to complement the activities of building societies, or to serve as a 'lender of last resort'. Each of the authorities adhere strictly to the categories set out in circular 22/71 when deciding whether or not to make an advance, and in several cases the actual groups are set out as part of the explanatory leaflet provided for would-be borrowers.

Variations occur between the authorities under each of the headings set out in Table 2.5. Most remarkable, perhaps, is the wide difference evident in the upper valuation limit set for eligible property. The highest figure of £12,000 (West Bromwich) is more than double the lowest—£5,000 (Wolverhampton). It seems unlikely that the difference reflects a comparable variation in prices between the two areas.

It should be evident that detailed comparisons between authorities cannot be made in the same way as was done, for example, with waiting list priorities. While a basic framework of policies and rules are set down by the local authority for lending, within this each application is a special case, in which the unique combination of applicant's age, income and requirements and the property's age and condition have to be considered. Such detail was beyond the scope of this research. Rather it seems useful to see how the general policies outlined compare with those of building societies operating in the area.

In terms of the headings of Table 2.5, the findings for building societies are as follows:

(a) *Amount of advance*—normal maximum 80% valuation, but this may increase to 95% of valuation with a mortgage indemnity policy. The maximum percentage is affected by the age of the property, the amount the applicant wants to borrow and the term over which the money is lent.[1] For properties built before 1919 the maximum amount which will be lent can vary between 70% and 80% of valuation.

(b) *Relationship of advance and income*—normal ruling states $2\frac{1}{2}$ to 3 times applicant's income. There is some variation in the willingness to take wife's earnings into account, often depending on the nature of the husband's employment. Professional workers on incremental salary scales are more likely to have a generous limit set in terms of present day earnings.

(c) *Repayment period*—the maximum quoted varied between 25 and 35 years. A shorter period is often preferred for the original mortgage, allowing the term to be lengthened as interest rates rise in the future. The repayment period allowed obviously relates to the borrower's age (as well as the property age and term of unexpired lease with a leasehold property). Maximum ages quoted for the time at which repayments should be complete varied between 65 and 80 years, with several societies mentioning 70 years of age.

[1] Building Societies 1973 Part 1, in *Planned Savings*, Vol. 8, No. 13, June 27th, 1973.

(d) *Interest rates*—building societies operate variable interest rate schemes
    in which the level is set (as recent publicity indicates) by the overall
    financial situation and the ease with which they can attract the savings
    which enable them to lend.

In these terms, local authorities can be thought of as more generous in the
amount of advance they will make in relation to valuation, and the building
societies as more generous in the relationship of advance to income and the
length of repayment period. Local authority interest rates are fixed (in most of
the authorities), but higher than building society levels at the time the mortgage
is granted. For example, the Building Societies Association recommended
mortgage rate at June 1973 was 9·5%, while the Public Works Loan Board rate
for local authority loans over 25 years was 10·5% (Mortgage interest rates would
therefore be 10·75%).[1] There seems little advantage to the local authorities on
these criteria.

The chief advantage, of course, lies in the type and age of property which
will be lent on. Building societies prefer to lend on 'modern popular housing'—
defining this as built at least since 1930. While there is no absolute ban on older
terraced houses for lending purposes, great care is taken to avoid 'declining areas'
and terraced properties with attic and cellar, where there is a fear of multiple-
occupation. Older property in general (pre 1919) may suffer through conditions
being placed on the loans—the proportion of valuation lent is lower, and repayment periods are reduced. There is, apparently, considerable scope for local
authorities prepared to lend to applicants falling into categories (d) and (e) of
circular 22/71.

At the time of the survey local authorities may also have experienced increased
pressure from applicants because building societies were being forced to limit
lending. This normally took the form of granting loans to society investors
only—in some cases to investors who had saved at least sufficient for the deposit.
In conditions of shortage of supply of funds for lending, the number of loans
given for the purchase of older properties may be still more limited.

This rapid survey of local authority lending policies suggests that all the
councils studied accept the central government view that they should provide a
service complementary to, rather than competitive with, the service offered by
building societies. Regardless of variations in detail between authorities, this is
the common theme. How well they succeed in practice will be seen later.

Lending for Purchase of Council Houses

All the surveyed local authorities had at some time in the recent past sold
council houses, and all had made advances for their purchase. Despite the different
legislation under which these advances are made, policies in general seem very
similar to those operated for the purchase of private houses described above.
One difference is found in the scale of council involvement. While local authorities
accounted for under 9% of the loans made for house purchase during the second

[1] *Housing and Construction Statistics,* Number 6, 2nd quarter 1973. H.M.S.O. Table 42.

quarter of 1973 (by value), [1] the surveyed authorities estimated they provided the finance for about 90% of the council houses sold.

In detail, the schemes for advances for council houses seem slightly more generous than those for private houses:

(a) The relationships between advance and income, and the level of interest rates are the same for both types of advance.

(b) In all authorities the maximum repayment period for the loan is 30 years.

(c) Loans of near 100% of purchase price are more common. Usually a nominal deposit is requested—£10 in West Bromwich, £5 in Wolverhampton, Halesowen and Stafford, and 1% of purchase price in Warley.

(d) Advances may be given to elderly applicants if younger members of the family are willing to act as guarantors.

Rules governing the setting of purchase price and financial details of sales other than those related to the advances themselves are discussed in the following section.

COUNCIL HOUSE SALES

The 1957 Housing Act (section 104) gives local authorities powers to sell council houses. The actual wording is: 'Where a local authority have acquired or appropriated any land for the purposes of this Part of this Act (Part V—Provision of Housing Accommodation), then, . . ., the local authority may, with the consent of the Minister, sell or lease any houses on the land or erected by them on the land, subject to such covenants and conditions as they may think fit to impose in regard to the maintenance or use of the houses . . .'. Important features here are that a local authority *may* sell, not *must* sell, and that the Minister's (Secretary of State's) consent is required.

In fact a general consent has existed throughout the period since 1957, but the details of the consent have varied. The general consent given by MoHLG circular 54/70 applied to:

(a) Selling, or leasing for a term of 99 years or more, any house provided under or appropriated for the purposes of Part V of the Housing Act 1957 for a price . . . equal to the current market price . . . with vacant possession. Such sales may be made to:
    (i)   a sitting tenant
    (ii) in the case of a house which is unoccupied or has not been let, to a person who requires a house for his own exclusive use.

(b) Selling, or leasing for a term of 99 years or more any house as above at less than current market price subject to the following conditions:
    (i)   The price must not be more than 20% below what would be the current market price with vacant possession free from the conditions thus imposed (Provided that the price on sale shall in no case be less than the total cost incurred by the authority in providing the house)

[1] *Housing and Construction Statistics* Number 6, 2nd quarter 1973. H.M.S.O. Table 35.

(ii) The local authority shall impose conditions on the sale to provide that
—during a period of 5 years from the date of the completion of the
sale, the house shall not be resold at a price in excess of the amount
at which it was sold by the authority plus . . . increase for improvements (if any)
—the local authority reserve to themselves a right of pre-emption
precluding the sale or the grant of a lease of the house during that
period of 5 years unless the owner has first offered to resell the house
to the local authority and the authority have refused the offer.[1]

Such sales may be made to similar groups of persons as in (a) above.

DoE circular 56/72 draws particular attention to the 20% discount possible
for council house sales, and states: 'Councils will be aware that in special circumstances discounts of up to 30% have also been authorized.'

While the legislative possibilities of council house sales have remained almost
unchanged since before the Housing Act of 1936 (price setting bases have changed)
Ministerial consent has been alternately granted or withheld over time. In fact
the issue of the sale of council houses has become significant in party political
terms at both central and local government level. Since central government
exhortations both to restraint and to liberality may have influenced local councils
in their policies, it is relevant here to quote briefly from circulars which show the
divergence of thinking over a period of only 5 years.

First, the Labour Government circular 24/67 states: 'it would in the Minister's
view be wrong to contemplate any substantial development (in sales of existing
council houses) where there remained a pressing social need for more rented
housing. . . . In areas where there is still an unsatisfied demand for houses to let
at moderate rents, they should not sell their existing houses except where there are
special reasons in the case of a particular property. To do so would postpone the
time when an adequate supply of rented housing becomes available; and could
mean that families on the waiting list, who are among the most inadequately
housed, would have to wait longer for a vacancy . . . .Local authority tenants
who wish to move to a private house can be given every encouragement and
assistance to do so. The authority can then relet to a family in need'. Much of
the argument against excessive sales is couched in terms of the financial implications for the local authority. Specific examples of cases where sales would be
appropriate are also quoted; first where the present council housing stock is not
well balanced in relation to the needs of their area (in terms of dwelling size or
type), and secondly where the demand for rented housing is falling off or where
the authority can keep pace with demand with a very modest building
programme.

Circular 56/72 issued by a Conservative Government just five years later
paints a very different picture. It starts from the basic view that, 'unless the local
circumstances are quite exceptional, a local authority who deny their tenants
the opportunity to own the house which they have made their home would be

[1] Full details of the consent can be found in Appendix I of Ministry of Housing and Local
Government Circular 54/70.

failing to exercise their powers under section 104 of the Housing Act 1957 in a manner which is appropriate to present circumstances'. One by one the points raised by the earlier circular are dealt with. The mention of need prompts the following: '. . . these needs include those of the tenants of the authority who aspire to home ownership . . . it is possible for an authority to meet those needs in a way which is compatible with their responsibilities for meeting their area's requirements for dwellings to let'. The argument that tenants should be encouraged to move to the private sector is answered: 'many council tenants who are anxious to buy their home would not wish to move if they were denied this opportunity. Sales to such tenants would not therefore affect the supply of accommodation which the authority could let to prospective tenants. . . . . this argument (that tenants should move to the private sector) fails to do justice to the legitimate desire of many council tenants to remain in a house which they have made their home and not to sever their ties with a congenial neighbourhood. Moreover if council tenants can buy a house only in the private sector, their council needlessly creates additional demand for houses in that sector which can only aggravate the present pressure on house prices, particularly for houses in the lower price range.' Financial problems in a sales policy are to be remedied by the Housing Finance Bill—now the Housing Finance Act 1972.

Thus the arguments are set down in terms which are often emotive rather than based on fact. Many of the points stressed seem articles of faith stemming from basic ideologies with scant regard to objective conditions.[1] How have local authorities reacted to such conflicting 'guidance'?

Local Authority Policies for Council House Sales

First it is interesting to note that, while encouragement to sell has become stronger in recent years, three of the six local authorities surveyed had stopped selling council houses. Labour control the councils of the three which have discontinued sales—Warley, Wolverhampton and Stafford, but also hold the majority in West Bromwich. In Halesowen, the Conservatives have the largest number of members, and in Ludlow, Independents have control. Neither local party political composition nor size of authority is, therefore, the sole factor involved. Table 2.6 summarizes the council house sales policies of the surveyed authorities. The lower part of the table relates to the policy followed when sales were made for authorities which now no longer sell their houses.

It is interesting that longstanding tenants are favoured in so many authorities. This has never been part of ministry guidance, yet only in Warley is there neither a specified minimum tenancy for eligibility nor a sliding scale of discount with length of tenancy. This concern with tenancy means that many tenants may be paying more than the recommended 80% of market value, and in two instances total allowable discount never reaches the 20% level.

Limitations placed on the type of property sold are mainly the result of management considerations. This is particularly true of flats and maisonettes,

---

[1] For a fuller account of council house sales policies see A. S. Murie, *The Sale of Council Houses: A Study in Social Policy* (forthcoming).

Table 2.6. Council House Sales Policies, all Authorities: 1973

Policy:	West Bromwich	Warley	Wolverhampton	Halesowen	Stafford	Ludlow
Current policy	Sales	No sales	No sales	Sales	No sales	Sales
Dwellings sold	Houses only. 10% of total stock set as limit	Houses only. No limit set	All houses. Flats and maisonettes in approved cases. Limit of 12½% houses on any estate set	Houses only. No limit set	Houses only (except 4 bedroomed). No limit set	Houses and family bungalows only. No limit set
Purchasers	Any sitting tenant and those waiting for a house once an offer has been made	Any sitting tenant	Sitting tenants (other than service tenants), and applicants on the waiting list when an offer has been made	Local authority tenants of one year's standing	Sitting tenants who have been tenant of house to be bought for 2 years	Any sitting tenant
Purchase price	5-year pre-emption clause. Sale price is £50 below market value. Additional discount for length of tenancy of 10 years or more: 10 years—5% then ½% for each completed year to 10% for 20 years	5-year pre-emption clause. 20% discount on market value regardless of length of tenancy	5-year pre-emption clause where reduction in price because of tenancy discount; 5 years—10% then 1% for each completed year to 20% for 15 years	5-year pre-emption clause. 20% discount on market value regardless of length of tenancy	5-year pre-emption clause. 15% discount on market value regardless of length of tenancy	5-year pre-emption clause where reduction in price because of tenancy discount: 5 years—5% then 1% for each completed year to 20% for 20 years

In all authorities the basic price is calculated from full market value with vacant possession. The minimum sale price is always set by the total cost of providing the dwelling. In each case the pre-emption clause may be waived, in which case the price is full market value.

but in the case of old persons' bungalows the reason seems equally to be pressure of demand for that type of accommodation. It might, of course, be argued that by restricting sales to houses only, the local authorities will be accommodating the great majority of purchase demands. Overall limits for sales were set only in West Bromwich and Wolverhampton, and it may be that the figures chosen here were arbitrary rather than reasoned from the full implications of an unlimited sales policy. Only Stafford explicitly excluded the sale of four-bedroomed houses, and elsewhere the limit was not specifically broken into different house size groups.

Reasons for selling council houses, or for failing to sell them, were not made clear by the surveyed authorities. It seems to be an issue of policy where aims are particularly ill-defined, though the actual resulting policy is extremely clear cut and precise. It would be true to say that differences of opinion at central government level are fully reflected at the local level.

CONCLUSIONS—LOCAL AUTHORITY POLICIES

The conclusions to be drawn from the material presented here can be briefly stated. There are two important points.

First, as was assumed at the outset, there is considerable scope for local discretion in the legislation considered, and local authorities make considerable use of that discretion. Each of the authorities surveyed has its own interpretation of its powers, and its own set of policies and procedures conceived within that framework. In almost every policy field examined, each authority is unique. The exception, where variation is much less apparent, is in policies relating to discretionary improvement grants. In this particular policy field only Ludlow was seen to differ from the other authorities in general approach.

Having said this, the second point is in some ways a qualification. Variation—immense variation—does exist, but it is variation in details and not in fundamentals. Use of the term 'fundamentals' can be justified by quoting examples. Thus, although all the council house allocation systems were different, and produced different priority orderings, there was a general consensus on the purpose of council housing, who should be eligible for a tenancy, and the elements to be taken into account in considering and defining housing need. Equally, although specific requirements for council loans, the amount advanced or the length of the repayment period varied, the same groups of potential borrowers were considered, and the same general function was perceived for council lending. The exception to prove this particular rule may be found in the approaches to the sale of council houses. Here, as usual, the details differed, but the fundamentals varied too. A basic yes/no decision divided the surveyed local authorities.

Within the particular policy fields examined, then, the present system of discretion and guidance appears to produce consensus regarding the general orientation of policies. The system does not produce local uniformity, and on issues of considerable political or ideological impact, even strong exhortations from central government can go unheeded. Perhaps the true significance of local differences can be seen by comparing performance rather than policies. This is done in the following two chapters.

3. Local Authority Housing Performance

INTRODUCTION

For the purposes of this research, local authority housing performance has been defined in simple terms. The measures are, for example, who is applying for a council house, and who is being allocated one; who is buying their council house; or who is using a council mortgage advance to buy a private house. There are two types of comparison which might be made using such information—comparisons between local authorities over a particular policy field, and comparisons of the groups of households helped by a particular local authority through its various policies. For convenience, the two types have been separated, and this chapter deals with between-authority comparisons.

Housing policies have been found to vary in detail between the surveyed authorities. To return to the research questions posed in the Introduction: 'to what extent do apparently different policies produce different end results, or apparently similar policies produce similar end results?' The different fields of housing policy are taken in the same order as followed in the previous chapter; that is, council house allocations, improvement grants, council mortgages and, finally, council house sales.

COUNCIL HOUSE ALLOCATIONS

The Pattern of Allocations

Council houses are allocated to applicants from the waiting list or the transfer list, to mutual exchanges, to households displaced by clearance, and to other 'special cases' which fall outside the more normal lettings group. Table 3.1 shows how total lettings made during the year 1972-3 were divided between these groups in the surveyed authorities. The table also shows the proportion of all lettings made to new council tenants which went to waiting list applicants, and the ratio between 'new' lettings and those made to existing council tenants through transfers and exchanges.

Table 3.1. The Pattern of Allocations, all Authorities: 1972-3

Group:	West Bromwich	Warley	Wolverhampton	Halesowen	Stafford	Ludlow
Sample number	510	435	679	124	190	118
	%	%	%	%	%	%
Waiting list	28	36	37	47	56	48
Transfer list	39	40	49	29	27	40
Mutual exchanges	12	6	7	7	14	11
Clearance	14	16	3	10	1	1
Other	8	2	3	6	3	—
Waiting list as % all 'new' lettings	57%	67%	84%	73%	94%	98%
Ratio of 'new' lettings to 'transfer' lettings	1:1·03	1:0·87	1:1·27	1:0·57	1:0·68	1:1·03

Source: Local authority records.

There are two points of difference between authorities of particular interest here. The first is the differing significance of clearance rehousing. Clearance needs were given priority in the lettings policies of all the authorities, yet they account for a tenth or more of allocations in three areas only. In West Bromwich, clearance rehousing could, in theory, take up to 90% of vacancies, but in fact accounted for only 14% of all lettings, and for 27% of all 'new' lettings. Here and elsewhere it seems the absolute priority given to clearance needs reflects the historical rather than the present situation, in which slum clearance programmes are greatly reduced. This means, of course, that waiting list applicants can be rehoused in considerable numbers. The distinction between 'new' lettings and all lettings leads us to the second point. Total allocations are inflated in some authorities by a very well-developed transfer system. That transfers can have a multiplier effect on lettings is obvious. If 100 vacancies occurring in the housing stock were all let to waiting list applicants, only 100 lettings would be made in all. If, however, all those 100 vacancies were let first to transfer applicants, and the houses which they in turn vacated were let to the waiting list applicants, there would be 200 lettings made. Clearly this could be extended almost indefinitely, with considerable chains of movement growing in the council house sector before a vacancy was offered to a 'new' tenant from the list. The authorities surveyed avoid either theoretical extreme (nought or near infinity), but still show considerable differences; ranging from Halesowen, with a relatively small multiplier effect, to Wolverhampton, where each naturally occurring vacancy in effect generates a further 1·25 vacancies. These differences cannot be linked directly to explicit allocation policies. Again, transfers were given some degree of priority in lettings in all authorities, yet the observed variations still arise. It is also interesting that size of authority seems to have little influence, since Ludlow *and* two of the larger county boroughs have high transfer ratios. Later in this chapter reference will be made to relative strength of demand for transfers in the different authorities which may, of course, influence the number of transfers allowed. Here it is sufficient to add that, since discretion was so often claimed as the basis for all transfer allocations, this, and the beliefs of the individual officers concerned, might be important in determining the importance of transfers among all allocations.

The underlying pattern of allocations described sets a framework within which waiting list and transfer lettings can be examined in greater detail. Mutual exchanges, clearance rehousing and special cases are not discussed here because sample numbers are rarely adequate for full analysis in all authorities. Such details as are available on these minority groups are presented in the case study chapters of the report (Chapters 6 to 11).

The Waiting List and Allocations

As explained in the previous chapter, waiting list allocation policies operate at two levels. First they determine who shall be eligible for consideration for a council house, and secondly they determine the order of priority among those eligible. The first effect might be expected to show in the composition of the waiting list, and the second in the pattern of allocations made from those eligible.

The waiting lists vary greatly in length between the surveyed local authorities; from over 6000 in Wolverhampton, to just over 400 in Ludlow. Since the authorities also vary greatly in size this is not surprising. If, however, the number on the list is expressed per thousand of the enumerated population in 1971 for each authority, the variation is much reduced. The figures now range from 27 per 1000 in West Bromwich to 18 per 1000 in Ludlow. (Note that the waiting list figures relate to applicants and not to total persons on the list, so the ratio is not a true one in population terms). These figures have been calculated from the total waiting lists, and thus include all registered applicants. However, in West Bromwich, Warley and Wolverhampton separate 'live lists' are maintained, which include all those eligible for consideration for a council tenancy. The live list in these authorities is considerably shorter than the total list. In terms of those eligible for consideration these three authorities have the shortest lists relative to the total population size. (Table 3.2.)

Table 3.2. Relative Length of Waiting List, all Authorities: 1973

Authority:	Total list per 1000 population	Live list per 1000 population
West Bromwich	27	9
Warley	25	6
Wolverhampton	23	17
Halesowen	21	21
Stafford	25	25
Ludlow	18	18

Source: Local authority records and 1971 census.

The effects of the relative strictness of eligibility requirements on the length of the waiting list can be shown. The degree of association between length of list and various other variables has been measured using the Spearman rank co-efficient of correlation. Table 3.3 shows the five variables most strongly correlated with the length of the total waiting list and with the length of the live waiting list only. (A full list of the variables used in the analysis and an outline of the method is given in Appendix V). The higher the correlation co-efficient, the stronger is the relationship indicated. A minus figure indicates an inverse relationship.

Table 3.3. Factors Associated with Length of Waiting List, all Authorities: 1973

Total list		Live list	
Variable:	Co-efficient of correlation	Variable:	Co-efficient of correlation
Proportion of council houses in total stock 1971	+ ·743	Growth in total population 1961–71	+ ·914★
Growth in total population 1961–71	— ·657	Restrictiveness of eligibility rules	— ·829★
Average house price 1973	— ·571	Average house price 1973	+ ·771
Total population 1971	+ ·571	Council house completions 1968–72	— ·771
Proportion of allocations going to clearance rehousing 1972–73	+ ·543	Proportion of council houses in total stock 1971	—·600

★Significant at the 5% level of significance.

Relatively unrestricted demand for a council house, as shown by the total waiting list is mainly associated with the size of the public sector in the housing stock of the local authority concerned. While no causal relationship is inferred by the method, in this case it may be reasonable to assume some such relationship is present. Some of the other results are more surprising, since a long list is associated with slow population growth or population decline, and low average house prices. Other variables which might be expected to have some effect— the number of young people or elderly households in the population, and the number of households lacking standard amenities—fail to show strong relationships with the length of waiting list. The relative restrictiveness of eligibility rules (scaled subjectivity from Table 2.1—see Appendix V) has a striking effect when live lists only are considered. This is shown both by the appearance of the factor as an important variable in its own right, and by great differences between the findings for all lists and live lists in Table 3.3.

Restrictions on access to the list operate mainly through some form of residential qualification and tenure. The effect of the first cannot be checked through the information available here. Tenure can be examined. In none of the authorities are more than 3% of all owner-occupiers (from 1971 Census figures) on the waiting list. In those authorities where a live list is maintained, the proportion reduces when the live list is considered, but total numbers involved are so small as to make analysis difficult. The impact of eligibility restriction on private tenant households is easier to check. Again the restrictions particularly affect the composition of the live list of applicants eligible for active consideration for a tenancy. In West Bromwich, for example, about 50% of all private tenant households are registered on the waiting list, but only 5% are on the live list. The comparable figures for *all* households on the waiting list and the live list are 11% and 3% respectively. Tenants are those particularly subject to exclusion from consideration for a tenancy. (Of course, the proportion of tenants on the dormant list can be expected to increase with greater restrictions on access to the live list, since a backlog of applications will build up over time).

The combination of the basic demographic structure, household aspirations and desires, and eligibility regulations as they are perceived, and as they operate, produces in each local authority a unique waiting list structure. This structure can be expressed in terms of household type and different elements of housing need. These are shown in Tables 3.4 and 3.5. The main figures in these tables relate to all waiting lists, those in brackets under West Bromwich, Warley and Wolverhampton, to the live lists only.

Table 3.4. Household Type—Waiting List, all Authorities: 1973

Household type:	West Bromwich	Warley	Wolverhampton	Halesowen	Stafford	Ludlow
Sample number	592 (153)	412 (102)	630 (448)	114	164	207
	%	%	%	%	%	%
Single person	7 (7)	8 (10)	16 (19)	8	9	8
Small adult	27 (30)	26 (31)	24 (23)	42	24	15
Small family	33 (36)	28 (17)	24 (23)	28	31	27
Large family	9 (15)	10 (12)	7 (7)	4	12	4
Large adult	13 (3)	10 (4)	8 (6)	7	5	6
Small elderly	13 (9)	18 (27)	20 (22)	11	20	40

Source: Local authority records.

Table 3.5. Indices of Housing Need—Waiting List, all Authorities: 1973

% of sample who are:	West Bromwich	Warley	Wolverhampton	Halesowen	Stafford	Ludlow
Lodging with family	40 (63)	25 (17)	26 (31)	54	19	16
Lodging, other	10 (20)	8 (12)	16 (20)	4	9	2
Without own living room	41 (70)	26 (38)	44 (53)	49	31	20
Sharing with 5 or more persons	7 (18)	4 (8)	10 (13)	3	3	1
Living at a density of more than 2 persons per bedroom	22 (42)	14 (16)	18 (22)	17	17	12
Living at a density of 0·3 persons per bedroom or less	2 (2)	6 (13)	6 (8)	3	5	10
Claiming medical priority	9 (13)	4 (5)	15 (19)	2	7	30
Lone parent families	10 (14)	11 (10)	12 (11)	7	8	6

Source: Local authority records.

Allocations are made from amongst those registered on the waiting lists. It is on these lists, then, that the second set of selection policies—those which decide priorities—operate. Structures of allocations, directly comparable to those of the lists presented above are found in Tables 3.6 and 3.7.

Table 3.6. Household Type—Waiting List Allocations, all Authorities: 1972-73

Household type:	West Bromwich	Warley	Wolverhampton	Halesowen	Stafford	Ludlow
Sample number	166	138	230	58	101	57
	%	%	%	%	%	%
Single person	3	8	6	16	9	4
Small adult	19	28	15	38	19	11
Small family	56	38	58	19	39	32
Large family	10	13	7	2	14	9
Large adult	6	7	4	3	5	2
Small elderly	7	7	10	22	15	44

Source: Local authority records.

Table 3.7.   Indices of Housing Need—Waiting List Allocations, all Authorities: 1972-73

% of sample who are:	West Bromwich	Warley	Wolverhampton	Halesowen	Stafford	Ludlow
Lodging with family	66	59	51	55	28	33
Lodging—other	11	14	18	9	14	4
Without own living room	73	62	73	64	40	39
Sharing with 5 or more persons	20	17	15	12	7	7
Living at a density of more than 2 persons per bedroom	53	36	52	31	25	28
Living at a density of 0·3 persons per bedroom or less	2	1	2	7	7	2
Claiming medical priority	13	1	22	16	5	40
Lone parent families	9	17	12	3	17	16
On list before 1971	33	17	17	14	23	28

Source: Local authority records.

Although the correspondence between the waiting list and allocations structures in each authority is not exact, there are clear relationships. For example, small adult households are the largest single group both on the list and among allocations in Halesowen. Similarly, small elderly households are most numerous in Ludlow. In fact, chi-square analysis shows that, for most authorities, there is a greater similarity between the household type structures of their own waiting list and allocations, than between their allocation structure and the allocation structures of the other authorities.[1] Wolverhampton is the exception to this generalisation, for here list and allocations are very different. Allocations, then, to some extent reflect the nature of the waiting list in each authority. There are differences, however, which must be explained.

The effect of lettings policies at this stage can be checked by comparing those on the list with those allocated a tenancy in each authority—a measure of the selectivity of allocations. Throughout the analyses which follow comparisons are made between those on the waiting list in 1973, and those allocated a house from the waiting list during the survey year 1972–73. Clearly this is not an ideal form of comparison, but details of the waiting lists from which the allocations were actually made are not available. The analysis in this form assumes that new registrations have been similar to those made in the past, or at least, when

[1] See Appendix V for details of the analysis.

authorities are being compared, that any changes in the nature of recent applicants will have been similar in all authorities. This underlying assumption must be borne in mind when reading the following paragraphs.

It is, perhaps, appropriate at the outset to illustrate the effects a selective allocation policy can have. This is done by means of an example in Table 3.8. Suppose that, in year 1, the waiting list of 100 applicants is evenly divided between four different household groups: A, B, C and D. It is assumed that 20 households a year are allocated a dwelling, and, in accordance with lettings priorities, these are divided as shown in column 2—that is with category B being particularly favoured. Each year there are 20 new applications registered, falling into household groups in similar proportions to the original waiting list—i.e. evenly divided. Table 3.8 shows the structure of the waiting list after 5 years of the operation of such a lettings policy. Groups B and D have been favoured and show smaller proportions than at the beginning of the period, while a backlog of applicants in groups A and C has built up. The one set of figures decreases as the other increases. This makes the difference between list (column 4) and allocation structures (column 2) the more extreme.

Table 3.8. An Example of the Effects of Selectivity

Household group:	(1) Initial list Year 1	(2) Allocations p.a.	(3) New registrations p.a.	(4) List Year 5
Sample number	100	20	20	100
	%	%	%	%
A	25	10	25	37
B	25	40	25	13
C	25	20	25	29
D	25	30	25	21

An idea of the degree of selectivity in the lettings process, or the difference between the structure of allocations and waiting list, is given by the number of standard errors by which any two figures are separated.[1] For example, in Table 3.8, the standard error for group B, comparing allocations and list in Year 5, is 11·4. Since the difference between the percentages is 27, there are more than 2 standard errors between the figures. This measure of selectivity is shown in Table 3.9 for various indices of housing need in the surveyed authorities. A distinction is made only between cases where there is less than one standard error difference, where there is one SE, and where there are 2 or more SEs difference.

The figures which were compared to produce Table 3.9 were those for all waiting lists and allocations. Thus, in every authority, allocations are selective of the majority of the need categories. The indices of need apparently most favoured by the allocation procedure are overcrowding (over 2 persons per bedroom) and lack of a separate living room—usually associated with living in

[1] See Appendix V for more detailed account of the method.

Table 3.9.   Selectivity of Need Items—Waiting List and Allocation, all Authorities

Need item:	West Bromwich	Warley	Wolverhampton	Halesowen	Stafford	Ludlow
Lodging with family	2SE	2SE	2SE	—	1SE	2SE
Lodging—other	—	1SE	—	1SE	2SE	—
Without own living room	2SE	2SE	2SE	1SE	1SE	2SE
Sharing with 5 or more persons	2SE	2SE	1SE	2SE	1SE	1SE
Living at a density of more than 2 persons per bedroom	2SE	2SE	2SE	2SE	1SE	2SE
Living at a density of 0·3 persons per bedroom or less	—	—	—	1SE	—	—
Claiming medical priority	1SE	—	2SE	2SE	—	1SE
Lone parent families	—	1SE	—	—	2SE	2SE
Children aged 5 or under	2SE	2SE	2SE	—	1SE	1SE
Applicants aged over 70	—	—	—	2SE	—	—

lodgings of some form. This applies to all authorities regardless of allocation procedure.

Table 3.10 shows exactly the same selectivity measurement calculated on the basis of the live waiting list only, and allocations. Of course, the figures for Halesowen, Stafford and Ludlow are exactly the same since no separate live list is maintained.

Something quite surprising emerges from a closer examination of Tables 3.9 and 3.10. West Bromwich operates a fairly sophisticated points scheme for determining priorities between those registered on the live list. However, Table 3.9 shows that the majority of selectivity occurs not at this stage, but when access to the live list is decided. There are considerable differences between the structure of the total waiting list and allocations, but relatively few differences between the structures of live list and allocations. The points system has apparently little effect. In contrast, Warley, which operates a *date order* allocation scheme, achieves almost all its selectivity at the allocation stage, and comparatively little by the determination of access to the live list.

This extreme example reinforces the more general conclusion from Table 3.9 that the formal allocation policy has little effect on the degree of selectivity of the allocation process. Some other powerful force must be at work which can make a date order allocation scheme as selective as a points order scheme designed specifi-

Table 3.10. Selectivity of Need Items—Live Waiting Lists and Allocations, all Authorities

Need item:	West Bromwich	Warley	Wolverhampton	Halesowen	Stafford	Ludlow
Lodging with family	—	2SE	2SE	—	1SE	2SE
Lodging—other	—	—	—	1SE	2SE	—
Without own living room	—	2SE	2SE	1SE	1SE	2SE
Sharing with 5 or more persons	—	2SE	—	2SE	1SE	1SE
Living at a density of more than 2 persons per bedroom	1SE	2SE	2SE	2SE	1SE	2SE
Living at a density of 0·3 persons per bedroom or less	—	—	—	1SE	—	—
Claiming medical priority	—	—	—	2SE	—	1SE
Lone parent families	—	1SE	—	—	2SE	2SE
Children aged 5 or under	2SE	2SE	2SE	—	1SE	1SE
Applicants aged over 70	—	—	—	2SE	—	—

cally to favour just such items of housing need as have been included in this analysis.

Before moving on, it is relevant to note that a date order allocation system may result in a shorter wait for some at least of the successful applicants. Table 3.7 showed that only 14% of those allocated a tenancy in Halesowen during the survey year had registered their application before 1971. The comparable figure for Warley, the other date order authority, was 17%. Only Wolverhampton of the authorities operating a points scheme achieved a similarly low figure (17% again), and the West Bromwich proportion was 33%. This does not, however, reflect the length of time any applicant may expect to wait for a tenancy offer. In fact, the evidence suggests that, while many allocations are made to relatively recent applicants, a backlog of long-standing applicants is collecting on both the live list, and particularly (of course) on dormant lists where these exist.[1] This, surprisingly, seems to be true particularly of authorities operating date order schemes.

Although none of the allocation systems in the surveyed authorities seem specifically designed to favour one type of household relative to another,[2] in fact

[1] See the Tables *Indices of Housing Need—Waiting List* in the case study chapters.

[2] An exception to this is found in West Bromwich, where points are given for family size.

such differences do occur. This can be shown by calculating the number of allocations made to a particular household group in relation to the number of applicants in that group on the waiting list. Table 3.11 show the 'queues' for different household type groups in each authority. The queue is calculated as follows. Suppose there were 100 small family households on the waiting list in authority A, and 40 allocations in A were made to small family households during the survey year. In this case the queue for small family households in A would be 2·5. Thus a small number in Table 3.11 indicates a short queue, and a relatively favourable situation for that household type group in that local authority. The main figures in the table relate allocations to all waiting lists; those in brackets for West Bromwich, Warley and Wolverhampton relate allocations to numbers on the live lists only.

Table 3.11. Waiting List Queue Lengths—Household Type, all Authorities

Household type:	West Bromwich Queue	Warley Queue	Wolverhampton Queue	Halesowen Queue	Stafford Queue	Ludlow Queue
Single person	28·0 (4·4)	6·0 (1·8)	16·5 (14·0)	2·5	3·5	16·0
Small adult	10·3 (3·0)	5·7 (1·7)	9·0 (6·2)	5·5	4·7	10·3
Small family	4·2 (1·2)	4·5 (0·7)	2·3 (1·6)	7·3	2·9	6·3
Large family	6·9 (2·9)	4·3 (1·3)	5·6 (3·8)	10·0	3·1	3·2
Large adult	15·2 (1·0)	8·9 (0·9)	12·4 (5·6)	10·0	3·6	26·0
Small elderly	11·2 (2·2)	15·0 (5·4)	10·3 (8·2)	2·5	5·0	6·6
Total	6·6 (1·8)	6·0 (1·5)	5·5 (3·9)	4·9	3·7	7·3

There are three points in particular to note from this table. First, when all lists are considered there are relatively small differences between the total queues (all household type groups) for the different authorities—Ludlow has the longest, and Stafford the shortest queues. The larger county boroughs, therefore, fall into intermediate positions. When, however, live lists are considered, the access restrictions imposed have the effect of considerably reducing the eligible queues in West Bromwich and Warley. (Note that queues calculated in this way differ from the length of list measures in Table 3.2).

Secondly, the same household type groups are favourably treated, on this measure, in most of the authorities, and for both live and total lists. In general, small and large families have short queues, while single persons and small elderly households are much less well placed.

Finally, variations between household types favoured do not seem to be related to the type of allocation procedure followed. For example, in Warley (date order), Wolverhampton (points scheme) and Stafford (Housing Manager's discretion) small and large families show shorter queues than other groups, and particularly than small elderly households. Halesowen, which like Warley, operates a date order allocation system, stands out as quite distinct from all the other authorities in favouring single person and small elderly households.

To summarize the findings so far it seems that, while lettings policies which restrict access to the waiting list have a noticeable effect on both the length of list for consideration (live list) and the characteristics of those on the live list (tenure), the policies for ordering priorities and deciding allocations from among those eligible have little value in explaining the different selectivities discovered. Certain broad similarities seem to exist between authorities regardless of letting procedures, while the markedly different situation in Halesowen cannot be accounted for simply in terms of policy adopted. In particular it seems relevant to enquire how a date order priority scheme can prove so selective of some need items. There are two factors which might account for these phenomena.

First, it is in some ways an over-simplification to compare waiting lists with allocations since there is, in fact, an intermediate stage when an offer of a tenancy is made. A local authority can merely make an offer to an applicant when their turn is reached. There is no guarantee the offer will be accepted. (Authorities can attempt to reduce the number of refusals by a policy decision that each applicant will receive only a certain number of offers. While this was avowed policy in certain of the surveyed authorities, the evidence suggests it is not always strictly applied.) The argument then runs as follows. Offers are made to applicants in accordance with the priority ordering achieved by the lettings policy. In a date order scheme offers might be expected to show a structure, in terms of housing need measures, similar to that of the live waiting list as a whole. Applicants in less housing need (as they themselves perceive it) might then be more likely to turn down a first offer made, feeling themselves able to wait until a property more precisely to their taste is offered. Applicants in extreme housing need would accept the first offer made, being desperate for any improvement of their housing conditions. Allocations thus become automatically selective of those in need, not through any policy decisions, but through the response of the applicants themselves.

This factor certainly seems to have some effect. The authorities vary widely in the number of applicants still on the live waiting list who have already received and refused at least one offer of accommodation. The figures range from 30% of all applicants in Warley, to only 5% in Stafford and Ludlow. In both Warley and Halesowen (date order allocations), applicants who had received offers included relatively small proportions of households in most of the housing need categories defined in Table 3.10. For example, while 50% of those allocated a house in Warley were lodgers with relatives, only 7% of those refusing an offer were in this category. Households in different kinds of housing need are more likely to refuse a tenancy—again in Warley, although only 1% of those allocated a house had been living at a density of less than 0·3 persons per bedroom, no less than 27% of those refusing an offer were in this group. This suggests that underoccupation is perceived as a less severe form of housing need than overcrowding, and may lend support to priority schemes which favour the latter.

A study of offers alone cannot, however, fully account for allocation selectivity in a date order scheme. In both Warley and Halesowen, while the inclusion of offers with allocations reduces the differential between 'successful' applicants and live list applicants, the successful group still includes higher proportions of those in need. Offers as well as allocations are selective of the usual items of housing need.

This leaves a second factor to be examined in an attempt to account for the basic similarities observed in the operation of different allocation systems, and the differences which occur regardless of system. It is quite obvious that offers can only be made when a vacancy arises and becomes available for letting to a waiting list applicant. (Vacancies available for the waiting list depend not only on the stock in the authority and the naturally occurring voids, but also on the transfer policy in operation. This point is discussed in a later section, and here the stock on offer to general needs applicants is taken as an externally determined factor.)

Table 3.12 shows the size of dwelling allocated to waiting list applicants in the surveyed authorities in the year 1972–73. Two features stand out. First, there is a basic similarity between the size distributions in West Bromwich, Warley, Wolverhampton and Stafford, with two-bedroomed accommodation taking the largest share. Secondly, Halesowen and Ludlow stand out with their emphasis on one-bedroomed units.

Table 3.12.   Size of Accommodation Allocated to Waiting Lists, all Authorities: 1972–73

Size:	West Bromwich	Warley	Wolverhampton	Halesowen	Stafford	Ludlow
Sample number	143	155	253	58	106	57
	%	%	%	%	%	%
1 bedroom	15	14	14	50	14	42
2 bedrooms	50	48	46	33	52	28
3 bedrooms	35	38	39	18	32	30
4 bedrooms	1	1	1	—	2	—

Source: Local authority records.

Halesowen was distinct from the other authorities in the need selectivity analysis (Table 3.10) since allocations there favoured households underoccupying their accommodation, and applicants aged over 70. It was also unique in having the shortest 'queue' for small elderly and single persons households (Table 3.11). The emphasis on one-bedroomed accommodation allocated (due to new building completions during the survey year) clearly accounts for this. In Ludlow, the waiting list includes a very high proportion of small elderly households, and the Rural District is unusual because of the composition of initial applicants (with a considerable bias in favour of the elderly: Table 3.4), rather than because of selectivity at the allocation stage.

Among the remaining authorities it is interesting to look at West Bromwich, Warley and Stafford since these operate completely different allocation systems. Not only are the size distributions in Table 3.12 very similar, but the type of accommodation allocated is also similar. The proportion of allocations made to two-bedroomed flats or maisonettes fell between 46% and 49% in all three authorities. Now two-bedroomed flats and maisonettes are most usually offered to couples with or without small children—a typical family being husband, wife and one young child. Small families had short queues in each authority. Similarly, when a small family of this kind is found on the waiting list, they are very often living with in-laws—hence are classed as lodgers with family. Having the use of only one bedroom, the birth of the child has brought the density of occupation of their accommodation above the 2 person per bedroom level. The child is aged under 5. These are precisely the measures of housing need that all three authorities were found to favour in their lettings in Table 3.9. A chain from the type of accommodation being offered to the type of housing need being relieved can be established.

The conclusions of all this are very simple, and may be self-evident. The question of who is allocated a council house from the waiting list is not solely, or even chiefly dependent on the allocation policy in use. It is also a function of the composition of the waiting list (itself influenced by the demography of the area, the desires and aspirations of the population and the perceived chances of actually being allocated a tenancy); the pattern of refusals of offers of tenancy; and the accommodation available for allocation. Each of these factors has been shown to have an effect on the operation of lettings performance. There is, apparently, no need to have identical waiting list allocation policies to achieve similar results, nor any guarantee that uniform policies would, in practice, achieve any less diversity than is apparent at present.

The Transfer List and Allocations

Analysis of the relations between transfer policies and practice cannot be so complete as for general needs allocations. This is because, as was outlined in the previous chapter, transfer policies are generally ill-defined in the surveyed authorities. In spite of this it is still interesting to compare their performance.

Some restrictions are made on eligibility for a transfer in West Bromwich, Warley and Halesowen, where some form of need for a transfer must be proved. This does not seem to have any effect on the length of the list however—as is shown in Table 3.13. Here the length of transfer list is expressed per 1000 local authority dwellings in 1971 to give a comparable figure between authorities.

Table 3.13.   Relative Length of Transfer List, all Authorities: 1973

Authority:	Total list per 1000 council dwellings
West Bromwich	143
Warley	175
Wolverhampton	93
Halesowen	87
Stafford	59
Ludlow	93

Source: Local authority records.

A correlation analysis (similar to that done for the length of waiting list) was used to see which variables are particularly associated with the length of the transfer list. The results are presented in Table 3.14, where the five variables with the highest correlation coefficients are shown.[1]

[1] A list of all the variables used can be found in Appendix V.

Table 3.14.   Factors Associated with Length of Transfer List, all Authorities: 1973

Variable:	Rank co-efficient of correlation
Proportion of waiting list applicants allocated a flat or maisonette 1972–73	+ ·743
Proportion of small elderly households in population 1971	+ ·714
Proportion of pre-war houses in council stock 1971	+ ·714
Proportion of owner-occupied in total stock 1971	— ·657
Proportion of flats and maisonettes in council stock 1971	+ ·600

The effect that flats and maisonettes have in producing pressure for mobility is clearly seen, though it is interesting that the use to which this type of property is put has more influence than the absolute numbers involved. The size of the owner-occupied sector was included as an index of the chance a council tenant has to improve his housing situation by moving out of the council sector, rather than within it. In these local authorities at least, this factor appears to have little effect on the pressure of demand for transfer. The analysis shows there to be some association between the length of list and the proportion of all allocations which are made to transfers (correlation coefficient +·571). This could be interpreted in two ways—either the number of transfers granted reflects demand, or more tenants apply for a transfer because they see a greater chance of it being granted.

The nature of the transfer lists which result in each authority can be seen in Tables 3.15 and 3.16. The figures in all cases relate to all applicants registered on a transfer list.

Table 3.15.   Household Type—Transfer List, all Authorities: 1973

Household type:	West Bromwich	Warley	Wolverhampton	Halesowen	Stafford	Ludlow
Sample number	413	380	355	113	110	149
	%	%	%	%	%	%
Single person	4	6	3	1	2	1
Small adult	11	15	9	5	9	13
Small family	21	31	28	36	36	31
Large family	15	14	19	13	17	15
Large adult	23	10	18	23	26	15
Small elderly	26	25	24	21	11	25

Source: Local authority records.

Table 3.16. Indices of Housing Need—Transfer List, all Authorities: 1973

% of sample who are:	West Bromwich	Warley	Wolverhampton	Halesowen	Stafford	Ludlow
Living at a density of more than 2 persons per bedroom	8	7	6	11	4	5
Living at a density of 0·3 persons per bedroom or less	5	8	5	—	3	2
Claiming medical priority	22	20	10	26	11	36

Source: Local authority records.

Comparable details of transfer allocations are given in Tables 3.17 and 3.18.

Table 3.17. Household Type—Transfer Allocations, all Authorities: 1972-73

Household type:	West Bromwich	Warley	Wolverhampton	Halesowen	Stafford	Ludlow
Sample number	185	169	321	36	51	47
	%	%	%	%	%	%
Single person	1	3	3	6	4	—
Small adult	8	8	10	3	8	17
Small family	28	40	33	14	29	34
Large family	25	15	21	17	20	15
Large adult	16	14	16	8	10	15
Small elderly	21	20	17	53	29	19

Source: Local authority records.

Table 3.18. Indices of Housing Need—Transfer Allocations, all Authorities: 1972-73

% of sample who are:	West Bromwich	Warley	Wolverhampton	Halesowen	Stafford	Ludlow
Living at a density of more than 2 persons per bedroom	8	11	12	—	—	9
Living at a density of 0·3 persons per bedroom or less	9	5	5	14	14	—
Claiming medical priority	37	12	12	44	20	32
On list before 1971	43	41	24	37	36	40

Source: Local authority records.

When the household type structure of lists and allocations are considered, both visual inspection of the Tables and the evidence of chi-square tests[1] show the following:

(a) The differences between list and allocations within each authority is generally less among transfers than among waiting list applicants. (Halesowen is an exception to this rule). The pattern of transfer allocations thus more directly reflects the pattern of demand.

(b) There are greater similarities between authorities in the composition of both transfer lists and allocations than was found among general needs applicants. This suggests that certain common influences are at work in determining the composition of the list and in deciding who shall be allocated a house.

So far as the first point is concerned, it is reasonable to suppose, and the evidence supports the view, that development through the family cycle is responsible for many transfer demands. More large family, large adult and small elderly households are found on transfer lists than on waiting lists. The average age of transfer applicants is generally greater, there are more, and older, children in the families. Need for more space to accommodate a growing family, or the desire for a house rather than a flat for a home with children, and then the desire for a smaller house when the families have left, are understandable and generally occurring phenomena. It is not surprising then, that broad similarity between authorities is evident. (That these features of family growth and decline are important can be seen from the reasons given for making a transfer application, which are presented in the case study chapters).

Allocations in each authority have been found to reflect demand in terms of household type. However, if the details of selection are examined, some interesting features emerge. Table 3.19 shows the selectivity measure for housing need indices, calculated by means of the standard error technique used for waiting list applicants.

Table 3.19. Selectivity of Need Items—Transfer List and Allocations, all Authorities

Need item:	West Bromwich	Warley	Wolverhampton	Halesowen	Stafford	Ludlow
Living at a density of more than 2 persons per bedroom	—	1SE	2SE	—	—	1SE
Living at a density of 0·3 persons per bedroom or less	1SE	—	—	2SE	1SE	—
Claiming medical priority	2SE	—	—	1SE	1SE	—

[1] See Appendix V.

Unlike the waiting list analysis, which suggested that most authorities were selective of most items of need in their allocation procedures, with transfer allocations the authorities fall into two distinct groups. There are those where relief of overcrowding is the main concern—Warley, Wolverhampton and Ludlow—and those where the emphasis is on relief of underoccupation and meeting medical needs—West Bromwich, Halesowen and Stafford. This simple distinction does not, of course, mean that in Warley, for example, underoccupation is not relieved by means of transfers. It does mean that relatively more allocations were made to applicants in overcrowded circumstances and relatively fewer to applicants in underoccupied dwellings than would have been the case if all needs had been met in the proportions found on the transfer list. It is simply a question of degree and emphasis. Only in West Bromwich is this apparently the outcome of an openly stated policy, since here transfer priorities were said to be given to the relief of underoccupation. It must be pointed out that these findings relate only to the survey year—in a situation where transfer priorities depend so much on discretion, it would be perfectly reasonable to expect that the balance might change from year to year. This is one danger of a survey undertaken at a single point in time.

The number of transfer applicants on the list to each allocation made (the queue) is shown in Table 3.20 for each household type group.

Table 3.20.   Transfer List Queue Lengths—Household Type, all Authorities

Household type:	West Bromwich	Warley	Wolverhampton	Halesowen	Stafford	Ludlow
	Queue	Queue	Queue	Queue	Queue	Queue
Single person	17·0	8·9	1·6	0·5	0·8	—
Small adult	6·1	9·2	1·9	6·0	1·9	2·5
Small family	3·5	3·5	1·9	8·2	2·0	2·9
Large family	2·8	4·0	2·1	2·5	1·4	3·1
Large adult	6·7	3·2	2·4	8·7	4·2	3·1
Small elderly	5·8	5·8	3·2	1·3	0·6	4·1
Total	4·5	4·5	2·2	3·2	1·6	3·2

Overall, the length of queue is shorter for transfer than for waiting list applicants. (In West Bromwich and Warley the maintenance of a live waiting list reduces the queue of those eligible for consideration to a lower level than among transfers). Of the large authorities, Wolverhampton has a notably short total queue length which suggests that the importance given to transfers among all allocations speeds turnover among applicants (see also Table 3.18 where the small number of successful applicants who had registered before 1971 was shown).

The total variability of queue lengths for each household type group is rather less than for waiting list applicants. This suggests that a transfer applicant has a more even chance of an allocation regardless of household type.

A less consistent pattern of groups favoured by most authorities emerges than was found among waiting list cases. A pattern of a sort can be described, in which the queues for small family and large adult households are relatively short amongst the authorities favouring relief of overcrowding, while the queues for small elderly households are relatively short amongst the authorities favouring relief of underoccupation. But even this holds true only in general terms.

The distinction between authorities favouring the relief of overcrowding or of underoccupation can also be traced in the type of accommodation being allocated to transfer applicants. Table 3.21 shows the size of dwelling going to transfers in the different authorities. West Bromwich, Halesowen and Stafford have the greatest proportion of one-bedroomed units; Warley, Wolverhampton and Ludlow the larger numbers of three- and four-bedroomed dwellings.

Table 3.21. Size of Accommodation Allocated to Transfer List, all Authorities: 1972-73

Size:	West Bromwich	Warley	Wolverhampton	Halesowen	Stafford	Ludlow
Sample number	196	175	335	36	57	47
	%	%	%	%	%	%
1 bedroom	29	19	16	50	26	8
2 bedrooms	22	16	29	14	16	29
3 bedrooms	42	61	51	36	57	59
4 bedrooms or more	7	3	4	—	2	2

Source: Local authority records.

In all authorities surveyed the current transfer list represents unsatisfied demand for one-bedroomed accommodation, and to a much lesser extent, demand for four-bedroomed units. In most cases two- and three-bedroomed dwellings would be released if the transfer demands could be accommodated. It is important to remember that this refers to the net results only. Many transfer requests are for accommodation of the same size, and gross flows between different sizes are almost balanced.

The whole question of stock availability, and the use of vacancies (whether for transfer or waiting list applicants) is clearly of central importance. Lettings procedures are extremely complex. The decision to offer a property to a transfer applicant has implications for all waiting list applicants. The ramifications of any particular action are almost endless. The section which follows attempts to show some of the interrelationships which exist.

Council Stock and Turnover

The size of the council stock varies greatly between the surveyed authorities, as does its composition in terms of dwelling size and age. Table 3.22 shows this, and also includes two measures of provision relative to the population of the authorities. Rather more variation is seen in the provision of accommodation potentially suitable for the elderly than in all accommodation, and the level of provision is consistently lower (except in Halesowen). Details of the stock are, however, of much less concern than the vacancies which occur. Dwellings became available for letting through new building, through deaths, tenants moving out of the council sector, and through transfers within the council stock.

Table 3.22. Details of the Council Stock, all Authorities: 1973

Characteristics:	West Bromwich	Warley	Wolverhampton	Halesowen	Stafford	Ludlow
Sample number	30,523	24,898	39,222	5,263	5,619	1,595
	%	%	%	%	%	%
1 bedroom	16	9	15	26	10	12
2 bedrooms	26	28	27	20	22	19
3 bedrooms	56	61	54	51	65	66
4 bedrooms or more	3	2	4	3	3	4
Built before 1945	38	40	35	34	21	24
1945–1964	41	34	50	43	66	59
Built after 1964	21	26	16	23	14	17
Bungalows	2	1	1	19	3	14
Flats, maisonettes	34	32	30	28	21	9
Houses	65	66	65	53	70	73
Other (acquired)	1	*	4	1	7	3
Total households to each LA house	1·8	2·3	2·2	3·6	3·1	5·1
Small elderly households to each bungalow or 1 bed. flat	2·5	6·9	3·6	3·1	6·2	8·6

Source: I.M.T.A. *Housing Statistics (England and Wales)* 1971 and *Census 1971.*

Some new dwellings were let in the survey year in all authorities. The proportion of all lettings made to new houses was 22% in Halesowen, 18% in Warley, 15% in Wolverhampton, 10% in Ludlow, 9% in West Bromwich and 6% in Stafford. Most usually the new dwellings being provided were bungalows or flatlets for the elderly, although some houses and maisonettes were also being built.

Unfortunately, complete information is not available on the way all vacancies arise in the stock. In general terms, such evidence as there is, suggests that deaths release relatively more one-bedroomed flats and bungalows, while movement out of the council sector releases all house types, but particularly flats and maisonettes. The number of vacancies occurring through transfers is, of course, directly related to the number of transfer allocations being made (see Table 3.1). The type of property being released by transfers varies from authority to authority; for example, over 60% of the dwellings vacated by transfers in West Bromwich, Warley and Halesowen were flats and maisonettes, while the comparable figure in Ludlow was 50% and in Wolverhampton and Stafford 39%. This apparently reflects the policies adopted towards allocation in general.

Vacancies arising from all these causes produce the turnover figures shown in Table 3.23. Turnover in this sense is measured by expressing the allocations made in the survey year as a percentage of the 1971 total stock in that house type/size category. The very high figures for bungalows in some cases are due to new building rather than excessive relets. The total turnover figure at the bottom of the table excludes new building, but includes mutual exchanges.

Table 3.23.   Turnover Rates by House Type, all Authorities: 1972-73

House type:	West Bromwich Index	Warley Index	Wolverhampton Index	Halesowen Index	Stafford Index	Ludlow Index
Bungalow	38*	15*	11	26*	8	9
1 bed. flat	9	17	9	19	22	15
2 bed. flat, maisonette	13	12	16	23	35	22
2 bed. house	8	5	7	4	13	11
3 bed. flat, maisonette	21	14	37*	14	80	40
3 bed. house	5	6	6	14	9	5
4 bed. house	10	9	8	—	7	2
Total (excluding new)	8	7	7	7	13	7

*Particularly inflated by new building.

Source: Local authority records and I.M.T.A. *Housing Statistics (England and Wales) 1971.*

Several features of this table are worthy of notice. First, in all authorities the turnover rate among flats and maisonettes is higher than among houses of comparable size. As was said earlier, this seems to be the result of above average movement from this dwelling type both to the private sector and to other council houses through transfers. This could be either because of the inherent characteristics of the house type (unsuitability for children), or because of the use made of them in the allocation process (young families tend to be more mobile than older). In fact it is likely that both factors are involved.

The second point is the apparently similar turnover rates found in all authorities except Stafford. This is particularly interesting because the *total* turnover is the result of naturally occurring voids *and* transfer vacancies. The authorities varied considerably in the number of transfers granted as a proportion of all allocations (Table 3.1). In Wolverhampton, West Bromwich and Ludlow where the transfer systems are relatively well-developed, turnover due to other relets must be correspondingly much lower. In Halesowen, and particularly in Stafford, other relets are relatively higher. It is not clear if the similarity apparent (again excluding Stafford) occurs by chance, or if there is some feeling that a certain level of turnover in any year is 'about right' in terms of estate disruption or administrative procedures.

The type of property being allocated to waiting list and transfer applicants is different, as can be seen in Tables 3.24 and 3.25. Regardless of the precise nature of the stock available, in every authority many more houses and bungalows are allocated to transfers, and relatively more flats and maisonettes to waiting list applicants. This is true whether the authorities were found to favour relief of overcrowding or underoccupation in the transfer allocations, and whatever the stated policy of priorities between transfer and waiting list allocations.

Table 3.24. Type of House Allocated to Waiting List Applicants, all authorities: 1972-73

House type:	West Bromwich	Warley	Wolverhampton	Halesowen	Stafford	Ludlow
Sample number	179	155	253	58	106	57
	%	%	%	%	%	%
Bungalow	2	—	*	22	—	28
1 bed. flat	13	14	14	28	14	14
2 bed. flat, maisonette	49	46	30	33	47	19
2 bed. house	1	2	16	—	5	9
3 bed. flat, maisonette	19	25	19	16	1	5
3 bed. house	16	13	20	2	31	25
4 bed. house	1	1	1	—	2	—

Source: Local authority records.

Table 3.25. Type of House Allocated to Transfer Applicants, all Authorities: 1972-73

	West Bromwich	Warley	Wolverhampton	Halesowen	Stafford	Ludlow
Sample number	196	175	335	36	51	47
	%	%	%	%	%	%
Bungalow	12	3	2	44	6	6
1 bed. flat	17	16	14	6	20	2
2 bed. flat, maisonette	7	10	22	6	6	6
2 bed. house	15	6	7	8	10	23
3 bed. flat, maisonette	2	1	13	14	2	8
3 bed. house	41	60	38	22	55	51
4 bed. house	7	3	4	—	2	2

Source: Local authority records.

Rather than attempting to disentangle all the strands of policy and procedure which lie behind these findings, two points only will be discussed. First, it is important to remember that the pattern of transfers, in part at least, determines which waiting list applicants will be housed. It is possible to design all sorts of imaginary transfer systems which would relieve overcrowding or underoccupation; or reflect equally all needs; or any combination of policies required.

The results of these 'doodlings' may be useful in emphasising the importance of the pattern of transfers in the whole allocation process. Table 3.26 shows one such example. One hundred initial vacancies are assumed to arise, distributed between house sizes as shown in the first column. In every case half these vacancies are allocated to transfers leaving half free for direct allocation to general needs applicants (only the two groups are considered). Just which houses will be allocated to transfers depends on the policy followed. In case A, transfers are primarily aimed at the relief of underoccupation; case B aims at relief of overcrowding; and case C, a little of both. The final columns headed A, B and C show the distribution of resulting vacancies which would be available for offer to waiting list applicants as a result of each transfer policy. Considerable variations have resulted, yet the example is immeasurably simpler than the real-life situations where whole chains of transfer allocations occur.

Table 3.26. An Example of the Effects of Transfer Policies

Dwelling size:	Initial vacancies	Resulting vacancies		
		A	B	C
Sample number	100	100	100	100
	%	%	%	%
1 bedroom	20	9	33	12
2 bedrooms	30	40	52	61
3 bedrooms	50	51	15	27

In reality, an emphasis on two-bedroomed accommodation on offer to waiting list applicants was revealed in Table 3.12, reminiscent of the results of policy C (which aimed at the relief of both overcrowding and underoccupation). In the majority of the local authorities, relatively more of the vacancies occurring in one- and three-bedroomed accommodation are allocated to transfer applicants, and relatively more of the two-bedroomed voids to waiting list applicants. This is true regardless of the apparent selectivity of transfer allocations shown in Table 3.19. (Ludlow is an exception since very few of the one-bedroomed vacancies go to transfers; here the emphasis on relief of overcrowding is clear from this evidence as well.) The surveyed authorities seem to operate well balanced transfer allocations, with only slight variations in emphasis.

The second point is that once a certain pattern of waiting list and transfer allocations has become established, it will be difficult to change. The most usual pattern observed is as follows: (the starting point is chosen for convenience and is not especially significant—the process is a cycle). Two- and three-bedroomed flats and maisonettes are allocated to young families from the waiting list. The family size increases as more children are born, until the accommodation is seen as too small, or of unsuitable type. A transfer application is made for a three- (or two-) bedroomed house. When a three-bedroomed house becomes vacant, it is let to the family. The flat left empty is not attractive for transfer applicants, so it must be let again to the waiting list—only to perpetuate the cycle. There are two critical policy decisions which ensure the process will be repeated; that young families are allocated flats, and that houses are offered to the transfer list. These are common to all the authorities, and it is easy to see why. If houses were to be offered directly to waiting list applicants and since only so many vacancies occur among houses, a backlog of frustrated demand from unsuitably housed transfer applicants would build up. Any change in the pattern could only be achieved gradually by offering the vacancies in flats and maisonettes which occur through moves into the private sector to applicants who are without children and who are likely to remain without children. However, by implication, any break in the cycle which has the effect of reducing mobility, will reduce the total number of waiting list applicants who can be rehoused in a given period. At present, turnover rates in houses are relatively low, and the volume of vacancies would be reduced overall. It is arguable that the move to a flat constitutes an improvement in living conditions for the waiting list applicant which it is not justifiable to delay. Whether the present situation arises through a conscious recognition of this argument, or simply because it is the way the system works, is by no means clear.

The second major type of transfer movement may have provided the vacancy in the three-bedroomed house postulated in the ideal cycle. This is the move at the later stage in the family cycle when the home becomes too big and a move to a smaller house is requested. A typical chain of transfers could be imagined set off by the building of an old person's bungalow: Bungalow—four-bedroomed house—two-bedroomed house—two-bedroomed maisonette; or bungalow—three-bedroomed house—three-bedroomed house—two-bedroomed maisonette. In each case the intermediate stages are by transfer, in the first case to relieve overcrowding, and in the second simply to change area. In both cases the end result is a maisonette for offer to a waiting list applicant.

Council House Allocations—General

Allocation procedures are complicated. All the different strands interrelate, and any action has a whole chain of implications and reactions. Apart from the rules concerning waiting list applicants, policies cannot be tested since they are not closely defined. It is never clear if the end result observed is the result of conscious intent, or a relatively chance outcome of a series of individual ad hoc decisions.

These are the main conclusions of this section. Where possible performance has been checked against known policies. Sometimes the policy is seen to have a predictable effect, sometimes it does not. Basic similarities between local authorities have been discussed which cannot be accounted for by detailed policies. Equally, differences occur which are due to demographic factors, pressures on the housing market and the basic nature of the local authority stock, which again override detailed policies. Similarity or difference of detailed policies by no means guarantee similarity or difference in performance.

But perhaps this should not come as a great surprise. The fundamentals of the policy approaches to council housing policy were found to be similar in all the surveyed authorities. The same concepts of housing 'need' were adopted, and the operational definitions of 'need' were similar. This means, in practice, that households of similar type, and living in similar housing conditions are favoured by the allocation procedures of each authority. At some point in each allocation system a filter is applied which distinguishes applicants with 'legitimate' needs from those whom the council have decided they cannot help. In the date order schemes examined, this filtering is achieved by the rules which govern access to the live list. In authorities operating a points scheme, the filter can be found either in rules for access to the list, or in the priorities set by the weightings within the points scheme itself. (In terms of eventual outcome, an ineligible applicant fares very much the same as one with a very low priority claim.)

Provided this basic filter is designed to select households showing similar sorts of housing need (as was the case in the surveyed authorities), the detail of the priority schemes seem relatively unimportant. This, of course, implies that any attempt to change a priority system, or to affect its outcome, must be concerned with the underlying philosophy and intentions of the scheme as well as with details of points or procedures.

So far the analysis of performance in the allocation of council housing has been satisfactory, in that the broad intentions of the authorities, as embodied in their policies, are being fulfilled. However, the survey material also suggests that the satisfactory outcome may not be due entirely, or explicitly, to the policies operated. The decision, common to all the authorities studied, to give priority to transfer applicants in the allocation of houses has a tremendous effect, and this decision apparently influences the type of waiting list applicant who will be housed by determining the type of property available for letting to 'new' tenants. This research has not been able to show if the authorities concerned are fully aware of this interrelationship; if they are consciously using the transfer system to create the vacancies required to accommodate 'priority' applicants from the waiting list more quickly; or if this is simply the outcome of the working of an established system triggered by previous allocation policies and transfer demands, and thus divorced from policy intentions. In any case the moral is clear. Separate parts of the allocation system cannot be seen in isolation; change in one part will have repercussions elsewhere; and attempts to influence priorities must take account of this. For example, a decision to give greater priority to single person households on the waiting list could not be made effective simply by giving the group more points. Complementary changes in the new building programme, occupancy regulations and the transfer system might all be necessary before the group can benefit as intended.

Many of the questions relating to allocation policies and performance remain open. It is always dangerous to interpret a pattern by looking back at past events, particularly when a single year is taken to establish this pattern. There seems to be a particularly fruitful line for research in looking at decisions as they are made, and at change as it occurs. Only in this way will observed patterns really be understood and interpreted.

IMPROVEMENT GRANTS

Improvement Grants and Type of Work

Both discretionary and standard improvement grants are given to owners of private houses in all the surveyed local authorities, though the proportion in each category varies quite considerably. The number of grants being given each year has increased during the period 1970 to 1972 after the passing of the Housing Act 1969 which introduced the present improvement grant code. The share of discretionary grants has also grown. Again the rates of growth differ between the authorities. All this is shown in Table 3.27.

Table 3.27. Number and Type of Grants Given, all Authorities: 1970–72

Authority:	Total grants 1970–72	Proportion of which were discretionary 1970–72	1972 only	Grants 1972 as % grants 1970
	Number	%	%	%
West Bromwich	877	29	85	289
Warley	1173	43	65	162
Wolverhampton	960	82	91	337
Halesowen	244	61	78	305
Stafford	189	27	47	134
Ludlow	387	69	78	142

Source: *Local Housing Statistics*. H.M.S.O. 1970–72.

The survey material is particularly useful because it allows authorities to be compared in terms of the type of work being done with the help of grants, which is not available in published statistics. The results are presented in Tables 3.28 (all grants) and 3.29 (discretionary grants only).

Table 3.28. Work Done by Improvement Grants, all Authorities: 1972–73

Work involved:	West Bromwich	Warley	Wolverhampton	Halesowen	Stafford	Ludlow
Sample number	219	190	207	104	114	165
	%	%	%	%	%	%
Installation of missing amenities	5	25	6	14	17	4
Provision of bathroom	16	24	8	14	60	33
Provision of bathroom and kitchen work	2	37	30	20	3	31
Kitchen extension	65	11	42	38	3	—
General improvement	9	—	11	11	11	14
Conversion to flats	3	3	3	4	7	10
Conversion to dwelling	—	—	—	—	—	8

Source: Local authority records.

It is interesting that in West Bromwich, Wolverhampton and Halesowen less than half of all grants (and of discretionary grants) are for work falling into the first three categories, which represent the installation of basic amenities previously missing in the dwelling. Since improvement grants are often spoken of as a valuable tool in providing amenities in older houses to complement clearance policies, this is particularly important. The extremes of the spectrum found in these authorities are represented by the neighbouring authorities of Warley, where 78% of discretionary grants are used for installing basic amenities, and West Bromwich, where 78% of discretionary grants are used for kitchen

Table 3.29. Work Done by Discretionary Grants, all Authorities: 1972–73

Work involved:	West Bromwich	Warley	Wolverhampton	Halesowen	Stafford	Ludlow
Sample number	184	118	189	81	52	126
	%	%	%	%	%	%
Installation of missing amenities	1	14	2	—	4	—
Provision of bathroom	2	4	4	7	44	17
Provision of bathroom and kitchen work	3	60	36	26	6	40
Kitchen extension	78	17	46	48	6	—
General improvement	11	—	12	14	25	19
Conversion to flats	3	4	3	5	15	13
Conversion to dwelling	—	—	—	—	—	10

Source: Local authority records.

extension work in otherwise sound houses. The authorities showing fast rates of increase in grants given in Table 3.27 are those where non-standard-amenity work is important, especially kitchen extensions.

Some more realistic measure of performance than simple grant numbers and growth rates is required. In the first column of Table 3.30, the number of improvement grants given in each authority in 1971 and 1972 is expressed as a percentage of the total number of households lacking exclusive use of one or more of the basic amenities in the 1971 Census. In the second column the number of grants is weighted to take account of the proportions which were actually for basic amenity installation. The introduction of this factor affects the picture, particularly in West Bromwich and Halesowen. Ludlow stands apart from the other authorities by its very high scoring on each measure.

Table 3.30. Relative Performance in Improvement Grants, all Authorites: 1971–72

Authority:	All grants 1971–72 as % households lacking amenities	Bathroom grants 1971–72 as % households lacking amenities
	%	%
West Bromwich	11	3
Warley	6	5
Wolverhampton	5	2
Halesowen	9	4
Stafford	7	6
Ludlow	17	12

Source: Local authority records, *Local Housing Statistics* and *Census 1971*.

In common with all the other features described so far, the authorities also show quite large differences in the average costs approved for the different types of grants and the different works involved, as can be seen in Table 3.31.

Table 3.31. Average Grant Approved, all Authorities: 1972-73

Authority:	Standard grant	Discretionary grant	All grants	For bathroom provision with or without kitchen work	For kitchen extension
	£	£	£	£	£
West Bromwich	210	670	600	420	650
Warley	178	355	288	349	230
Wolverhampton	160	420	400	531	285
Halesowen	120	555	460	715	390
Stafford	152	486	304	312	—
Ludlow	280	850	715	700	—

Source: Local authority records.

An average level of expenditure is involved in Ludlow which is appreciably higher than elsewhere. If Ludlow is not considered for the moment, there is a remarkably close association between the average amount approved for all grants and the proportion of all grants which are not used for the provision of amenities. Thus in West Bromwich, with an average grant approved of £600, 77% of all grants do not involve the simple installation of amenities. In Warley— average grant £288—only 14% of the grants are not for amenities. Another scale is established with West Bromwich and Warley at the opposite end.

West Bromwich is unique among the authorities in that expenditure approved on kitchen extension work is greater than that for bathroom provision—a feature due in part to the very small proportion of bathroom work which is helped by discretionary grants. This is not the only factor involved however. West Bromwich also seems more generous in the proportion of total estimated costs which are allowable for grant purposes. The grant approved represented over 40% of total estimated costs for kitchen extension work in 78% of cases in West Bromwich, in 49% of cases in Wolverhampton and in only 18% of cases in Warley. Variation observed in the approved costs for bathroom and amenity installation works is considerably less, though West Bromwich is still the most generous.

Property Being Improved

The information on the type of property being improved is not always complete, and Table 3.32 should be considered as generally indicative rather than accurate in detail. At this general level it is clear that the findings correspond closely to the type of work involved in the grants. Where basic amenities are important, terraced property and houses built before 1919 are found in greater numbers. Kitchen extension work is particularly associated with semi-detached houses built during the inter-war period—hence the importance of this age group in West Bromwich and Halesowen. The proportion of grants going to owner-occupiers is consistently higher in the authorities where basic amenity improvements are less important.

Table 3.32.   Property being Improved with Grants, all Authorities: 1972-73

Characteristics:	West Bromwich	Warley	Wolverhampton	Halesowen	Stafford	Ludlow
Tenure	225	139	206	104	114	164
Sample number	%	%	%	%	%	%
Owner-occupied	90	64	70	75	60	38
Private rented	10	23	23	25	29	15
Other, Vacant	—	13	8	—	11	47
House type						
Sample number	—	74	179	55	73	154
	%	%	%	%	%	%
Terraced	—	70	40	42	80	21
Semi-detached	—	26	60	42	11	12
Other	—	4	—	16	9	68
Age of property						
Sample number						
(discretionary)	165	71	53	70	39	96
	%	%	%	%	%	%
Before 1919	20	62	61	40	77	90
1919–44	75	37	37	56	23	5
1945 onwards	4	—	2	4	—	5

Source: Local authority records.

The question of improvement and tenure merits closer attention since the Census shows that the worst problems of lack of amenities are to be found among private renting households and research repeatedly shows that private landlords are less likely to make improvements than owner-occupiers. In Table 3.33 the first column shows the percentage of tenants among all private sector households; the second, the percentage of all private sector households lacking amenities in 1971 who were tenants; and the third, the percentage of all improvement grants going to private landlords. The final column shows the percentage of 'bathroom' grants going to private landlords. The best comparison of performance can be got from looking at columns (2) and (4) since these relate specifically to the lack of amenities and standard amenity grants.

Table 3.33.   Private Landlords and Improvement Grants, all Authorities

Authority:	(1) % of private sector households who are tenants 1971	(2) % of private sector households who lack amenities who are tenants 1971	(3) % of all grants going to landlords	(4) % of all bathroom grants going to landlords
West Bromwich	21	58	10	27
Warley	29	54	23	33
Wolverhampton	25	61	23	37
Halesowen	13	53	25	43
Stafford	25	64	29	28
Ludlow	35	57	15	22

Source: Local authority records and *Census 1971*.

In each local authority, private landlords are failing to make use of improvement grants even at a rate which would take account of their share of the problem of lack of amenities. Of course, even a *pro-rata* share of grants would not be sufficient to improve conditions in rented property relative to owner-occupied, but at present the gap must be progressively widening. Of the surveyed authorities Halesowen shows the smallest gap between grants and 'need' proportions, followed by Warley and Wolverhampton. In the remaining authorities, the gap is of a size which casts serious doubts on the viability of improvement grants in tackling the problem at all.

Improvement Grants—General

In the previous chapter it was found to be difficult to describe clear policies and policy differences between the local authorities. It was suggested that, in all authorities, the implicit aims of improvement grant policies were to save houses from clearance, upgrade the stock generally, and to provide additional units of accommodation. The three strands can also be identified in practice, though with variations in relative importance. All the authorities approved grants for conversion of houses to flats. In Ludlow in particular, conversions are significant, involving not just the creation of flats from an existing dwelling, but also the conversion of other buildings to dwellings.

It is more difficult to draw the line between grants which might save houses from clearance and those designed to modernise the stock. The former are almost certain to involve the installation of standard amenities in houses built before 1919. In West Bromwich and Halesowen, relatively few grants are of this type, and the aim of upgrading inter-war houses is more satisfactorily achieved. Stafford and Warley show the opposite emphasis. In all the authorities (except Ludlow), regardless of emphasis, the contribution grants are making to the solution of problems of lack of amenities is small. Even in Stafford, where the figure is at its highest, grants for standard amenity installation given in two years, represented only 6% of households lacking amenities. At this rate of progress it will take a very long time to complete provision of even basic amenities through improvement grants alone. (It is not known of course how much improvement and installation of amenities is done *without* grant aid.) Table 3.33 showed how much slower progress is when private landlords are considered—again in all authorities.

The only clear policy difference in the nature of works allowable for grant purposes is the refusal to include kitchen extension work in Ludlow. Yet other, very considerable, differences in the type of work involved in grant applications have been shown. These could be due to differences in advice given at the stage of initial contact between prospective improver and local authority officer, and could thus be attributable to policy working at a detailed level. Equally, the differences could be the result of differences in housing stock, pressure on the housing market, information, aspirations, and not least, the established pattern of improvement grants. The knowledge that grant money is available for extending a small kitchen, and the chance to see the end result in a neighbour's house is likely to stimulate further applications. Any pattern can thus become self-reinforcing almost regardless of the policy intentions of the local authority.

The final point raised in considering policies was the impressions given on the importance of achieving high standards in improvement work. Warley and Stafford were identified as authorities where there was a realisation that insistence on the highest standards might mean no improvement, and that there might be social reasons to outweigh any purely physical approach to the standards required. Consistently these authorities have been found to be similar to each other. They have the highest proportion of standard to discretionary grants, and the smallest average expenditure per grant. They also have the highest proportion of grants for the provision of basic amenities and show favourably in the contribution grants are making to solving the overall problem of lack of amenities. Old terraced housing is benefiting most from the grant system. In all these respects West Bromwich and Halesowen are found to be at the opposite extreme.

It would be quite unjustifiable to say, on the basis of this evidence, that toleration of lower standards boosts an authority's improvement record—there are many more factors which cannot be considered here. However, the very consistency of the distinction is interesting, and perhaps does suggest that an authority's basic philosophy can have a pervasive influence in practice.

Most of these general conclusions do not apply to Ludlow. The whole orientation of the grant system here is different. Maximum grants are usual, and virtual rebuilding rather than improvement is quite common. The sheer dissimilarity with the other authorities makes useful comment difficult. The whole housing market situation in a pleasant rural district with attractive houses and cottages suitable for improvement, is quite different to that of conurbation authorities or towns such as Stafford. It is not surprising that the pattern of grants is quite different, whether policies are ostensibly similar or not.

MORTGAGE LENDING FOR PRIVATE HOUSE PURCHASE

Introduction

All the authorities surveyed make advances for the purchase of houses in the private sector. In general, however, the number of loans made in any year is small. Lending reaches the highest levels in Warley where 132 advances for house purchase were made in 1972. In West Bromwich, by contrast, only 95 loans were made between 1968 and 1973. In Stafford, 73 loans were made in 1972–73, which represents a much higher level than in Warley when considered in relation to the total housing stock of the areas, though still representing less than 1% of the owner-occupied dwellings. In all the authorities the number of loans made for the purchase of council houses has, in recent years, greatly exceeded those for private houses.

Rather than attempt to examine in detail the effect of the different lending policies set out in the previous chapter, which would be quite beyond the scope of the survey evidence, a more general approach will be adopted. All the authorities aimed in their lending policies to provide a service complementary to that offered by building societies. Do they achieve this in practice, and in what particular aspects do their loans differ from those of building societies? Are there observable differences between the authorities in these terms?

Local Authority Mortgage Advances

Table 3.34 shows a number of mortgage details for each of the local authorities and for the Nationwide Building Society (Midland Region). Average figures only are included because they have been weighted to be comparable between the authorities[1]—necessary because the advances included in some of the samples were made some years ago. Local authority and building society lending is clearly different.

Table 3.34.   Mortgage Details—Private Houses, all Authorities and Building Society

Authority:	Average Advance* £	Average deposit* £	Average advance as % average price %	Average term of loan Years
West Bromwich	2620	680	79	18
Warley	1870	470	80	13
Wolverhampton	1420	530	73	20
Halesowen	2170	700	76	20
Stafford	2270	500	82	18
Ludlow	2830	670	81	17
Building Society	4520	1290	77	23

*The figures are weighted to 1972 levels.

Source: Local authority records and Nationwide Building Society (Midland Region).

While variations occur between the authorities, their average size of advance and deposit are consistently lower than the building society figure. In terms of the proportion of purchase price which the loan represents, the building society is not much less generous than the local authorities in many cases. The average term of local authority loan is consistently less than that of the building society.

The annual repayments incurred through advances are shown in Table 3.35. The table also shows what repayments mean to the borrower in terms of the proportion of his income committed.

Local authority repayments are lower than building society repayments, and usually represent a smaller commitment in terms of the applicant's income. The local authorities themselves vary considerably when repayments are considered—ranging from Wolverhampton where very small average advances are made over relatively long repayment periods, to Ludlow where advances are higher, and the periods shorter.

[1] See Appendix III

Table 3.35. Mortgage Repayments and Income, all Authorities and Building Society

	West Bromwich	Warley	Wolverhampton	Halesowen	Stafford	Ludlow	Building Society
Average annual repayments £*	330	270	240	280	310	390	430
Repayments as % income:							
Sample number	45	85	89	61	86	72	1536
	%	%	%	%	%	%	%
Less than 10%	9	8	19	11	5	1	—
10–17%	38	54	57	54	30	27	—
18–25%	45	29	24	33	44	41	—
Over 25%	9	9	1	2	21	33	—
Average percentage	18	16	13	15	20	23	22

*The figures are weighted to 1972 levels.

Source: Local authority records and Nationwide Building Society (Midland Region).

This very brief summary of mortgage lending suggests that the local authorities do in fact differ from the building society in the type of lending undertaken; and also differ between themselves. The differences could be attributable to the type of property being lent on, or the characteristics of the borrowers.

Property Bought with Mortgage Loans

Table 3.36 shows what type of houses are being bought with local authority and building society loans.

Table 3.36. Houses Bought with Loans, all Authorities and Building Society

Characteristics:	West Bromwich	Warley	Wolverhampton	Halesowen	Stafford	Ludlow	Building Society
Average price†	£3250	£3240	£1950	£2870	£2770	£3500	£5810
Dwelling size:							
Sample number	40	84	79	66	88	61	1536
	%	%	%	%	%	%	%
1,2 bedrooms	45	46	25	38	38	41	20
3 bedrooms	53	48	70	56	61	39	70
4 bedrooms or more	2	6	5	6	1	20	9
% of dwellings:							
Terraced	65	95	61	*	85	34	18
Built before 1919	55	88	60	94	86	68	15
Rateable value £50 or less	53	80	*	*	36	75	*

*Information not available.   †The figures are weighted to 1972 levels.

Source: Local authority records and Nationwide Building Society (Midland Region)

The pattern emerges quite clearly. Relative to the building society, local authority loans are made on lower priced houses, many of which are terraced, built before 1919 and have low rateable values. The average house size is smaller as more two-bedroomed dwellings are involved and, except in Ludlow, fewer four-bedroomed. The contrast in terms of price, size, type and age between property bought with council advances and a sample of houses advertised for sale in each of the authorities is even more marked than that with the building society. (The details of comparison for each authority are found in the case study chapters.)

Variations between authorities do exist, though they are insufficient to cloud the basic distinction set out above. The higher average price in Ludlow may be associated with the relatively high proportion of four-bedroomed houses, and with the generally higher price levels found to exist in the Rural District (see Chapter 11). In West Bromwich, higher prices could be due to the slightly more recent date of building for a proportion of the sample. Average house price levels were found to be particularly low in Wolverhampton (see Chapter 8), though the lower average loan could well be due to the £5,000 valuation ceiling which will automatically cut out any higher priced property which would raise the average. On the basis of these average levels, the valuation limits set elsewhere (£12,000 in West Bromwich, £10,000 in Halesowen, and £7000 in Warley) seem adequate and even generous. Fifteen per cent of the houses bought with a council loan in Ludlow had a purchase price of over £5000. Comparable figures in Stafford, West Bromwich and Halesowen were 11%, 8% and 2% respectively. None of the houses in Warley and Wolverhampton cost over £5000. The emphasis on cheap, small, old houses is clear.

Characteristics of Borrowers

Some of the income and household characteristics of borrowers are set out in Table 3.37. Comparable information for building society borrowers is unfortunately not always available.

Again there is a fairly consistent pattern. Local authority borrowers are on average older than building society borrowers, and include a higher proportion aged over 45 years. Average borrowers' income is never so high as among the building society sample. Although comparable building society figures are not available, it is interesting to note the high average household size among borrowers. Family commitments in addition to mortgage repayments must be considerable. In every local authority, skilled manual workers make up the largest single social class group. This in part reflects the employment structure of the areas, but the emphasis is much greater among borrowers. Except in Ludlow, over two-thirds of all borrowers in each authority were classified as skilled manual or semi-skilled or unskilled workers.

The number of Asian purchasers is also significant. The proportions observed here are far in excess of numbers in the total population, which never exceeds 4%. The percentage in a particular local authority does not reflect the total number present; Halesowen is a striking example, since the borough had a total

Table 3.37. Household Characteristics of Borrowers, all Authorities and Building Society

Characteristics:	West Bromwich	Warley	Wolverhampton	Halesowen	Stafford	Ludlow	Building Society
Average age (years)	36	31	34	36	29	35	30
% borrowers aged over 45	15	11	8	12	9	10	8
Average household size	3·4	3·5	3·6	3·7	★	3·3	★
% Asians†	11	35	12	51	12	—	★
Average income £	1880	1640	1840	1860	1550	1660	1980
% skilled manual workers	61	60	41	60	53	43	★
% semi- or un-skilled workers	22	21	28	36	17	14	★

★Information not available.

†Estimated from name of applicant only in Warley, Halesowen, Stafford.

Source: Local authority records and Nationwide Building Society (Midland Region).

New Commonwealth population totalling only 1·1% of population at the Census in 1971. A council mortgage may have become the accepted path to owner-occupation for Asians here.

Average incomes in Stafford seem surprisingly low. This might be accounted for by the lower average age (since earnings often rise with age) and the number of non-manual jobs held by borrowers. At the lower levels of qualifications, non-manual posts are often less well paid than manual jobs.

Local Authority Mortgages—General

From the evidence briefly expressed above, a list of the ways in which local authority lending complements that of the building societies can be drawn up. Some of the points are inferred rather than proven.

Local authorities are more likely to lend:

(a)   For the purchase of houses built before 1919.

(b)   For the purchase of terraced houses.

(c)   For the purchase of cheap, relatively low-valued houses.

(d)   To applicants with rather lower than average incomes.

(e)   To applicants aged over 45.

(f)   To immigrant households.

(g)   To skilled manual and semi-skilled workers.

Some of these features are the natural consequence of building society policies. As described in the previous chapter, building societies are reluctant to lend on some older types of terraced property, and will make more generous provision for professional or white-collar employees with rising salary scales.

Guidance given to local authorities on the particular priority areas they should consider for lending purposes (Circular 22/71) covers categories related to applicant and property. In only two of the surveyed authorities, Halesowen and Stafford, was the lending category recorded on the application form. Table 3.38 shows which categories were used in these authorities. The overwhelming importance of 'older and smaller property' is clear. The similarity found between Halesowen and Stafford and the other authorities suggests the same categories will be important in all. The categories which are not used so much—notably help for self-build groups, larger property for conversion and persons moving to the area for employment reasons—are equally interesting, since it is apparently national policy that local authorities should lend for these purposes as well.

Table 3.38. Categories for Mortgage Lending, Halesowen and Stafford

Categories: (Circular 22/71)	Halesowen	Stafford
Sample number	58	71
	%	%
(a) Local authority tenants, those on the waiting list, etc.	5	6
(b) Homeless or those threatened with homelessness, or overcrowded	9	14
(c) Individual members of self-build groups	—	1
(d) Older, smaller houses	84	78
(e) Larger property for conversion	—	—
(f) Development or overspill area	—	—
(g) Staff urgently required	2	1

Source: Local authority records.

Property characteristics are more important than characteristics of borrowers in determining local authority lending patterns. This is suggested by Table 3.38. It is also supported by the figures in Table 3.39. Here in the first column, the average price of house bought with a council loan is expressed as a percentage of the average price of house bought with a building society loan. The second column lists precisely the same calculation for applicants' income. The difference between local authority and building society is very much greater in terms of house price than income.

The chief conclusion reached is that the bulk of local authority lending is, in fact, of a type which building societies might regard as marginal. The two services *are* complementary. A council, by acting as a lender of last resort so far as a particular type of property is concerned, may incidentally be helping purchasers who also have rather different characteristics from those of the average building society borrower. The significance of their role in keeping the property

Table 3.39.   Council and Building Society Lending—Price and Income, all Authorities

Authority:	Council average price as % building society average price	Council average income as % building society average income
West Bromwich	56	95
Warley	40	83
Wolverhampton	34	93
Halesowen	49	94
Stafford	48	78
Ludlow	60	84

Source: Local authority records and Nationwide Building Society (Midland Region).

market buoyant in areas of older housing in conjunction with other renewal policies cannot be overstated. This is a very obvious field where the comprehensive approach to housing policy and practice is essential.

COUNCIL HOUSE SALES

Introduction

Warley, Wolverhampton and Stafford no longer sell council houses, but in all cases the decision to stop selling was taken very recently. For the purposes of this section, sales which actually have taken place will be considered, whether or not the authority is still selling houses. In Ludlow, very few houses have been sold, and the Rural District is excluded from the discussion which follows. Sales in the remaining five authorities are analysed. The survey samples were drawn from houses which had been bought with a council advance. Since about 90% of all sales, on average, were financed in this way, the limitation should not prove too serious.

As in the case of private sector mortgage advances, general rather than detailed issues are examined—first the number of houses sold, their character and the broad approach to sales and pricing policies in the authorities; second a comparison of the lending policies for council house purchase; and finally the broad similarities and differences observed among the tenants who are actually buying their houses in the surveyed authorities.

Council Houses Sold and Pricing Policies

The number of houses sold varies between the authorities. Table 3.40 shows the number of sales completed by a date in early 1973. It shows what this total means in terms of the council stock, and the stock of council *houses* (as opposed to flats and maisonettes) in each authority. There is apparently little correspondence between numbers sold and the decision to discontinue sales. An overall limit to sales was set only in West Bromwich (10%) and Wolverhampton (12·5% on any estate), and in neither case has the limit been reached.

Table 3.40. Council Houses Sold by Spring 1973, all Authorities except Ludlow

Authority:	Number sold	Houses sold as % 1971 stock	Houses sold as % 1971 stock of houses
West Bromwich	1400	4	7
Warley	1500	6	9 sales discontinued
Wolverhampton	800	2	3 sales discontinued
Halesowen	300	6	11
Stafford	200	4	5 sales discontinued

Source: Local authority records.

Since turnover rates among council houses (houses as opposed to flats) were found to run at about 5% a year (Table 3.23), over a long time scale the loss of 1000 houses through sales could result in the loss of 50 vacancies a year. (This includes vacancies through transfers and exchanges). Losses of this order may seem acceptable, though the significance obviously increases with the proportion of houses lost, and thus the proportion of all potential vacancies lost.

The type of house being sold is shown in Table 3.41. The distributions in terms of size and age vary slightly between authorities, just as the character of the total stock varies. As the case study chapters show, there is considerable consistency in the pattern of houses sold—in terms of size they are very little different to the whole stock of houses in the authority, but post-war houses usually prove more popular for purchase. The houses sold are also relatively likely to be found on attractive estates—the proportions classed as attractive or very attractive among those sold are higher than the proportions found among waiting list or transfer allocations, for example.

Table 3.41. Size and Age of Council Houses Sold, all Authorities except Ludlow

Characteristics:	West Bromwich	Warley	Wolverhampton	Halesowen	Stafford
Sample number	100	65	66	71	100
	%	%	%	%	%
2 bedrooms	22	9	20	13	8
3 bedrooms	76	89	75	83	91
4 bedrooms	2	2	5	4	1
Pre-war	30	57	15	27	16
Post-war	70	43	86	73	84

Source: Local authority records.

It is interesting to see from Table 3.41 that the number of pre-war houses sold (relative to the total number of pre-war houses in the stock) increases as the proportion of the stock sold rises. Thus in Halesowen and Warley, where high proportions of all houses have been sold, the relative selectiveness of sales of post-war houses is reduced. This might suggest either that a really large number of sales can only be achieved where pre-war houses are attractive for purchase, or that the most attractive (post-war) houses are sold first, and that the proportion of less attractive (pre-war) houses rises only when the first rush of sales has been completed. Of course, general considerations of estate attractiveness and pressure on the housing market cannot be ignored in accounting for high sales. Whatever the reasons, the conclusion remains that sales are selective of the most popular elements of the local authority stock—houses as opposed to flats or maisonettes (limited by policy) and moden houses on attractive estates (the self-selection process of applicants). This increases the significance of sales beyond purely numerical consideration, and has important implications for transfer and other allocation policies in the remaining stock.

Pricing policy as suggested by the central government seems designed to make purchase attractive to tenants. In return for a 5 year pre-emption clause and limitation on sale price during that 5 year period, the purchaser may receive a 20% discount on full market valuation. Only two of the authorities surveyed adopted the straight discount arrangement in determining sale price—the others had a lower total discount (Stafford) or a discount dependent on length of tenancy. Table 3.42 shows the valuations set in the different authorities and the resulting average purchase prices when discounts are allowed.

Table 3.42. Valuation and Purchase Price—Council Houses, all Authorities except Ludlow

Valuation:	West Bromwich	Warley	Wolverhampton	Halesowen	Stafford
Sample number	49	83	66	72	100
	%	%	%	%	%
Under £3000	20	7	9	—	10
£3000–£3490	49	11	32	11	23
£3500–£3990	27	29	38	28	52
£4000–£4490	2	28	14	32	6
£4500 and over	2	25	8	28	9
Average price (1972 levels)	£2690	£2860	£2940	£3350	£2860
Discount available	£50+ 10% possible	20%	20% possible	20%	15%

Source: Local authority records.

Despite discount variations average prices are very similar. In fact the lowest price is found in West Bromwich with the least generous discount possibilities, and the highest in Halesowen, where the standard 20% discount is applied. The combination of valuation levels and discount together produce the small range in prices observed. Valuation levels seem higher in Warley and Halesowen, and significantly lower in West Bromwich. Since all valuations are by independent valuers this may not reflect council policy, but may affect the discount it is felt right to offer.

It is interesting to see that the highest valuations are found in the authorities where the greatest proportions of stock have been sold. Higher prices do not seem to discourage sales. Both Halesowen and Warley operate the straight 20% discount arrangements. The simplicity of the calculations, and the feeling that the tenant is getting a 'bargain' could explain in part the higher sales in these authorities.

Undoubtedly the tenants in each local authority *are* getting a bargain in many respects. The average price of the council houses sold in all authorities was just £300 higher than the average price of the private houses financed by council loans. On the one hand the typical dwelling is a two/three-bedroomed terraced house built before 1919 and often requiring repairs, and on the other the typical dwelling is a three-bedroomed house built since 1945 presumably well-maintained and in a good state of repair. The restrictions on resale within a 5 year period, and the necessity of living among 'council tenants' seem at least adequately compensated. While pricing policies may not be designed specifically to encourage sales, in no authority were they particularly discouraging.

Council Lending for Purchase of Council Houses

Just as prices are relatively favourable to council house as compared to private house purchasers, so lending arrangements seem more generous. Table 3.43 gives information directly comparable to that found in Table 3.34 earlier.

Table 3.43.   Mortgage Details—Council Houses, all Authorities except Ludlow

Authority:	Average advance	Average deposit	Average advance as % average price	Average term of loan
	£	£	%	Years
West Bromwich	*	*	*	22
Warley	2700	160	94	22
Wolverhampton	2620	320	89	18
Halesowen	3150	200	94	20
Stafford	2690	150	94	22

*Information not available.

Source: Local authority records.

In every case the loan represents a larger proportion of purchase price and (except in Wolverhampton) the advance is made with a longer repayment period. The council faces less possible risk in making a high percentage loan when price is less than valuation, and where they could presumably recommence letting in the case of repossession. Again a combination of circumstances creates a favourable situation for the tenant.

Mortgage repayments do however constitute a greater commitment in terms of the proportion of applicants' income involved for council house purchasers than for council mortgagors in private houses. (This is not true in Stafford where the average proportion committed is noticeably less.)

The pattern of repayments and commitments shows much less variation than was seen in respect of private house buyers in Table 3.35. In the case study chapters, it is suggested that the earnings of additional household members among

Table 3.44. Mortgage Repayments and Income—Council Houses, all Authorities except Ludlow

	West Bromwich	Warley	Wolverhampton	Halesowen	Stafford
Average annual repayments £	330	330	340	390	320
Repayment as % income					
Sample number	*	81	63	72	99
	%	%	%	%	%
Less than 10%	—	1	3	1	1
10–17%	—	52	50	27	54
18–25%	—	39	33	61	43
Over 25%	—	7	14	11	1
Average percentage	—	17	18	19	17

*Information not available.

Source: Local authority records.

council house buyers have the effect of cushioning the impact of mortgage repayments when household rather than applicants' income is considered. In this, council house buyers are again fortunate relative to the private house buyers.

In Warley, information was available which allowed the mortgage repayments incurred by purchase to be compared with the last rent payments for the council house when tenanted. In only 2% of cases were the mortgage payments the same or lower than rent. In a further 23% of cases, repayments represented between 101% and 130% of rent levels. Nearly half, 48%, had repayments between 131% and 150% of previous rent levels. Thus over a quarter, 27%, were paying more than half as much again after buying their council house. The direct comparison between rent and repayments is an over-simplification. Rates and maintenance and repair costs will increase housing expenditure above mortgage repayment levels alone. Housing costs rise as a result of purchase, but the beneficial purchase price reduces the total amount of that rise. Still, households are prepared to make extra payments, whether for the privileges of ownership, or in expectation of capital gain at some future date, or to achieve security for families or any other reason.

Households Buying Council Houses

The household characteristics of tenants buying their council houses are shown in Table 3.45 in summary form. Greater detail is presented in the case study chapters. (Chapters 6 to 11.)

The really remarkable feature of this table is the marked similarity between the local authorities which it reveals. There is a variation of only 3 years in average ages, and less than £200 between average income figures. Admittedly there is greater variation in household size figures, but even here the pattern of larger than average households is maintained.

The average age of council house buyers as a group is much higher than that of purchasers in the private sector with either a building society or a council mortgage. Presumably this kind of purchase is undertaken at quite a different stage in the family cycle, since the object is not to establish a home, but merely to buy the house already lived in. The tenancy figures show that well-established tenants are most likely to buy. This seems likely to reflect a combination of three factors: middle-aged council tenants are more likely to *want* to buy their house, they are more likely to be in a financial situation where they can consider purchase, and they are more likely to be living in a house attractive for purchase. Present allocation policies, by which waiting list applicants are first allocated a flat or maisonette and only later transfer to a house they may wish to buy, effectively render minimum tenancy requirements for purchase unnecessary.

Table 3.45. Household Characteristics of Council House Buyers, all Authorities except Ludlow

Characteristics:	West Bromwich	Warley	Wolverhampton	Halesowen	Stafford
Average age (years)	45	42	45	45	42
% purchasers aged over 45	45	31	42	51	40
Average household size	★	4·3	3·9	3·2	★
Average income (£)	★	1910	1880	2060	1890
% skilled manual workers	★	68	57	59	47
% semi- or un-skilled workers	★	18	13	23	22
% tenants for over 10 years	60	52	73	61	66
% tenants for over 20 years	20	10	25	21	23

★Information not available.

Source: Local authority records.

Variable discount rates with length of tenancy do not appear to influence the number of long-standing tenants among purchasers to any marked degree. More tenants of 20 years standing are found among purchasers in Stafford (where no variable element is included) than in West Bromwich where discount increases with tenancy.

The other point to note in relation to the purchaser's age is the number aged over 45. Between a third and a half of all purchasers fell into this group in most authorities. Yet the average term of loan granted was over 20 years, which implies that the repayment period must extend beyond 65 years for some purchasers. Local authorities take specific account of this by allowing younger relatives to act as guarantors for the loan. It is not clear if, in fact, these younger relatives would themselves be buying the house, if sales were not specifically limited to *tenants*. It is interesting that while a proportion of purchasers in each authority were aged over 60, there were very few small elderly households buying their house. Tenancies are not always automatically transferred to family members on a tenant's death, and maybe purchase is seen as a kind of insurance.

The average incomes shown in Table 3.45 are higher than those of private house buyers using a council advance. In addition the larger, older families give more scope for additional earners to supplement household income. In comparison with the incomes of all council tenants from the Family Expenditure Survey, the samples of buyers are seen to include relatively fewer households with very low and very high incomes. Average purchasers' earnings are very near to the national average earnings level for a full-time employed male worker in 1972, which was £1870.[1]

Council House Sales—General

Although it is not the intention of this report to argue the pros and cons of a council house sales policy, it does seem appropriate to examine some of the issues involved in the light of the survey evidence. This is particularly important because so many of the arguments have been made on political and philosophical grounds, and so few on any factual basis. Leaving aside the financial questions which have been modified by the introduction of the Housing Finance Act 1972, four points are raised by the conflicting circulars produced by Labour and Conservative governments. These are: (argument against) the inappropriateness of sales where demand for rented accommodation continues, and the fact that tenants who want to become owner-occupiers can be encouraged to move to the private sector; and (argument for) every tenant has a right to buy the house he has made his home, and even if he cannot buy, he will not move and create a vacancy.

In all the authorities surveyed the waiting list provides evidence of a continuing demand for rented accommodation. Eligibility rules are introduced, and 'live' and 'dormant' lists maintained in conscious recognition of the fact that demands cannot be met. Clearance is continuing to require lettings each year in the larger authorities, and these same authorities are facing land availability problems with new building programmes other than on redevelopment sites. But in fact the situation is still more complex. *Houses* are sold. A supply of *houses* is essential to accommodate transfer applicants who in turn create vacancies available for the waiting list applicants—as the system works at present. Dwellings on attractive estates, favoured for purchase, are also sought by transfer applicants. So it can be argued that demand for rented accommodation is continuing, and that demand for houses is significant in the functioning of the present public sector system.

The argument that prospective owners could, or should, be encouraged to move to the private sector depends very much on local housing market situations, availability of mortgages and other 'external' factors. From the evidence of the surveys, those currently buying their council houses would not be barred from buying in the private sector by means of income, since their average income levels were higher than those of people buying private houses with the help of council mortgages. Age might present problems unless the lending agency were prepared to accept guarantors to cover loans beyond retirement age. It seems very

[1]*Department of Employment Gazette.* Vol. LXXI No. 12, Dec. 1973, Table 128.

unlikely that prospective owners could find in the private sector houses of comparable size and condition without paying a very much higher price, and being committed to much higher repayments than current purchasers of council houses.

The 'right' of a tenant to buy his house is debatable in a philosophical sense only. However the contention is that the house has been made 'home', and that ties have been made with a 'congenial neighbourhood'. Certainly in the surveyed authorities purchasers *are* long-term established tenants, and local bonds among other tenants of attractive estates have no doubt been forged.

The really critical point in the arguments on both sides is whether the prospective purchaser would in fact move if his wish to buy his house were denied. The same evidence of long-standing tenancy and age (usually associated with reduced mobility) argues that, in the short term, a vacancy is not being lost through a sale. The whole argument concerning continuing demand for property for renting then becomes irrelevant. But this is in the short term only. In the long term a vacancy must be lost, and over a long enough period of years the loss will be comparable to the number of houses sold. The whole question of the function of public sector houses in the future—will demand increase as the private rented sector decreases, or will demand decline as incomes rise and owner-occupation becomes the norm?—then becomes relevant. Short term solutions can often lead to long term problems—on the other hand the future can take care of itself.

Without much more evidence on motivation for the purchase of council houses, and the movement out of the council sector by potential purchasing groups, a firm conclusion cannot be reached. In the short term, a moderate sales policy might not be as harmful as appears from a superficial examination of numbers. However no continuing policy can remain 'short term' and 'moderate' indefinitely—both time and numbers are cumulative.

LOCAL AUTHORITY HOUSING PERFORMANCE—GENERAL

Rather than attempting anything in the way of a comprehensive summary or set of conclusions from this chapter, a single simple statement seems appropriate. In terms of the initial question, it can be stated definitely that apparently similar local authority policies can lead to very different end results, and that different policies can produce similar patterns. It would be virtually impossible to infer from any given result which detailed policies had been in operation. Local policies are just one strand in a whole range of factors affecting housing performance, from the death rate to the mortgage rate.

In the previous chapter it was concluded that local discretion was important, and made full use of, in detailed issues only—with broad consensus achieved over the fundamentals which are the essence of central government policy. The present chapter suggests that fundamental similarities also occur between authorities in terms of housing practice and performance, and, in addition, that the detailed variations in policy need not produce any consistent results in different authorities. Local conditions are equally, or more, important. In these circumstances there is no apparent merit in arguing for a change in the present legislative system in favour of greater central government direction and greater local uniformity of policies.

In fact the argument in favour of conformity lies in any applicant having *de jure* equality of opportunity regardless of the local authority he happens to live in, and regardless of the *actual* chance he has as determined here. Housing opportunities offered by local authorities, and the influence they have on access to housing or to better housing are the theme of the following chapter.

4. Access to Housing

INTRODUCTION

All the evidence has now been presented on housing policies and practice followed by the surveyed local authorities. Rather than using any new evidence this chapter looks at what has already been said in a rather different way. One of the original research questions was concerned with the influence local authorities have on the access an individual household enjoys to housing—to any house, or to a better house. The fields of policy selected clearly do influence access—to a house (waiting list and clearance allocations to council houses and private sector mortgages) and to a better house, or one more suited to the household needs or wishes (transfer allocations, improvement grants, and council house sales).

The chapter is divided into three parts, each of which examines the question of access from a slightly different viewpoint. First those excluded from help by their local authority in the chosen policy fields, in theory and in practice, are described. Second, the corollary of the previous point—those actually helped are described by means of the 'stereotype' of households aided by each housing activity. Finally, and by way of a general conclusion, the 'strategy' is described which would seem most appropriate for a household to adopt to ensure the maximum council help in its housing situation. The emphasis throughout is on generalisation between authorities and not on differences between them.

ACCESS—THOSE EXCLUDED

Introduction

It should be clear that practice does not always directly reflect avowed policy in housing matters. A particular household may be perfectly eligible in theory for housing aid, but in practice may stand no chance of receiving that aid. Thus there are three categories of household which can be identified for each policy field; those absolutely excluded by policy statements, those eligible but unlikely to be helped, and those eligible and likely to receive help. This section concentrates on the first two categories, and the next section on the third.

Council House Allocation

The following list shows those most vulnerable to exclusion from council housing. All the authorities did not exclude all groups, and as was seen in Chapter 2, even those explicitly excluded by waiting list requirements might be considered as special cases for rehousing. Medical priority might outweigh many of the following exclusions even within the normal list framework.

A. General needs applicants:

(1) Persons likely to be excluded from active consideration by policy

—Those living outside the area of the authority in question.

—Recent movers to the authority in question where some minimum residential period is required for eligibility.

—Owner-occupiers of self-contained, adequately sized accommodation.

—Tenants of privately owned self-contained, adequately sized accommodation with all standard amenities.

—Young single persons without dependants (relatively rare category for exclusion through policy).

—Engaged couples prior to marriage.

—Households living in areas scheduled for clearance in the near future (consideration for rehousing is likely to be delayed until the Orders have been confirmed and rehousing takes place through clearance rather than waiting list procedures).

—Applicants with rent arrears outstanding from a previous Council tenancy.

(2) Persons likely to be excluded, or accorded very low priority by the practical workings of the allocation system.

—Owner-occupiers of self-contained, adequately sized accommodation with all amenities (where these are eligible for consideration).

—Tenants of privately owned self-contained, adequately sized accommodation with all amenities (where these are eligible for consideration.

—Single persons without dependants and below retiring age. While usually eligible, single persons have low priority relative to elderly households for the allocation of small units of accommodation.

—Small elderly households. Elderly households often have to wait some time for an allocation (though to a much lesser extent than single persons). This is due, not to lack of priority, but to shortage of vacancies in appropriate accommodation.

—Any person unable to remain within the local authority while the application is moving towards allocation levels.

—All those not registered on the waiting list, regardless of housing need.

B. *Transfer Applicants:*

(1) Tenants likely to be excluded from active consideration by policy.

—Tenants who have not lived in their present house for a minimum time period, unless medical or overcrowding grounds outweigh this.

—Tenants who are in arrears, or have a poor recent rent record, or who are considered to have very poor housekeeping and maintenance standards.

—Tenants who have already occupied several local authority houses (Warley only); again unless medical or overcrowding grounds exist.

—Tenants who are not in 'need' of a transfer in terms of definitions which usually centre on overcrowding, underoccupation, and ill health. (Only a minority of authorities set such a limitation on eligibility for consideration in theory).

(2) Tenants likely to be excluded, or accorded low priority by the practical workings of the allocation system.

—Applicants who are not adjudged to be in need of a transfer—i.e. are not living under conditions of overcrowding or underoccupation, nor suffering ill health, nor having 'valid reasons' for wishing to change area.

—Tenants of flats or maisonettes who wish to transfer to a house but who have not lived in the flat for a minimum specified period.

—Applicants not 'in need' of a transfer, and whose transfer would not particularly help the Housing Department in other allocation or management situations.

—Tenants who might be eligible, but have not applied for a transfer.

C. Clearance Rehousing. Exclusions here seem less well defined, and the research has not been particularly concerned to distinguish between statements of policy and practice. The following groups of households would seem vulnerable to exclusion from housing, though in any particular local authority, rehousing might in fact take place.

—Households moving into affected property after the appointed day in relation to the Clearance Order.

—Lodgers and sub-tenants. While these would rarely be totally excluded, they are more likely to be offered accommodation with the household they presently live with, than accommodation in their own right.

—Single persons without dependants and not of pensionable age. This group seems particularly vulnerable if found in circumstances described in the two cases above. While a family with children moving into the area after the set date, or living as sub-tenants might be offered accommodation of their own, a young single person would be unlikely to receive such an offer.

—Any otherwise eligible owner or tenant not wishing to be rehoused by the local authority.

Improvement Grants

In this case there is no equivalent to an allocation system. Any applicant who satisfies the basic requirements may receive a grant, so there is no distinction set by the local council between those eligible and those in practice helped—any distinction which arises is due to differences in the character of those applying. Those specifically excluded from receiving discretionary grants include:

—Owners of modern houses, usually those built since 1961.

—Owners of houses which meet the 12 point standard in all respects, including adequately sized kitchen.

—Owners of houses which could not be brought up to the 12 point standard by improvement.

—Owners of houses which are thought not to be capable of a 30 year life after improvement. This may be due either to the condition of the house itself, the area in which it is located, or any planning or other proposals affecting the property.

—Owners of second homes (Ludlow only).

—Owners of rented property not tenanted at the time of application who fail to convince the Committee that they are not 'profiteers' (Wolverhampton only).

—Any person who is not the owner of the property concerned (through the legislative requirements).

—Those owners of otherwise eligible houses not making an application.

Council Mortgage Advances

Again there is no particular distinction between exclusions in theory and practice. The list of those unlikely to receive a council mortgage is as follows:

—Those buying a house outside the area of the local authority in question.

—Those buying a house above a certain value, which can vary between £5000 and £12,000. This does not always apply. In Stafford no upper limit is set.

—Those applicants who are unable to satisfy the Council that they will be able to provide the deposit payment, and meet monthly repayments.

—Those who are not intending to live in the house they buy.

—Those buying a house which is not in all respects fit for human habitation, or which cannot satisfy certain minimum life requirements.

—Persons who do not themselves fall within one of the Circular 22/71 categories (i.e. are not on the waiting list or a council tenant etc.), or who are intending to buy a house which does not fall within one of these categories (i.e. is not a small old house, or a larger property suitable for conversion).

—Persons who do not apply for local authority help.

Council House Sales

Ultimately, eligibility to buy a council house may depend on the ability to raise finance for its purchase. However, leaving these considerations aside, the following exclusions apply: (obviously these points apply only in authorities where sales are allowed at all).

—Any person not a sitting tenant in a council house, or due to be allocated one from the waiting list. In some cases a minimum length of tenancy, either in any local authority dwelling, or in the house to be bought, is required.

—Any tenants of property other than houses (or such other property that is sold).

—Any tenant otherwise eligible who does not apply.

Access and Exclusions—General

There are three main conclusions to be drawn from the lists shown above—all of some significance.

First of all, it may have seemed pedantic to have included those who have not applied to the local authority *for* help among those who are excluded *from* help. This is a truism almost too obvious to mention, yet it is important to consider in relation to the second conclusion.

The second point is this. In nearly every policy field the criterion for eligibility, both in theory and practice, is a degree of housing need. There are exceptions to this principle—a residential qualification for council housing bears no relationship to housing need, and, most striking of all, council house sales rules seem designed to help those living in a most advantageous position, that is, in council *houses*. This major exception really emphasizes the general rule in other policy fields—that those in housing need are being selected for help, and that at least an attempt is made to give most help to those in greatest need.

Thirdly, it is apparent that those excluded are not always excluded by conscious intent. Thus young single people are in effect barred from council housing not through a specific policy decision, but through a lack of suitable accommodation available to offer them. The same is true, to a lesser extent, for small elderly households on the waiting list. Vacancies in suitable dwellings occur relatively rarely, and are often required for the prior claims of transfer applicants. In these cases current performance is being limited by past priorities as revealed in building programmes, and thus in the dwelling stock, and by the way the whole allocation system is working.

Major criticism can be made of local authorities that they are failing in their housing duties in a social sense, and that they are not preventing all hardships to households which arise from the inadequate workings of the private housing market. If the three conclusions above are accepted, they suggest that these criticisms should be aimed at three particular points: the definitions of housing need adopted by authorities, the workings of the system in *practice* as opposed to policy statements, and the extent to which eligible persons in 'need' are failing to register applications for help.

The definitions of housing need for a council house is usually judged in terms of the tenure, condition and occupancy of present accommodation, and any particular health problem the applicant has. Need for a council mortgage to enable a household to buy a house in the private sector is judged in a negative way. Those unlikely to attract a commercial mortgage may be helped by the Council, but the applicant must still satisfy basic financial requirements which may not be very different from those of the commercial lending agencies. Need is more likely to relate to the property to be bought than to the characteristics of the applicant. These particular fields have been selected because they involve access to a *house*, not merely a change in dwelling quality or tenure. In each case it is physical rather than social elements which are considered in the definition of need. Amongst applicants for a council house there is little effort to take account of social need in the sense of an inability to improve housing conditions in other ways.[1] Amongst applicants for a mortgage there is less concern for problems relating to personal circumstances than for property details.

Housing policies may, therefore, be missing those in great hardship because definitions of need in operation are not those most appropriate.

Examples of the ways in which inherited policies, and current practice can limit present opportunities for access to housing have already been given. It is possible to illustrate this point again from another policy field. When improvement grant applications were discussed in Chapter 3, it was suggested that the pattern could, under some circumstances, become self-reinforcing. The knowledge that grants are available, and the possibility of seeing the end results encourages applications, regardless of policy intentions in the local authority. If this type of impetus builds up for grants for kitchen extension work, it may act to the disadvantage of applicants seeking grants for the installation of amenities since delays can occur in the internal administrative procedures of the local authority concerned, and further pressure is put on the building firms who will undertake grant work. Again it is the system as much as any specific policy which is to blame.

Those in very great housing need, of a type fully recognized by the local authority, may fail to register an application for appropriate aid. Ignorance of eligibility rules, the services available and the procedures to be adopted are partly responsible. Mistrust of the local council, fear of 'charity' and a hundred and one other reasons may contribute, but basically ignorance, lack of information, or too much misinformation seem the chief culprits. In many social surveys where households are found to be living in 'bad' housing conditions, and are found not to have registered for council help, the 'I didn't think I was eligible' reason crops up.[2] Just the same principle applies to improvement grants and loans. Housing aid and advice centres are specifically aimed at these problems. None of the surveyed local authorities had set up such a centre, so the current research can shed no light on their usefulness and effectiveness—it can, however, suggest the need for some further means for ensuring that members of the public know what is available and how they might be helped.

Thus, on the basis of these research findings, the course for improving local authority housing performance is not seen to lie in detailed tinkering with present systems of priority and procedure, but in always ensuring that the needs being met are the appropriate ones, that housing performance is not being unnecessarily distorted or limited, and that those in need are availing themselves of the services provided. Some sort of continuous monitoring system, concerned with all aspects of local authority housing involvement, is essential if these conclusions are granted.

---

[1] See Chapter 2 for a much fuller discussion.

[2] See, for example, Pat Niner et al, *The Beeches Road Area Study*. University of Birmingham, Centre for Urban and Regional Studies (forthcoming).

ACCESS—THOSE HELPED AND THE MEANS OF AID

Introduction

Having seen those excluded, it is now time to look at those who are being helped by current local authority practice. This is done first by means of describing typical households helped in each policy area, and secondly, by selecting specific groups of households (the elderly, large families etc.), and seeing through which local authority policy they are most helped. Because this discussion centres on households, very few references are made to improvement grant policies, because information on the *people* helped in this way is not available.

Typical Households

Maybe one of the most interesting results of this research is that it is quite possible to identify 'typical' households who are allocated council houses, get transfers, receive local authority mortgages and buy their council houses. Some authorities stand out as different in these respects, and differences can usually be accounted for—the similarities seem to express the general rule, and the differences exceptions to it.

Some of the basic differences between different policy groups—waiting list allocations or tenants buying council houses—are shown by the average age and household size figures, which are presented in Table 4.1.

Table 4.1.   Average Age and Household Size, all Authorities

Applicant's age—average:

Policy group	Age in years
Receiving mortgages for private houses	34
Waiting list allocations	37
Waiting list applicants	41
Tenants buying council houses	44
Transfer applicants	47
Transfer allocations	47

Household size—average:

Policy group	Household size in persons
Waiting list applicants	2·46
Waiting list allocations	2·65
Transfer allocations	3·18
Transfer applicants	3·24
Receiving mortgages for private houses	3·49
Tenants buying council houses	3·77

Source: Local authority records.

Several very interesting features emerge from this. Note for instance the similarity between those receiving mortgages and waiting list allocations in terms of average age, and the great dissimilarity in terms of household size; and the similar relationship between transfer applications and those buying council houses. Relative to those on the list, waiting list allocations are slightly younger, and have slightly larger families, while just the reverse relationship exists between transfer applicants and allocations. Perhaps the relatively high average age of those helped by local authorities is worthy of note—the average is never in the twenties when the first household is being established and housing needs are extreme.

All this, of course, stresses the dangers of relying on average figures—waiting list allocations cannot really be younger than applicants—they simply include fewer of the elderly who are found on the waiting lists. Similar dangers, though not so extreme, apply to the stereotypes which follow. By definition they are generalizations and abstractions from the complexity of reality.

Waiting list applicants I. Young couples or small families with young children. The applicant is usually under 30, and if children are present, there is normally one child only, aged 5 or under. The application was made within a year of the date of marriage. The applicants are lodging, most usually with in-laws, and if there are children, accommodation is overcrowded. Much less usually the family may be living in rooms or a small flat.

Waiting list applicants II. Small elderly households, where the applicant is aged over 65. Most usually these households are tenants of privately owned self-contained accommodation which is now too large for the applicants, and which may lack the basic plumbing arrangements and be in a poor state of repair.

Waiting list allocations I. This group represents the first group of applicants when their application is successful. Small families are more usual than childless couples, and two children aged 5 or under are often present. The applicant is usually in his late 20's. Tenure arrangements are just as in the applicants group I.

Waiting list allocations II. Small elderly households, living in rented accommodation, and often having a medical claim in support of their application. In some authorities this group is virtually absent.

Transfer applicants I. Small and large families—including numbers of children aged 16 or below. The applicant is aged between 25 and 35. Most typically this group represents households allocated a flat or mainsonette from the waiting list about 5 years previously, and who now either wish to transfer to a larger dwelling or to a house rather than a flat or maisonette.

Transfer applicants II. Small elderly households, often with the applicant aged over 70. The long-term council tenants now find the house they have been living in, and the garden, too much to manage, and want a transfer to an old person's flat or bungalow.

Transfer applicants III. A group of adult households intermediate to the two preceding groups. Here couples, often aged in their 50's, have children over 16 who may be on the point of leaving home. In some cases the applicant is seeking a larger house to accommodate the older children—maybe larger in terms of an additional living room rather than extra bedrooms. In other cases older children have already left home, and the present three- or four-bedroomed accommodation is too big and a two-bedroomed house, for example, is being sought.

Transfer allocation groups I, II and III. These correspond directly to the groups described above for applicants, and are present in roughly comparable proportions. There tend to be more large families, and more children among group I, and more persons aged over 70 among group II allocations than among the respective applicant groups.

Persons buying a private house with council mortgage. The stereotype presents a highly distinctive group of applicants aged in the mid-thirties, with well-established small or large families including children aged 16 or under. The applicant may be an Asian immigrant. He is likely to be earning wages rather below the national average at a skilled manual or semi-skilled job. He is buying a terraced house built before 1919.

Tenants buying a council house. Again this group is highly distinctive, com-posed of well-established council tenants aged between 35 and 45 having large families including numbers of children, now usually aged over 5. Household composition is such that there are several persons earning to contribute to the household income. In addition the applicant himself is usually earning near or above national average wages in a skilled manual job. The dwelling being bought is typically a post-war house on an attractive estate.

These stereotypes might usefully be compared with the theoretical 'housing stages' that households are often assumed to pass through.[1] These are:

(a) For the first twenty years or so they live in their parents' homes.

(b) A growing proportion spend a brief period on their own or with friends after leaving home to study or work. The first year or two of marriage, when wives generally remain at work, may be regarded as a continuation of this phase.

(c) As soon as their first baby is born the household's needs change and become, during this expanding phase, increasingly extensive and de-manding.

(d) In time, all or most of their children leave home, and where there are no elderly relations living with them, the household is again small. A home has been established and filled with possessions, roots have been put down, and people are less likely to move than in earlier years.

(e) Finally, in old age, households shrink still further, they become even less mobile, and their comfort and peace of mind depend increasingly on security of tenure, upon design and equipment of the house, the services available in the neighbourhood and the support of nearby relatives and friends.

[1] D. V. Donnison *The Government of Housing,* Penguin Books, London, 1967, page 215.

There are obvious similarities and differences between this 'ideal' framework and the stereotypes defined. So far as council housing is concerned, taking allocations from both the waiting list and the transfer list, it is apparent that stage (b) is often omitted and groups (a) and (c) expand into each other. The usual pattern may be to apply for a council house on marriage or in expectation of marriage, while resident in the parental home, but an allocation is not then made until at least one baby has been born—well into stage (c), while the applicant is still living in the parental home. Once a council house is achieved, the first type of transfer represents the expansion phase of stage (c), quite in accordance with theory. Stages (d) and (e) are represented by transfers II and III and waiting list II. While theory suggests these groups are less mobile, with the implication that they will remain in 'unsuitable' family accommodation, their presence on both waiting and transfer lists suggests some mobility is possible and desired, if suitable accommodation is thought to be available. In some authorities (Ludlow) this group of shrinking and small households may constitute the largest single group among applicants. Some modification of the groups would be needed to really make them correspond to the public sector 'system'.

Private mortgage applicants do not really seem to fit into this framework very well. They would fall squarely within stage (c), but there is no evidence that it is household change *per se* which has prompted the change in housing situation represented by the purchase financed by the council loan. A full picture could only be built up if more information were available on the previous housing situation of these purchasers.[1] Much the same is true of tenants buying their council houses. Here the purchasers would seem to fall between stages (c) and (d)—possibly when the family has reached maximum size and can be expected to decline in size in the future. The phrases 'a home has been established' and 'roots have been put down' relating to stage (d) are very reminiscent of the DoE circular of the early 1970s encouraging council house sales. Just why households at this stage should decide to make a change in *tenure* is not clear. A different type of mobility is implied involving ownership rather than geography. Thus both types of purchase can be located within the different household development stages, though the precise trigger to action would seem to be outside this sort of explanatory framework.

Ways in which Different Groups are Helped

Several special groups in the population can be identified who have particular housing needs. The following are simply a selection of all those which might have been considered, and are included for illustration of the different focuses of local authority policy.

[1] Survey work undertaken by Valerie Karn in Birmingham concerned specifically with local authority mortgages shows that the majority of borrowers are using the council loan to buy their first self-contained accommodation. Prior to the purchase they were living either with parents or in lodgings.

The elderly. Elderly persons living alone, that is in small elderly households, are virtually excluded from help through council mortgages either for a private house or a council house, because of income and repayment regulations. Elderly tenants with younger relatives may be able to buy their council houses if these younger persons can act as guarantors for their loans. Undoubtedly the chief means by which the elderly are helped is through the direct provision of council housing. Small elderly households are found amongst those allocated a house from the waiting and transfer lists, and amongst clearance rehousing (though the details of this have not been fully presented here). The position of the elderly on transfer lists tends to be more favourable relative to other household groups than on the waiting list. Vacancies occurring in small accommodation suitable for the elderly or new building of old persons' dwellings tend to be allocated to transfer applicants rather than waiting list applicants, since this releases a family-sized house which can, in turn, be allocated for some other purpose.

Young families. Young families are the group most favoured by council policies. In most authorities they form the largest single group among both successful waiting list and transfer applicants. Definitions of need employed tend to relate to the housing conditions in which young families find themselves; lodging in relatively overcrowded conditions on the waiting list, or again, in relatively overcrowded conditions caused by family growth on the transfer list. Young families most usually require either two- or three-bedroomed accommodation, in which the great bulk of vacancies occur.

Young families are also the chief group helped by the council mortgages given for the purchase of private houses. The youth of the household head allows the full possible repayment period to be allowed. Fewer young families are found among the purchasers of council houses, though not in any way debarred by policy requirements. Young families are rather less likely to live in the houses suitable for purchase than slightly older households because of the allocation system in operation whereby waiting list applicants are first allocated a flat or maisonette, and must reach a house through the transfer and exchange procedures —implying a lapse of time during which a young family has ceased to be young. Equally, family financial commitments are high, and the advantage of ownership at the cost of higher expenditure may well be delayed until additional earners can boost family income.

Large families. If large families are defined as households including seven or more persons, they are found to constitute a small minority of households in any field of housing activity—and, as might be expected when dealing with very small numbers, the different authorities were found to vary considerably in terms both of the demands made of them, and their ability to meet those demands. Transfer allocations represent the largest single means through which large families are helped. Higher proportions of large families are found among transfer allocations than among waiting list allocations, reflecting a similar distinction among the respective applicants. However, in both cases there is evidence, in some authorities at least, that allocations are not fully meeting demands. The supply of vacancies in four-bedroomed or larger accommodation is small—

the total numbers in the stocks are relatively small and turnover is not rapid. Few vacancies, which because of their very scarcity are likely to occur irregularly over time, mean full needs cannot be satisfied adequately. In addition, in most of the authorities surveyed, the largest form of council house has four bedrooms. When dealing with a family of ten, eleven or twelve persons, which do occur on transfer lists, the space standards in *any* accommodation available will be inadequate. Where six-bedroomed houses exist, vacancies are so few, that any really effective lettings policy is virtually impossible to achieve.

Large families also receive a certain number of the mortgages given for private purchase—rising to a maximum of 9% of all mortgages in Halesowen. Once again the space standards resulting may be less than perfect, though the survey is unable to show whether they constitute an improvement on previous living standards.

Large families are helped by the local authorities, but the character and composition of the housing stock means that there can be no positive discrimination in favour of these households however extreme their needs may be.

Students. Students are not treated as a separate group in any of the authorities. Thus they receive treatment which is no less or more favourable than that accorded to other persons. Young single people without dependants have already been shown to be one of the groups most vulnerable to exclusion from council house allocations, in practice if not in theory. The problem for students would be made worse if they were involved in a recent move to the authority and if minimum residential qualifications exist. The short term nature (in terms of a waiting list time scale) of student needs means that a council house is unlikely to be available when needed. While not specifically excluded from house purchase, the non-orthodox financial arrangements which might be necessary makes it unlikely that this will be successful either on any scale. Only in Stafford, where a separate waiting list was maintained for multi-storey flats, was there any evidence that single people living with friends in non-family households were being considered and actually being allocated accommodation. Elsewhere, the priority demand from the elderly outweighed the demands of younger people. Students, and single people in general are not helped very much by any of the housing policies studied.

Immigrants. Full information on birthplace is rarely available, since ethnic origin is not considered to be a significant factor in determining housing needs or weighing priorities. Much of what follows is based on implications rather than facts, on surnames rather than knowledge of country of origin. However, there is no reason to believe that the general conclusions are inaccurate.

Persons with Asian names appear in greatest numbers among those receiving mortgages to buy a private house. Here 'immigrants' are helped in numbers far exceeding their representation in the total population. This rises to a peak in Halesowen where one half the mortgage applicants are immigrants. The very tendency of immigrants to become owner-occupiers acts against their chances of becoming council tenants. Where the information is available, persons born in the West Indies, India and Pakistan are found on the council house waiting lists in slightly greater numbers than would be expected from their representation in the total population. In most authorities, allocations keep step with applications in proportional terms, without favouring or avoiding immigrant applications. The nature and timing of immigration means that it is relatively rare for a situation to arise where young immigrant couples can apply for a council house while living with in-laws. Potential applicants are forced to find some interim accommodation. If this is owned, or rented, and is of reasonable condition, the immigrant could well find himself no longer eligible for consideration for a council house— just as a native-born family would in comparable circumstances. In the future this situation may change; at present mortgages represent the chief type of housing aid sought from local authorities by Commonwealth immigrants.

Persons living in old sub-standard accommodation. In theory at least, local authorities make a four-pronged attack on older housing within the policy fields examined— through clearance, through improvement grants, by rehousing applicants in council houses and by giving loans for the purchase and improvement of older houses. Clearance obviously has a direct impact on households living in unfit property, and households affected in the surveyed authorities enjoy somewhat preferential treatment. Clearance rehousing has absolute priority for allocations in most authorities, and the evidence suggests that clearance households are offered relatively attractive accommodation and may refuse several offers to wait for a house they really want. The majority of mortgage loans were also found to be channelled to older houses, though in this case they are less likely to be sub-standard, and cannot, by the nature of the legislation, be unfit. Some improvement or repairs were often insisted on as a condition of the mortgage loan—in accordance both with ensuring the maintenance of value of the asset, and with general renewal policies. By maintaining a market for older property, the provision of mortgages constitutes an essential part of any general renewal strategy, and may indirectly help other households in similar areas.

Improvement grants contributions to the core problems of older housing were found to vary from authority to authority. In half the areas surveyed, grants for the provision of amenities were the more important element among all grants, and in half they were the less important element. Within this last group at least, it is misleading to take improvement grant numbers alone as any index of the impact they will be making on the older stock.

Owner-occupiers of old houses, even when lacking basic amenities are not favoured by any of the authorities in their allocation policies. The position of tenant households is rather better. In general terms however, the lack of amenities is seen as a much lower priority element of housing need than overcrowding or lack of a separate house. Individual households in old, sub-standard accommodation may be helped by rehousing—particularly if the applicant is elderly and in ill-health—but the numbers are not as great as other more 'orthodox' need groups. In fact, where information on the provision of amenities is available, larger proportions of households lacking a bath are found on the waiting lists than among allocations. Allocations are not keeping pace with demand, even where the applicants are eligible, for consideration.

Of course, local authorities are in a rather paradoxical position when considering rehousing from old houses. Unless the property is actually unfit, rehousing one household will simply allow another household to move in and apply for a council tenancy. If they in turn succeed, the same process can be repeated. This situation can arise particularly in multi-occupied premises, where the very seriousness of housing conditions ensures the authority must take notice of the application and accord it some priority. This has three implications. First, it can create a never-ending demand for local authority housing. This in itself is not too serious because the households being rehoused would, presumably, be potential tenants wherever else they found to live, and the authority is rehousing them under one need heading rather than another. The second point is that the process in no way encourages improvement of the housing stock. If the landlord can be assured of a constant stream of tenants there is no incentive to make improvements, and the cause of renewal is not advanced. Which leads to the third point, which argues that the system, as it now exists, not only fails to encourage, but actively discourages improvement, either of the housing stock, or of an individual household's living conditions within it. While points (or priority) are awarded for crowded conditions and absent or shared amenities there will be a continuing demand for such sub-standard accommodation. In every town there is some 'waiting area' used as a stepping-stone to a local authority tenancy. A renewal policy which aims to remove all sub-standard accommodation must also ensure that the eligibility and priority rules for a council tenancy are altered accordingly to make the continuation of poor conditions unnecessary.

Groups Helped—General Points. This last explicit recognition of the links between renewal and allocation policies suggests a broader conclusion. Each local authority is operating an embryonic form of comprehensive housing service. Different groups are already being helped most in different ways—and this must also be true of all the housing authorities not covered by this research. The comprehensive approach is only described as embryonic because there is no evidence to suggest that the local authorities are actually aware of the ways in which their activities, carried out by different departments, are complementary or competitive. Every policy has implications for others, but there is no guarantee that inter-departmental or inter-committee aspects will be examined. The development of a more consciously comprehensive approach seems advisable for providing a service in which all needs can be met in the least wasteful manner. Once again this suggests the importance of monitoring needs and performance, and of basic research to show what the local authority as a whole is seeking to achieve, and what it is actually achieving. Comprehensiveness also implies a management structure capable of taking account of all aspects. This need not fall within one department—in fact the specialist aspects of the housing services provided in different departments in the surveyed authorities seemed particularly good. A commitment to concern with interrelationships and linkages, and an avoidance of strict departmental divisions and responsibilities is highly desirable, however achieved.

ACCESS—PLAYING THE SYSTEM

This final section provides a short, and relatively light-hearted guide to the housing system from the point of view of a household trying to get housing help from a local authority. Since the ground rules for getting an improvement grant (buy a house which is structurally sound and not in the track of a major highway development but which lacks some amenity included in the 12 point standard) and a council mortgage (have an adequate income to make repayments, choose a house which is fit and has an adequate minimum life but which no building society will touch, and approach the Council when it has funds available for lending) are relatively simple, the bulk of this section will be devoted to council housing—applicants and transfers.

These then are the basic rules to be followed by a would-be council tenant:

(a) Apply for a house in the area you happen to live in. If possible arrange to be born where you want to live.

(b) Get married, make your application, and live with one set of inlaws—preferably the ones with the largest family in the smallest accommodation. *Never* on any account move into self-contained accommodation of any kind.

(c) Don't delay in starting a family. One or preferably two young children who must sleep in your bedroom will boost your points score very satisfactorily.

(d) If you have no parents in the area, or really couldn't stand living with them, move into rooms. Try to ensure that the whole house is fully occupied, and that you are sharing bathroom and kitchen facilities. Again babies will help to overcrowd your own accommodation.

(e) Don't bother to move to make your housing situation worse than it was at the time of application—local authorities are wise to this and refuse to take account of the extra points you score for some minimum time period. Don't, however, try to move to *improve* your housing situation, as you will lose the points you have already gained.

(f) If you are elderly, and have no children you can live with, preferably in overcrowded circumstances, be sure you are in accommodation which lacks the standard amenities. A brisk walk outside to the WC is helpful. A medical recommendation is really needed.

(g) Don't say that you will only live on one particularly attractive estate, or that you will only accept a house—vacancies of this kind occur rarely, and the chances of them being allocated to waiting list applicants are still less.

(h) Do be sure that you do not move outside the local authority you have applied to and stay away too long, or your application may be cancelled.

(i) Be sure you are dealing with a points scheme and not a date order scheme—or all your efforts will be wasted. If your authority operate a date order scheme, make sure of the conditions necessary for active consideration for a tenancy, and then live in the very best circumstances which make you eligible—ignore most of rules (a) to (f) for your own comfort.

(j)   Don't tell lies on the application form. They will be found out at the visit and the application may be cancelled.

(k)   Be sure to keep your application alive. If this means an annual renewal, with or without reminder from the housing department, *don't* forget.

(l)   It may help to visit the housing department once or twice, but pestering won't really do you much good in the long run.

(m)   You might think it better to by-pass the waiting list system altogether and try to be rehoused as a homeless family or other special case. This could help your chances of being housed quickly, but it may be necessary to accept any sort of dwelling in any sort of area. Be sure all your 'papers' are in order—you must be legally evicted, have evidence of a divorce, etc.

The rules for a successful transfer applicant are as follows:

(a)   Make sure you have enough children to qualify you for another bedroom.

(b)   Alternatively ensure you have too many bedrooms. If you have a particularly attractive house at present this will help greatly, especially if you are prepared to move to a less attractive area.

(c)   If you are living in a flat or maisonette, apply and be patient. The system works so that you can have a house after serving an apprenticeship in a flat for five years or so. Children help.

(d)   If you want to change area don't complain about the neighbours or the children, say you want to be nearer work or school, or to your mother who needs help with the shopping.

(e)   Make a medical claim, but you must have adequate grounds. 'Nerves' won't do.

(f)   Although a large number of children may help, it is not always wise to have so many that you need a four- or six-bedroomed house. Vacancies do not occur very often.

(g)   Try to be a good tenant. Pay your rent regularly and on the right week. Keep your house and garden (if any) in good condition, and be sure no decorations need doing. Be especially careful of your housekeeping standards when the housing visitor is due.

(h)   Be sure to keep your application alive. If this means annual renewal of your application be sure you don't forget.

(i)   Visit the housing department if requested to, and to explain your case carefully (by appointment) but don't pester them—it is unlikely to help in the long run.

These 'rules' as set out are undoubtedly flippant. They are not intended to be in any way contemptuous either of those in the types of genuine housing need described, or of the local authorities genuinely trying to meet those needs. They do, however, help to make two quite serious points.

First they show that it is possible for someone to 'play the system'. It is quite possible to imagine a household applying for a house as a lodger, being allocated a flat, biding their time and increasing their family until a successful transfer is achieved. The aim of a council *house* has been realised (In time if it is really attractive the house may be purchased). There are, however, innumerable steps where the family might miss its course; by moving while an applicant, and thus, inadvertently, rendering themselves ineligible, or by asking for a type of dwelling or an estate in which vacancies rarely arise, thus delaying their housing. Full information must be available, and in a simple form for prospective and actual applicants.

Secondly, the 'rules' show the extent to which self-help is discouraged by the current regulations. A family living in private rented accommodation may be similar in every way to one still living with in-laws, but their need is adjudged less serious. A wider consideration of need may be desirable.

These are, of course, the same conclusions reached earlier in this chapter when those excluded by council policies and practice were being considered. The chief findings of this survey suggest that local authorities are well-intentioned bodies in the housing field, concerned to meet the most serious needs as they see them. Performance is already good, but the main lines along which it might be improved are through the provision of more advice, aid, and information services and through the wider consideration of changing housing needs. These provide the main areas of emphasis for the future if local authorities are to provide a truly comprehensive housing service.

5. Some Implications for Local Authorities

INTRODUCTION

It has been a constant aim of this study to produce results which are useful to local authorities—not only to those directly involved in the case studies, but also, hopefully, to other authorities concerned with housing policy and practice. Several conclusions, implications and suggestions of particular significance for local authorities have already appeared, scattered through the three preceding chapters. This chapter tries to bring together the more important of these conclusions, and to suggest ways in which the present research approach might help authorities in reviewing their housing performance. The very length of the chapter (or rather, its shortness) indicates that the coverage is highly selective and brief.

SOME MAJOR CONCLUSIONS

Two broad themes recur throughout this report. They can best be illustrated by quoting directly from earlier sections.

First of all, there is the theme of concern with the fundamentals and intentions of housing policy; with the 'filter' which determines who is considered eligible for aid, and who is excluded; with, above all, the definitions of 'need' in use.

'. . . any attempt to change a priority system, or to affect its outcome, must be concerned with the underlying philosophy and intentions of the scheme as well as with details of points or procedures.' (page 68).

'Housing policies may . . . be missing those in great hardship because definitions of need in operation are not those most appropriate' (page 94). Basic intentions and definitions of need are vitally important in all the policy areas examined—whether set by central government recommendation (the Circular 22/71 categories for mortgage lending priorities) or by local discretion (priorities for council house allocation, or the type of work eligible for improvement grant aid) ' . . . the course for improving local authority housing performance is not seen to lie in detailed tinkering with present systems of priority and procedures, but in always ensuring that the needs being met are the appropriate ones . . .' (page 94).

This quotation runs on: '. . . that housing performance is not being unnecessarily distorted or limited, and that those in need are availing themselves of the services provided.' These points introduce the second major theme: that of interrelationships and linkages within the housing system, and the consequent necessity of a comprehensive response from the local authority. Housing performance can, under certain circumstances, be limited or distorted by the workings of other housing policies; local councils must be as concerned with those failing to register applications as with those whose needs are better known. 'Separate parts of the allocation system cannot be seen in isolation; change in one part will have repercussions elsewhere; and attempts to influence priorities must take account of this.' (page 68).

'It (does) however, suggest the need for some further means for ensuring that members of the public know what is available and how they might be helped.' (page 94.) 'The significance of this role (local authority mortgages) in keeping the property market buoyant in areas of older housing in conjunction with other renewal policies cannot be overstated. This is a very obvious field where the comprehensive approach to housing policy and practice is essential.' (page 79). 'Each local authority is operating an embryonic form of comprehensive housing service. Different groups are already being helped most in different ways . . . . Every policy has implications for others, but there is no guarantee that the inter-department or inter-committee aspects will be examined. The development of a more consciously comprehensive approach seems advisable for providing a service in which all needs can be met in the least wasteful manner'. (page 102).

If these conclusions are accepted as valid the obvious implication is that local authorities must know a great deal about the workings of the housing system in their area, about the impact (intended or otherwise) of their policies, and the extent to which their intentions are being achieved. This suggests a need for research, and above all, for a comprehensive monitoring system to show 'what the local authority as a whole is seeking to achieve, and what it is actually achieving.' (page 102). It is, of course, sound academic practice to conclude a study with a plea for more research. However, before doing this, the potential contribution of this present method of approach will be examined!

THE PRESENT APPROACH AND ITS USEFULNESS

The present research approach might be summarized as a comparison of housing policies with the outcome of housing procedures, in a form similar to that followed in the case study chapters (Chapters 6–11) together with subsequent analysis (along the lines of Chapter 4) to show which particular household groups are being helped, which are excluded, and how the different policies work to complement each other, or fail to do so. Doing this sort of analysis once provides an information base, repeating the analysis at regular intervals might form the basis for a rudimentary policy review or monitoring system. This section first suggests some of the merits of such an approach, then points out what it might mean in terms of local authority procedures and organization. Finally, some of the gaps and omissions which would result are described—the areas where more work is still required.

Some Merits of the Approach

Analysis of the records kept by local authority departments concerned with housing in rather greater detail than is usual at present has the following advantages and possibilities:

(a) At its simplest, the analysis can give an idea of what is happening at present, and how the local authority is performing in housing matters. By identifying *groups*, whether of households or dwellings, the impact of procedures and actions can be seen much more realistically than if only total figures are considered. A prime example of this is the analysis of improvement grant records according to type of work. Total figures of grants approved may suggest that improvement is making a satisfactory contribution to relieving the problems of lack of amenities in older housing, closer analysis of the actual numbers of grants going for such works may lead to a totally different picture. An emphasis on 'numbers' gives little indication of the *effectiveness* of any policy.

(b) These sorts of findings can be directly related to the policy intentions of the council. If policies and objectives are precisely defined, analysis could begin to show if the objectives are being achieved. If policies are framed in more general terms, analysis would at least show if performance is as intended, and the *practice* of the local authority is in accord with the *policy*.

(c) Where policy and performance do not seem entirely satisfactory, the understanding achieved by a detailed analysis of the situation may suggest remedies. The outcome of council performance could be unsatisfactory in two rather different ways. Firstly, stated policies and intentions may simply not be translated into actions—the groups policies are designed to help are not receiving that help. For example, suppose that it is council policy to rehouse elderly households through waiting list procedures, but that detailed analysis of allocations shows that very few are, in fact, being housed. The analysis should give clues to the reasons for this: are elderly households registering on the waiting list? If they are, are they in 'need' of housing as defined by their Council, that is, are they actually eligible for help? Is the sort of need typical of the elderly one given priority in allocation procedures? Are any vacancies in accommodation suitable for the elderly available to waiting list applicants? If not, is this due to an absolute shortage of suitable dwellings, or to the transfer system? According to the answers to these questions the remedy for this apparent shortfall in performance would be extra publicity, changes in eligibility rules, alteration of the points scheme, a new building or conversion programme, or a change in the whole allocation system, or any combination of these as necessary. Secondly, the pattern of performance revealed by analysis might be entirely in accord with policy intentions, but evidence might still show that the scale of the programme is simply not coping with the size of the problem. Local authority mortgage lending may prove a good example. Viewed within the confines of the policy itself, lending may be seen as fulfilling all requirements. Small old houses are being lent on almost exclusively, yet the total number of loans given may be so small that older areas of the town still experience the blight which results when finance is not available for house purchase. Improvement grant applications for the installation of basic amenities, particularly from landlords of private property provide an equally relevant example. Provided there are no bars on eligibility for help, the appropriate response in this case would seem to be publicity, better information and a conscious effort to spread knowledge of what is available as widely as possible.

(d) Any change in policies must be monitored in the future to ensure that it is having the intended (and expected) results. Not only policies change, external factors such as the economic situation and even the birth rate also change, with implications for a council seeking to provide a comprehensive housing service. Periodic repeats of the analysis could help show progress, and indicate possible new problem areas as they arise. To take a very simple example: many local authorities recently have experienced a lengthening of their waiting lists for council housing. Which groups are registering in greater numbers? Are there, in fact, more registrations, or fewer vacancies occurring? If the increase in registration is concentrated particularly among young married couples, could the council give help in some other form?

(e) Finally, feedback from analysis in a monitoring system could help a council to refine its concepts of 'housing need'. Are they still appropriate? Would some other measure be better? Do the measures of need used in different policy fields leave out some groups who may be suffering hardship?

Implications for a Local Authority

If it were decided that analysis on the lines set out above would be useful, what would this mean in practical terms? There are two important points—the system must be carefully planned and designed, but given this, it should be extremely simple to operate.

In the design of any survey, particularly one to be of direct use in future practice, certain basic questions must be asked and answered. In considering a performance analysis/monitoring system these would include:

(a) *Why* is the system required? i.e. what are the housing issues which need to be examined?

(b) *What* information should be collected?

(c) *Where* can this information be obtained?

(d) In *what form* is the information to be recorded and how is it to be analysed?

(e) *By whom* will the information be regularly collected and analysed, and how will the results be presented to and used by the Council?

Obviously, each of these questions must be answered by each local authority according to its particular requirements. The following points are simply general impressions gained as a result of doing the survey work presented in this report.

(a) The policy areas examined in this research were selected for a variety of reasons outlined in the Introduction and are more closely allied to the particular research aims and questions of local discretion than to issues of most significance for housing authorities. In spite of this, council house allocations, improvement grants, mortgages and council house sales *are* highly significant policy areas. The list could easily be extended to cover, for example, rent rebates and allowances, clearance and redevelopment, improvement area policies or treatment of houses in multi-occupation. Issues of particular concern would clearly be first choice as candidates for analysis.

(b) Put at its simplest, enough information should be collected to enable the impact of policies to be checked, and no more. Excessive data collection is wasteful, it makes analysis harder, and can lead to an early disillusionment with the system as a whole. If an objective of monitoring is to distinguish the impact of policy on different groups, sufficient information must be collected to allow those groups to be distinguished: for households this means demographic, employment and income details; for dwellings, age, value, size, type, and possibly location. If an objective of monitoring is to check the relevance of need measures, as many indices of housing hardship as possible should be included: occupancy, lack of amenities, sharing facilities, and ill health. Appendix VI provides a checklist of all the pieces of information collected and analyzed in this report. Obviously, this was constrained by what was available from local authority application forms and files. In the longer term, these forms themselves can be designed to provide information desirable for the monitoring system.

(c) In most authorities, it is likely that information to be collected will be held in several different departments. This clearly calls for a commitment to inter-departmental co-operation. It also suggests that information recording should be modified to ensure that as much detail as possible is held in a common form in different departments. For example, if income is to be considered, both mortgage *and* waiting list application forms should make it clear that gross applicant's income is being requested (or whatever definition is selected). In a comprehensive monitoring system, information from sources outside the local authority should be used. In the case study chapters, figures are quoted from the Census, Local Housing Statistics, Housing and Construction Statistics, and the Nationwide Building Society as well as more general comments from local estate agents and building societies. This is far from a complete list of potential sources.[1] The problems of integrating information on the private market through this approach are discussed later.

(d) An explanation of the method of recording information used in this research, and specimens of the recording sheets used are given in Appendix II. Information recorded in this way, and transferred to punched cards can be analysed by computer, and any cross-tabulations required can be produced. This approach requires the availability of facilities for card punching (or other input preparation) and computer time for analysis. The time involved in actually recording information from files on to the

---

[1] For a wider discussion, see C. J. Watson, et al., *Estimating Local Housing Needs*, University of Birmingham, Centre for Urban and Regional Studies, Occasional Paper No. 24, Ch. 11, 1973.

specially designed sheets is very short. It should be perfectly possible to introduce this type of recording as another short stage in the administrative procedure already followed when, for example, an improvement grant is approved, a council house let or a transfer application registered. Cards filled in in this way would be ready for subsequent punching and analysis when required. In an authority already operating a computer based system for the waiting list for example, the intermediate stage of data recording is omitted, and tabulations of specified variables can be produced as required.

(e) The procedures described under (d) above implies that data *collection* will be undertaken in the different departments by the people involved in day to day administrative processes.[1] However, analysis (and the planning of the system as a whole) should be in the hands of a single individual or team. Only in this way can a *local authority* as opposed to a *departmental* view result. It is as important to see the linkages or conflicts *between* policy areas as *within* policy areas. In which department this individual or team should be situated depends entirely on the management structure adopted by the local authority. (This, of course, accords entirely with the corporate management approach adopted by many of the new authorities since April 1974). If departments are to provide data, they must also receive feedback of the results in as detailed and useful a form as possible. The same is true of the Council and Committees; information must be widely distributed if it is to have an effect. A monitoring system is no substitute for policy making, but by taking account of its findings, a more sound basis should exist on which decisions can be made.

Limitations of the Present Approach

There are two fundamental limitations to the approach described in this report, and to any research method which attempts to compare council policies and performance from analysis of local authority records alone. Firstly, the procedures internal to the local authority departments concerned and the processes by which stated *policies* are transferred into recorded practical results, are virtually ignored. 'Informal' procedures have been mentioned frequently during the preceding chapters: what is the practical significance of different gradings in council house allocations, and how are gradings assessed? What happens at the interview between an applicant for an improvement grant and the public health inspector, how much is the application influenced? How much attention is paid to intangibles such as 'character' and 'reliability' in deciding whether a mortgage applicant with marginal income will receive his loan? Without further information it is not possible to say how important informal as opposed to formal policies and procedures are in affecting performance. This is a very significant

---

[1] This has the added advantage that personal files and information will only be seen by those in the specialist departments. The wider analysis is concerned with aggregated data rather than information pertaining to any single identifiable individual. The computer system can be designed to ensure confidentiality of information at this individual level.

area for further research. Only then will we be sure precisely how policy influences performance, which is vital knowledge if policies are to be changed effectively.

The second major limitation stems from the fact that the analysis is restricted to *council* policies and practice. There have been constant pleas for regarding 'need' as widely as possible, for seeing that groups suffering hardship are helped, and for regarding policy in a comprehensive framework, as concerned with the private sector as with 'orthodox' council housing. But this is exactly what is so difficult to do by examining existing policies. How are those *not* registering an application for help to be regarded—as not being in need? This is obviously not true as the presence of numbers of homeless families, households in multi-occupation and in clearance areas who are not on the waiting list, testifies. How, indeed, are need groups not registering an application to be identified? The Census provides some help by showing the number of households lacking, or sharing amenities, and the number living in overcrowded conditions, but it can give us no overall indication of housing need. This can be simply illustrated. A large proportion of housing need is generated by new households, young couples seeking to establish a home for the first time. The waiting lists in all the surveyed authorities included many applicants in this category, still living in the parental home. For Census purposes these households simply do not exist if the two families live together as a unit, and eat most of their meals together. How then, are all the hidden needs to be revealed so that a local authority can really plan to counter hardship effectively?

There is another danger in concentrating specifically on council policies and those helped thereby. Local authority policies can also have side-effects and unintended implications for households not themselves directly affected. For example, an improvement policy, vigorously pursued in an area of multi-occupation may aim at improving the standard of the dwelling stock, through conversion to self-contained flats, and at improving the housing opportunities of those already living in the area, through rehousing. But what happens in the future? Young single people at a future date may still find themselves excluded from council houses, and unable to afford the self-contained flats. Action in one area can spread multi-occupation elsewhere unless all the factors creating demand for such accommodation are understood and taken into account in a total policy approach. Analysis of council records alone is inadequate for such purposes.

There, then, are fields in which research is urgently needed. Social surveys can be used in particular circumstances, but these are expensive and time-consuming. Housing advice centres can provide information on households they help, and other voluntary bodies similarly can extend the coverage of those in need and of housing problems and stresses as they arise, but there is still no guarantee that all are included. At this point in time, the questions remain open.

Both the potentials and limitations of the research approach adopted here can be seen in more detail in the case study chapters which follow in Part III.

PART III
6. West Bromwich C.B.

BACKGROUND

West Bromwich is a county borough with a 1971 Census population of 166,600—the figure representing a small decrease (—0·16% per annum) from 1961 levels. The age structure of the population is shown in Table 6.1, and is compared to that of the West Midlands Region. The two structures are remarkably similar.

Table 6.1. Age Structure of Population, West Bromwich and Region: 1971

Age:	West Bromwich %	West Midland Region %
0–14	24	25
15–19	8	7
20–29	13	15
30–44	19	18
45–59	20	19
60 and over	16	17

Source: 1971 Census.

A higher proportion of the local than the regional population were born in New Commonwealth countries. The figures are 3·7% and 2·8% respectively.

There were nearly 53,600 private households in West Bromwich in 1971, giving an average household size of 3·08 persons. This is slightly larger than the regional average (2·98). Household size structure, and dwelling size structure are shown in Table 6.2. As can be seen, the number of small elderly households is again very similar in each case. The matching of households and dwellings results in 2·7% of households living at a density of more than $1\frac{1}{2}$ persons per room, and 29% living at a density of less than $\frac{1}{2}$ person per room. While this may apparently suggest some underoccupation, the situation is by no means unusual—no less than 34% of households in the Region live at the lower density.

Table 6.2. Household and Dwelling Size, West Bromwich and Region: 1971

Household size:	West Bromwich %	West Midland Region %	Dwelling size:	West Bromwich %	West Midland Region %
1 person	15	16	1–3 rooms	14	11
2 persons	30	31	4 rooms	22	21
3–4 persons	38	38	5 rooms	39	36
5–6 persons	13	13	6 rooms	23	25
7 persons and over	4	2	7 rooms and over	4	7
1 or 2 person households where one or both persons are of retiring age or over as % of all households	23	24			

Source: 1971 Census.

West Bromwich does stand out as distinct from the Region in terms of dwelling tenure. Fifty seven per cent of households were local authority tenants in 1971, compared to 34% in the Region, and only 34% were owner-occupiers, compared to 50%. Both locally and regionally the private rented sector was small, but particularly so in West Bromwich. The small size of the private rented sector accounts in part for the relatively high standard of amenity provision. Eighty-seven per cent of local households enjoyed exclusive use of bath, hot water supply and inside WC (Region 84%).

New house completions in West Bromwich have averaged just over 900 a year during the period 1968 to 1972,[1] with the public sector making up slightly over half the total. Even so demolitions, running at about 640 a year, have exceeded council house completions, and the net gain to the housing stock has been less than 270 dwellings a year.

West Bromwich emerges, then, as an area broadly similar to the region as a whole. Extremes in both demographic and housing characteristics are avoided, and maybe the chief distinguishing feature is the high proportion of council houses in the dwelling stock.

COUNCIL HOUSE ALLOCATION

Policies

Despite the high proportion of local authority houses in the total stock, demand still outstrips supply. In the shortage situation, rules are followed which first limit those eligible for consideration for a council tenancy, and then determine the order of priority among those eligible. A similar process is followed for general needs applicants, transfers and households affected by clearance action. Different priority scales exist within and between groups, and the rules are described in Table 6.3.

In addition to the bulk of general needs applicants, for whom allocations follow the rules set out, special cases can be considered by the Committee for rehousing. These include any marginal cases, owner-occupiers, single people or people living alone under pensionable age when their time for allocation has been reached, applicants against whom a possession order has been made for no fault of their own, and low priority medical cases who are registered on the Dormant List.

Priorities between groups are ordered as follows:

(a) Slum clearance rehousing, which may take up to 90% of vacancies.

(b) Improvement area rehousing.

(c) Transfers and exchanges.

(d) Housing applicants—general needs.

[1] *Local Housing Statistics England and Wales.* H.M.S.O.

At present clearance rehousing takes much less than its full possible allotment. The policy suggests that a vacancy will only be offered to a waiting list applicant if it is not needed for any other purpose. Since transfers, of course, release a vacancy for each allocation made, their priority over general needs does not reduce the total amount of accommodation available to waiting list applicants, but it does affect the type of property likely to be offered.

Practice—Allocations

It is estimated that about 2500 allocations were made during the year 1972–73. Of the total, 28% were made to persons on the general needs waiting list, 39% to transfer applicants, 12% were mutual exchanges, 14% went to clearance rehousing, and 8% to other lettings, special cases and service tenancies. Thus, lettings to existing tenants (transfers and exchanges) exceeded 'new' lettings (waiting list, clearance and other cases). The ratio of 'new' to 'existing' lettings was 1 to 1·03. General needs applicants took 57% of the 'new' lettings.

The type of property allocated to each lettings group is shown in Table 6.4. Some differences are clear, in terms both of house size and type. Size variations correspond to household size distribution—more one-bedroomed property being allocated to clearance needs where many one and two person households are being rehoused, and more three- and four-bedroomed property being allocated to transfer and exchange applicants, amongst whom are found relatively more five person households and larger. House type corresponds less well to apparent requirements; for example, children aged 5 or under were present in 57% of waiting list households allocated a dwelling, yet only 17% of waiting list applicants as a group were allocated a house. By contrast 56% of transfers got a house, while only 35% of transfer families included children of 5 or under.

Table 6.4. Types of Dwelling Allocated, West Bromwich: 1972–73

House type:	Waiting list and other cases	Transfers and mutual exchanges	Clearance	Total
Sample number	179	259	69	507
	%	%	%	%
Bungalows	2	10	20	8
1 bed. flat	13	16	15	15
2 bed. flat/maisonette	49	10	23	26
2 bed. house	1	13	10	8
3 bed. flat/maisonette	19	3	—	8
3 bed. house	16	43	32	32
4 bed. house	1	6	—	3

Source: Local authority records.

Vacancies are much more likely to arise in some dwelling types than others (Table 6.5). Nine per cent of the vacancies in the survey year were the result of new building (mainly bungalows). The high vacancy rates among flats and maisonettes were due mainly to flows of transfers away from this type of dwelling but relets for other causes were also high. Flats and maisonettes seem to generate mobility of many types.

Table 6.3. Eligibility and Priority Regulations, West Bromwich: 1973

Eligibility rules for application:	General Needs Applicants	Transfer Applicants	Clearance Rehousing	Improvement Areas
	Any person	Any council tenant	Not applicable	Not applicable
Eligibility for consideration:	Must be registered on the Live List. To be so registered, applicant must:	Certain basic conditions must be satisfied. Applicants must:	Any owner or tenant in residence before the date on which the Order was represented to Committees	In an Improvement Area the following rules apply:
	(a) Satisfy residential or employment qualifications	(a) Have held their present tenancy at least 12 months (unless medical priority)	No rehousing takes place until the Order has been confirmed by the Minister	(a) Families who live in multi-occupied dwellings are rehoused whether or not a housing application has been submitted
	(i) Applicant and wife reside in Borough and have so resided for at least 12 months; or	(b) Have a clear rent account for 13 weeks before transfer	Lodgers or sub-tenants may be rehoused separately if they have a registered application near allocation level. In other cases, lodgers are rehoused with their tenant/owner household.	(b) An elderly tenant is, if appropriate offered a 1-bedroomed flat, and the owner requested to take a nominated tenant
	(ii) Applicant is employed in Borough and has been so employed for at least 12 months; or	(c) Ensure the condition of the dwelling they vacate causes the Council no unnecessary expenditure	Single person lodgers are referred to Committee for individual consideration	(c) An elderly owner-occupier is offered a 1-bedroomed flat
	(iii) Applicant or wife lived 10 out of the previous 15 years in Borough; or	These conditions apply to transfer and mutual exchange applicants	Anyone moving into affected property after the date of representation will not normally be rehoused unless under Waiting List procedures	(d) An owner-occupier is rehoused if he is unable to afford improvements and:
	(iv) Applicant is a member of H.M. Forces who lived in Borough prior to enlistment	For consideration, applicants must also be in housing need defined as:		(i) is unable to afford second mortgage repayments
	(b) Be in housing need	(a) Underoccupation		(ii) is unable to obtain a second mortgage because of low income
	(i) Lodgers without a proper home of their own; or	(b) Overcrowding		
	(ii) Families living in overcrowded conditions; or	(c) Ill health		(iii) if the house is purchased by the Council for improvement and subsequent resale or letting
	(iii) Have lived in a flat for 5 years; or	(d) Having adequate accommodation, but have been in the present dwelling at least 5 years		
	(iv) Have lived in unsatisfactory dwelling (without bath) for 5 years; or	Families with children may apply to transfer from a flat to a house in this way		(iv) the owner will accept a nominated tenant
	(v) Have medical points			
	Those who do not satisfy these conditions, or are engaged couples, are put on the Dormant List.			

	Applicants eligible for inclusion on the Live List, but not requiring immediate rehousing have their application held In Abeyance. Live List applicants are eligible for consideration after a 6-month registration period which may be waived on medical grounds			

Method of determining priority:	Points scheme. Points awarded for:
	
	(a) Date of application
	
	(b) Housing need:
	   —bedroom deficiency
	   —size of family
	   —shared accommodation
	   —general overcrowding
	   —living apart
	   —sex overcrowding
	   —ill health or disability
	
	(c) Lack of amenities
		No formal system. Length of tenancy and need considered. Priority given to relief of underoccupation in houses	Date order (date of making the Order)	Not stated

Table 6.5.   Turnover Rates and House Type, West Bromwich: 1972-73

House type:	Number in Stock 1971 Number	Number among allocations Sample × 5 Number	Allocations as % stock % as index
Bungalows	555	210	38
1 bed. flat	4267	375	9
2 bed. flat/maisonette	4918	645	13
2 bed. house	2754	210	8
3 bed. flat/maisonette	998	205	21
3 bed. house	16070	810	5
4 bed. house	788	80	10
Total	30523	2535	8

Source: Local authority records and I.M.T.A. *Housing Statistics (England and Wales) Part 1*, 1971.

Practice—the Waiting List

As implied by the procedure described in Table 6.3, the waiting list in West Bromwich is maintained in three groupings: the Live List, from which allocations are made; the Dormant List; and applications held In Abeyance. Applications from engaged couples are also kept separately, but these are not included in the tabulations below. To this extent, the waiting list figures presented are an understatement of total recorded demand. The different waiting list groups are compared with the Successful List, that is, waiting list applicants allocated a house in the survey year.

Table 6.6 shows the household characteristics of waiting list applicants. Allocations are selective of families including young children, with young household heads. The Dormant List in particular includes a number of more elderly households, with markedly fewer young children.

Table 6.6.   Household Characteristics—Waiting List, West Bromwich: 1973

Household type:	Live List	Dormant List	In Abeyance	All Lists	Successful List
Sample number	153	288	151	592	166
	%	%	%	%	%
Single person	7	5	11	7	3
Small adult	30	24	28	27	19
Small family	36	28	38	33	56
Large family	15	7	7	9	10
Large adult	3	19	11	13	6
Small elderly	9	16	5	13	7
Average household size (persons)	2·82	2·82	2·70	2·79	3·06
Households with children aged 5 or under	39%	19%	13%	22%	58%
Average age of applicant (years)	34	44	39	40	31

Source: Local authority records.

Just one-fifth of applicants on the Live List had been born outside Great Britain—8% in the West Indies, and 7% in India and Pakistan. Only 11% of successful applicants had been born outside Great Britain.

Indices of housing need are listed in Table 6.7. The Successful List shows higher concentrations of households falling into many of the need categories. Very obvious exceptions to this are the number of households lacking amenities on the Dormant List, and the number of family lodgers among the applicants held In Abeyance. Allocations seem selective particularly of overcrowding.

Table 6.7. Indices of Housing Need—Waiting List, West Bromwich: 1973

% of sample who are:	Live List	Dormant List	In Abeyance	All Lists	Successful List
Lodging with family	63	8	76	40	66
Lodging—other	20	3	15	10	11
Without own living room	70	10	73	41	73
Sharing with 5 or more persons	18	2	10	7	20
Living at a density of more than 2 persons per bedroom	42	9	27	22	53
Living at a density of 0·3 persons per bedroom or less	2	4	—	2	2
Claiming medical priority	13	11	1	9	13
Without use of bath	11	21	8	15	5
Lone parent families	14	8	11	10	9
Registering within 1 year of marriage	46	17	31	29	60
Registering when baby expected	14	6	6	8	28
On list before 1971	25	71	86	63	33

Source: Local authority records.

The reasons given for making an application support the more objective measures of need (Table 6.8) very well. The desire for more space and independence are features of the Live List, while by definition, long-term 'insurance' elements are seen in the other groups.

Table 6.8. Reason for Application—Waiting List, West Bromwich: 1973

Reason:	Live List	Dormant List	In Abeyance	All Lists	Successful List
Sample number	150	280	152	582	178
	%	%	%	%	%
Seeking independence	26	7	19	15	28
Occupancy—					
Too little space	37	4	15	15	30
Too much space	1	5	—	3	1
Housing—					
Conditions	8	18	5	12	4
Expense	2	5	—	3	1
Location—					
Near work/relatives	3	13	5	9	3
Ill health	3	3	1	3	4
Insurance/tied accommodation	3	36	41	26	11
Other	17	9	14	14	18

Source: Local authority records.

Just under one-fifth (19%) of applicants on the Live List had already received at least one offer of a tenancy. Because details of offers made were not always kept, it is not possible to say how many of those on the Successful List received and refused offers prior to accepting a tenancy.

Practice—Transfers

Since all tenants can apply for a transfer, but only those meeting certain conditions are eligible, Live and Dormant Transfer Lists are maintained. In fact, the distinction as shown in the following tables may not always be correct due to recent changes in policy.

In terms of household characteristics, transfer applicants can be divided into two main groups. First there are the families, slightly older, larger and further through the development cycle than those found on the waiting list. Most usually these households want a larger dwelling, or a house as opposed to a flat or maisonette. Second, there are small elderly households already in a house, seeking a smaller dwelling. Allocations appear to favour the first group, in spite of the high proportion of small dwellings let to transfers, and the priority accorded the relief of underoccupation.

Table 6.9. Household Characteristics—Transfer List, West Bromwich: 1973

Household type:	Live List	Dormant List	All Lists	Successful List
Sample number	275	156	431	185
	%	%	%	%
Single person	4	3	4	1
Small adult	12	9	11	8
Small family	17	28	21	28
Large family	13	18	15	25
Large adult	21	28	23	16
Small elderly	32	15	26	21
Average household size (persons)	3·08	3·47	3·22	3·62
Households with children aged 5 or under	20%	24%	22%	36%
Average age of applicant (years)	54	47	51	47

Source: Local authority records.

Using the same indices of need for transfer as for waiting list applicants (where appropriate), transfers appear to be less in need in terms of occupancy, but in greater need because of ill health (Table 6.10). Despite this, a higher proportion of transfer than waiting list applicants gave occupancy reasons for making an application (Table 6.11). The 'low priority' reasons for transfer concerned with location and environmental quality show clearly among Dormant List applicants.

Table 6.10. Indices of Housing Need—Transfer List, West Bromwich: 1973

% of sample who are:	Live List	Dormant List	All Lists	Successful List
Living at a density of more than 2 persons per bedroom	12	3	8	8
Living at a density of 0·3 persons per bedroom or less	8	—	5	9
Claiming medical priority	32	5	22	37
On list before 1971	43	44	47	43

Source: Local authority records.

Table 6.11. Reason for Application—Transfer List, West Bromwich: 1973

Reason:	Live List	Dormant List	All Lists	Successful List
Sample number	258	127	385	173
Occupancy—	%	%	%	%
Too little space	16	6	12	23
Too much space	27	2	19	14
Housing—				
House type	6	24	12	21
Conditions	4	9	5	2
Location—				
Near work/relatives	12	23	15	8
Poor area/noise/ neighbours	6	21	11	5
Ill health	25	9	20	25
Other	4	6	6	2

Source: Local authority records.

Fourteen per cent of applicants on the Live List had already had at least one offer of a tenancy.

In terms of dwelling size, transfer applications imply a requirement for more small and large accommodation. The net result of granting all applications would be the release of 101 three-bedroomed dwellings, with demand for 68 one-, 8 two- and 23 four-bedroomed dwellings. (All the figures relate to sample numbers, and should be multiplied by 10 to give an idea of the total requirements.)

Practice—Clearance Housing

The household characteristics of families being rehoused through clearance procedures are shown in Table 6.12. A considerable mixture is evident, with a number of young households and a residual population of the elderly. Fifty-five per cent of the households had been living in the same house for over 20 years.

Nearly a quarter of the clearance households were owner-occupiers. It is interesting that only 23% were registered on the waiting list for a council house, and often they were not on the Live List.

Table 6.12. Household Characteristics—Clearance, West Bromwich: 1972-73

Household type:	Clearance rehousing
Sample number	67
	%
Single person	1
Small adult	7
Small family	21
Large family	7
Large adult	10
Small elderly	52
Average household size (persons)	2·57
Households with children aged 5 or under	18%
Average age of applicant (years)	55

Source: Local authority records.

IMPROVEMENT GRANTS

Policies

Improvement grant policies in West Bromwich must be set against the background of action for older housing in general. Over 6500 households were without exclusive use of all amenities at Census 1971. About 2500 houses are estimated to be statutorily unfit, and it is intended to represent about 450 houses a year in the future. One General Improvement Area has been declared which includes 375 dwellings, though progress is not seen as wholly satisfactory in implementation. A possible long-term programme of GIA action is proposed in the Structure Plan Report of Survey on Housing.[1] In addition, a scheme of modernization of inter-war council houses is in progress, and about 3500 have already been improved. The scheme is based on a voluntary principle—tenants apply for modernization of their houses—but has proved very popular. It is aimed to improve 600 houses a year in future.

Improvement grants to private owners are intended to assist in a general upgrading of as much of the housing stock as possible. High standards are aimed at where possible, and a discretionary grant is intended to give the house a 30 year life when the works are complete. Wherever possible applicants are urged to make use of a discretionary rather than a standard grant, to take advantage of the higher expenditure limit and repairs allowance.

Works defined as eligible for grant purposes include anything within the 12 point standard—for example, kitchen extensions are allowed since facilities for preparing and cooking food are mentioned, but the provision of an additional bedroom alone would not be allowed. In the case of conversions, self-contained flats meeting the 12 point standard are insisted on. (However it is policy to allow Special Grants for the provision of extra amenities in multi-occupied premises.) At present the only requirement for grant purposes is that the property should be at least 25 years old.

[1] *Structure Plan: Report of Survey—Housing.* West Bromwich CB 1972.

Practice—Improvement Grants and Work

Discretionary improvement grants were by far the more important during the survey period. Eighty-eight per cent of all grants were discretionary and only 12% standard, compared to figures for England and Wales (1972)[1] of 73% and 27% respectively.

Table 6.13 shows the type of work for which grants have been approved (for definition see Appendix IV). The great importance of kitchen extension work is clear. Less than a quarter of all grants in West Bromwich were for the installation of standard amenities.

Table 6.13.   Improvement Grants and Work, West Bromwich: 1972-73

Work involved:	Standard grant	Discretionary grant	All grants
Sample number	35	184	219
	%	%	%
Installation of missing amenities	26	1	5
Provision of bathroom	74	2	16
Provision of bathroom and kitchen	—	3	2
Kitchen extension	—	78	65
General improvement	—	11	9
Conversion to flats	—	3	3

Source: Local authority records.

Over 60% of the grants approved were for more than £500. The average amounts of grant in various categories are seen in Table 6.14. In West Bromwich, more is spent, on average, on kitchen extension work than on bathroom installation. In 52% of discretionary grants, repairs accounted for 40% or more of the approved costs. Unfortunately, national comparative figures are not available, even for the average amount of grant approved, since figures published in Housing and Construction Statistics are inflated by the higher levels of grant available in the Development and Intermediate Areas.

Table 6.14.   Average Grant Approved, West Bromwich: 1972-73

Type of grant:	West Bromwich £
Standard grant	210
Discretionary grant	670
All grants	600
For kitchen extension	650
For bathroom installation with or without kitchen work	420

Source: Local authority records.

In West Bromwich, over two-thirds of the houses being improved with a discretionary grant were built after 1930. Only 20% were built before 1919.

[1] *Housing and Construction Statistics No. 4.* H.M.S.O. 1972.

Owner-occupiers seem more likely to improve their property than private landlords. Overall, 90% of grants went to owner-occupiers, and 73% of the 'bathroom' grants were to owner-occupiers. In comparison, owner-occupiers only made up 42% of the households lacking exclusive use of amenities at the 1971 Census. Over half the houses being improved were mortgaged to a building society or other private lender. Thirty-nine per cent were owned outright, and only 6% mortgaged to the local authority.

COUNCIL HOUSE SALES AND COUNCIL MORTGAGES

Policy—Council House Sales

A scheme for selling council houses in West Bromwich has been in operation since 1967. Houses only are available for sale (as opposed to bungalows or flats). A limit of 10% of the total council stock has been set as an upper ceiling for sales. Any existing tenant of a pre- or post-war house is eligible for purchasing his house, including those waiting for a house once an offer has been made and accepted. Elderly tenants may require a guarantor before purchase can proceed.

Houses are sold subject to a standard 5 year pre-emption clause. The selling price is vacant possession market value (set by an independent valuer) less £50. There is also a discount given in respect of length of tenancy of the purchaser at his present and any previous council dwelling. No discount is given for tenancies of less than 10 years. Ten years tenancy earns a 5% reduction, and the percentage increases by $\frac{1}{2}$% for each completed year's tenancy to a maximum of 20 years (10%). The minimum sale price is always set by the original cost of construction, regardless of length of tenancy. In addition to the purchase price, the buyer is also required to meet charges to cover the Corporation's expenses in respect of legal and administrative work.

Policy—Council Mortgage Lending

West Bromwich operates schemes for lending money for the purchase of private houses and former council houses, and for improvement or alteration of existing property, using Housing Act powers. Some of the regulations governing mortgage lending for house purchase are set out in Table 6.15. The general intention behind the lending policy is to complement the service offered by building societies, and to provide finance for purchasers of council houses.

Practice—Mortgage Details

Only 95 loans for private house purchase were made during the period April 1968 to March 1973. During the same period, 1044 loans for council house purchase were made.

In general, the size of advances made by the local authority for house purchase is below that made by the building society. This can be seen in Table 6.16. Loans for purchase of council houses have been omitted because the information was not recorded in many cases. The table also shows, for private house loans, the

Table 6.15. Regulations for Mortgage Lending, West Bromwich: 1973

Regulation:	Private sector houses	Former council houses
Property and purchasers	The property or purchaser must fall within one of the categories of DoE Circular 22/71. The property valuation must not exceed £12,000	Any tenant buying his council house. Elderly tenants may require a guarantor
Amount of advance	The advance will not normally exceed 95% of valuation, or purchase price, whichever is the less. The Chairman of the Finance Committee may exercise discretion in special cases where a 100% loan is requested. The maximum advance on property with an estimated future life of less than 20 years is 85% of valuation. No advance will be made on property with an estimated life of 15 years or less The advance is limited by applicants' means. Repayments must not exceed one-fifth of average income. A wife's earnings are not usually taken into account	A minimum deposit of £10 is set The allowable repayments are calculated on the rule of thumb that total monthly outgoings on the property, together with other substantial commitments, should not exceed the applicant's weekly income. A wife's earnings are not usually taken into account
Period of the loan	The maximum repayment period is 25 years. In the case of leasehold property the term of the loan is limited to a period at least 10 years less than the lease has to run. Repayments must be complete 5 years before the estimated end of life of the property. Repayments must be complete when the borrower reaches 65 years of age	The maximum repayment period is 30 years Repayments must be complete when the borrower reached 65 years of age. Guarantors may be considered in certain circumstances where it is wished to extend the period beyond normal retiring age
Interest rates and repayment	Interest rates are set at pool rates, and are normally in line with those of the larger building societies. A variable rate is charged Repayments will normally be by equal monthly instalments of interest and principal, but on the request of the borrower, repayments may consist of equal instalments of principal, and interest on the diminishing amount outstanding	As for private houses

average size of deposit (i.e. the different between weighted average price and advance[1]). Although council balances seem much smaller, loans represented 79% of price in the local authority sample, and 77% of price in the building society sample.

In just over one-fifth of cases (21%) the advance made equalled over 90% of valuation. In a further 35% of cases, the advance was between 81% and 90% of valuation. This means that nearly half the advances made were for 80% or less of valuation. However, only in a single instance was the advance approved less than 90% of the advance requested.

Table 6.16.   Size of Mortgage and Advance, West Bromwich and Building Society

Advance:	Council loan— private house (1968–73)	Building Society[2] (1972)
Sample number	51	1536
	%	%
Under £2000	33	2
£2000–£2995	38	7
£3000–£3995	14	15
£4000–£4995	8	27
£5000 and over	8	50
Average advance	£2560	£4520
Weighted[1] average advance (1972 prices)	£2620	£4520
Weighted[1] average balance (1972 prices)	£680	£1290

Source: Nationwide Building Society (Midland Region) and local authority records.

[1] See Appendix III for method.

[2] Building Society figures here and in all other tables in this section relate to the Midland Region.

The average term of council loan for private house purchase was 18 years, and for council house purchase 22 years. The building society average term was 23 years. The private house average conceals a considerable spread, since a third of purchasers borrow over 10 years or less.

The average annual repayments for the council borrower for both private and council houses was £330 (1972 prices). The comparable building society figure is £430. Table 6.17 shows what repayments mean in terms of proportion of income spent by buyers of private houses (the council house data was again inadequate for analysis). On average, mortgage repayments represented 18% of applicant's income for council borrowers, and 22% for building society borrowers. The effect additional household income can have on reducing the impact of repayments is also clear from Table 6.17.

[1] Average figures have been weighted to 1972 levels.

Table 6.17.   Mortgage Repayments and Income, West Bromwich: 1968–73

Repayments as % income:	Applicant's income Council loan	Household income Council loan
Sample number	45	45
	%	%
9% and under	9	15
10–17%	38	56
18–25%	45	21
Over 25%	9	6

Source: Local authority records.

Practice—Households Buying Private Houses

Full household information is not available to allow comparison with council house applicants. Such details as are available are shown in Table 6.18. Households are usually established families; often, apparently with several children. Council borrowers are rather older than building society mortgagors.

Table 6.18.   Household Characteristics—Private House Buyers, West Bromwich and Building Society

Age:	Council loan (1968–73)	Building Society (1972)
Sample number	46	1536
	%	%
30 and under	35	63
31–45	50	28
46–60	11	8
Over 60	4	★
Average age (years)	36	30
Average household size (persons)	3·43	—

Source: Nationwide Building Society (Midland Region) and local authority records.

Eleven per cent of borrowers in West Bromwich were born in India. Altogether nearly a quarter of borrowers were born outside Great Britain. The great majority of applicants for a mortgage were in skilled manual occupations—in all 61%. A further 22% were in semi-skilled or unskilled jobs, leaving only 17% of applicants in non-manual, intermediate or professional occupations.

Applicant's income is shown in Table 6.19. The differential between the incomes of council and building society borrowers is considerably less than the differential between price of house financed by the two groups. Council incomes are 95% as high as building society incomes, while council prices are only 56% as high.

Table 6.19. Borrower's Income—Private House Buyers, West Bromwich and Building Society

Annual income:	Council loan (1968–73)	Weekly income:	Building Society (1972)
Sample number	46	Sample number	1536
	%		%
£1000 and under	6	£20 and under	3
£1005–£1500	37	£21–£30	28
£1505–£2000	35	£31–£40	36
£2005–£3000	17	£41–£60	27
Over £3000	4	Over £50	6
Average income	£1640	Average income	£1980
Weighted average (1972 prices)	£1880	Weighted average (1972 prices)	£1980

Source: Nationwide Building Society (Midland Region) and local authority records.

Practice—Households Buying Council Houses

Information on former tenants buying their council houses is less complete. Table 6.20 shows age details, and compares the structure with that of all council tenants in Great Britain. Purchasers show as being appreciably older than the private house sample, but less old than all council tenants, in average terms.

Table 6.20. Age Structure—Council House Buyers, West Bromwich and Great Britain

Age:	West Bromwich Council house buyers (1972–73)	Age:	Great Britain All council tenants (1971)
Sample number	100	Sample number	3668
	%		%
30 and under	10	Under 30	9
31–45	45	30–44	25
46–60	37	45–49	33
Over 60	8	60 and over	34
Average age	45 years		—

Source: *General Household Survey* and local authority records.

Many of the purchasers are not only middle-aged or elderly, but also long-established council tenants. One-fifth had been tenants for over 20 years, and only 17% for 5 years or less.

Practice—Private Houses Bought with Council Loans

The sort of house bought with a council loan differs quite considerably from that found among the building society sample, and from all houses for sale with estate agents in the West Bromwich area. This is particularly true of price.

Table 6.21. Price of House—Private Sector, West Bromwich and Building Society

Price:	West Bromwich		Midland Region
	Purchased with council loan (1968–73)	For sale with estate agents (1973)	Purchased with Building Society loan (1972)
Sample number	58	39	1536
	%	%	%
Under £2000	21	—	1
£2000–£2995	26	—	6
£3000–£3995	32	3	11
£4000–£4995	14	5	23
£5000 and over	8	92	59
Average price	£3240	£9000	£5810
Weighted average	£3250	£6970	£5810

Source: Nationwide Building Society (Midland Region), estate agents survey and local authority records.

The lower average price among the council group can be accounted for in part by the size and type of details given in Table 6.22. The number of terraced houses is undoubtedly related to the greater emphasis on two-bedroomed dwellings.

Table 6.22. Size and Type of Dwelling—Private Sector, West Bromwich and Building Society

House size:	West Bromwich		Midland Region
	Purchased with council loan (1968–73)	For sale with estate agents (1973)	Purchased with Building Society loan (1972)
Sample number	40	39	1536
	%	%	%
2 bedrooms	45	13	20
3 bedrooms	53	85	70
4 bedrooms or more	2	3	9
House type:			
Terraced	65	15	18
Semi-detached	24	59	40
Detached and other	11	26	42

Source: Nationwide Building Society (Midland Region), estate agents survey and local authority records.

Housing quality aspects are less easy to define. Over half the houses bought with a council loan (55%) were built before 1919, and a further 20% between the wars. Fifty-three per cent had a rateable value of £50 or less (before the 1973 revaluation), and repairs were required as a condition of the loan in just one-third of cases. While detailed figures for comparison with the building society do not exist, the general impression is that council advances are much more likely to go to older houses of rather lower quality.

Practice—Council Houses Sold

Up to the end of April 1973, nearly 1400 council houses had been sold in West Bromwich—representing about 4% of the total council stock, but about 7% of the stock of *houses*. In the size and age comparisons which follow (Table 6.23) the total figures refer to houses rather than the stock including flats and maisonettes. Two-bedroomed houses, and particularly houses built since 1944 are popular. The sale price of council houses shows little variation—nearly all cost between £2000 and £4000 to the purchaser.

Table 6.23.   Size and Age of Council Houses Sold, West Bromwich

Size:	Houses sold (1972–73)	Total stock of houses (1971)
Sample number	100	19,612
	%	%
2 bedrooms	22	14
3 bedrooms	76	82
4 bedrooms	2	4
Age:		
Pre-war	30	57
Post-war	70	43

Source: *I.M.T.A. Housing Statistics (England and Wales) Part 1,* and local authority records.

WEST BROMWICH—SUMMARY

West Bromwich emerges from this sketch as an authority with a population and household structure very similar to the regional average. It is distinct in having an above average proportion of council houses in the stock, and within the council sector, an above average number of flats and maisonettes. Inevitably council allocation policies, and council house sales policy are important. Local authority lending for private house purchase has been fairly restricted. The number of improvement grants given to private owners has increased very rapidly in recent years, at a rate significantly faster than in England and Wales as a whole.

In the council house allocation policy, considerable emphasis is given to transfers, so that a ratio of 1 to 1 for 'new' and existing tenancies results. Waiting list allocations are selective particularly of small families with young household heads and young children. Overcrowding and sharing of accommodation is being relieved particularly by allocations. Transfer allocations are again selective of families with children. Many transfers are given to elderly small households, but even so considerable unsatisfied demand exists for small (one-bedroomed) accommodation. Shortage of such dwellings may reduce the possibility of using the transfer system fully to release family accommodation for the waiting list. It also, of course, reduces the chances of small households on the waiting list being allocated a dwelling quickly. Clearance needs, while relatively small in total, have in the past also increased demand for small dwellings.

Households lacking amenities are not favoured for council allocation purposes. The improvement grant system, as it is operating at present, is equally having little impact on the problems of households living in older houses. The majority of all grants, and over 90% of discretionary grants, were going for some purpose other than the installation of basic amenities for the first time. Owner-occupiers, particularly of inter-war houses, are benefitting most from the grant system. Older houses, and private rented houses are not being improved to any great extent.

The purchase of older houses is being aided by council mortgages, but, as already said, activity on this front has not been marked. Lending that has taken place has been channelled chiefly to older, cheaper property; reflected in the fact that advances and repayments are below building society averages, and terms generally shorter. Households being helped are often established families (older than those allocated a council house), with the chief earner in a manual occupation and earning near national average wages. Property rather than borrowers can be regarded as marginal in a commercial sense.

Council houses being sold were mostly built during the post-war period. Discount for length of tenancy and pre-emption clause bring average prices to a level near that of the private houses bought with council loans. However amenity provision is rather better. Tenants buying their council houses are often middle-aged, and have been local authority tenants for several years. A rather different group of households may be following this path to owner-occupation than are found among purchasers of private houses either with local authority or building society advances.

7. Warley C.B.

BACKGROUND

Warley is a county borough with a 1971 Census population of 163,567. Population levels have been falling—by nearly 4% between 1961 and 1971—as out migration has exceeded natural increase. The age structure, though broadly similar to the regional average, shows slightly higher proportions of elderly people in the population (Table 7.1).

Table 7.1. Age Structure of Population, Warley and Region: 1971

Age:	Warley	West Midland Region
	%	%
0–14	24	25
15–19	7	7
20–29	14	15
30–44	17	18
45–59	20	19
60 and over	19	17

Source: 1971 Census.

Warley has a relatively high proportion of persons born in New Commonwealth countries. The total percentage is 5·7, over half having been born in India and a quarter in the West Indies.

There were just over 56,000 private households in Warley in 1971, giving an average household size of 2·91 (region 2·98). The household and dwelling size structures are shown in Table 7.2. Warley has relatively more small households, including elderly households, than the Region, and more medium sized dwellings. The match of households to houses results in 2·0% of households living at a density of more than $1\frac{1}{2}$ persons per room, and 37% at a density of less than $\frac{1}{2}$ person per room. Both overcrowding and 'under occupation' are slightly above the regional levels.

Table 7.2. Household and Dwelling Size, Warley and Region: 1971

Household size:	Warley	West Midland Region	Dwelling size:	Warley	West Midland Region
	%	%		%	%
1 person	18	16	1–3 rooms	9	11
2 persons	32	31	4 rooms	22	21
3–4 persons	36	38	5 rooms	39	36
5–6 persons	11	13	6 rooms	27	25
7 persons and over	3	2	7 rooms and over	4	7
1 or 2 person households in which one or both members are of retiring age as % all households	27	24			

Source: 1971 Census.

Table 7.3. Eligibility and Priority Regulations, Warley: 1973

	General Needs Applicants	Transfer Applicants	Clearance Rehousing

Eligibility rules for application:	To be registered on the waiting list an applicant must satisfy one of the following conditions:
	
	(a) Any person unless he is a single person under 25 without dependants or a divorced or separated person under 30 without dependants, provided such person:
	  (i) Lives in Warley; or
	  (ii) Has at any time lived for at least two years in Warley and has not been living outside the CB for a period of more than five years other than as a member of HM Forces;
	
	(b) Any person who has worked in Warley for a minimum period of ten years
	
	(c) Any applicant approved by Committee where there are exceptional circumstances
		Any tenant who has been the tenant of his present accommodation for two years, unless change in family circumstances has made the accommodation unsuitable
		
		A tenant may not apply if he has already been tenant of three council dwellings again unless a larger or smaller house is clearly necessary. To be eligible for registration on the list:
		One of the following reasons must also be proved:
		
		(a) Desire to change area or dwelling on the grounds that the present area or dwelling is detrimental to the health of one or more members of the applicant's family. (Must be supported by M.O.H.)
		
		(b) Need for a larger or smaller dwelling
		
		(c) Need for a house nearer the tenant's place of work, or nearer to the school where one or more of his children go.
		
		(d) Need for a house with a garage or garage space or near to Corporation grouped garages
		
		(e) Need to be nearer to aged or other relatives who are in need of supervision or other assistance the applicant intends to provide
		
		(f) Where a change in district or dwelling is desirable following a bereavement in the tenant's immediate family
		
		(g) Where there is a bona fide intention to adopt a child, and where such adoption is delayed or adversely prejudiced by the unsuitability of the applicant's present accommodation
			Not applicable

Eligibility for consideration:	Must be registered on the Live List. Applications may be transferred to a Suspense List: (a) The applicant declares he has no present need for Council accommodation but wishes to remain on the list (b) On the decision of the Housing Management Committee, being satisfied there is no present reason for the application to be given further consideration	All on this list	A tenancy is offered to any person who is a tenant or owner-occupier of a dwelling in a clearance or redevelopment area, or of an unfit house, provided that he has lived in the house at and since the date of the making of the appropriate Order Sub-tenants or lodgers in clearance property will usually be rehoused

	applicant on the waiting list, and whose turn has been reached on the list may be rehoused in a separate unit of accommodation if he so requests. A sub-tenant not satisfying these requirements but requesting separate accommodation will be referred to the Housing Management Committee for determination	Not specified
	A person refusing two suitable offers of accommodation will be reported to the Town Clerk	
	An offer will not be made under the normal system to: (a) applicants who are, or have been at any time during the three years immediately preceding allocation, owner-occupiers of self-contained accommodation (b) applicants who solely occupy adequate self-contained accommodation with all facilities and in good state of repair as tenants (c) family of an applicant serving in HM Forces prior to demobilization unless specified circumstances obtain (d) applicants who have not completed two years' residence in Warley (wife's residence can count). (e) applicants the Housing Estates Manager considers unsuitable to be granted a tenancy (f) applicants who have worked in Warley for a minimum of ten years shall be offered accommodation at the discretion of the Housing Estates Manager	Date order of application within house size and area groups. Exceptions to date order are as follows: (a) Where the M.O.H. evaluates a case as having the highest medical priority (A), the application shall be put at the top of the appropriate queue (b) Where the M.O.H. recommends a Medical B priority, a bonus of nine months waiting time shall automatically be given (c) Medical C will receive priority only if all other factors are equal (d) For every completed five years of tenancy over two, a bonus of three months waiting time shall be added at the time of registration. If two offers are refused, other than for good medical or social reasons, the application shall be cancelled and automatically reinstated at the date on which the offer was refused. Bonus points for length of residence and Medical B priority are lost
Method of determining priority:	Date order of application. Some exceptions exist: (a) An applicant who is a tenant of private property, and whose landlord has commenced Court proceedings for his eviction shall be rehoused providing his registration number is not more than 250 greater than the last person rehoused (b) An applicant who holds a service tenancy, and has to leave his accommodation because his employment has terminated will be rehoused if his registered number has been reached	

Council housing makes up a larger than average proportion of the total stock in Warley. Forty-four per cent of households were council tenants in 1971 and 40% owner-occupiers. The regional figures were 34% and 50% respectively. The private rented sector took a similar share in both cases.

Warley is particularly distinctive in figures for amenity provision. Only 75% of households had exclusive use of all amenities at the Census—despite the relatively high number of council houses. Nearly a fifth of owner-occupiers and over half the private renters were without exclusive use of one or more of the four basic amenities.

House completions averaged over 1000 a year in Warley between 1968 and 1972.[1] The public sector accounted for about four-fifths of houses built. An average of 563 houses a year were demolished or closed in the same period. The net gain to the housing stock has, therefore, been nearly 500 a year.

Warley then emerges as a town of declining population, with above average proportions of elderly and small households. The housing stock contains above average numbers of council houses and private sector dwellings lacking basic amenities.

COUNCIL HOUSE ALLOCATIONS

Policies

Demand for council housing in Warley exceeds supply. The rules of eligibility for application and consideration are given in Table 7.3. The methods of ordering priority within the groups are also shown. As a general rule, waiting list applicants in Warley who have registered on the list since January 1st 1966 will be offered a flat or maisonette only. For an applicant to be eligible for a house, he must have Committee approval as an overcrowding or medical case, or there must be sound management grounds why a house should be offered.

Special cases may be considered by the Committee falling outside the normal waiting list procedures. For example, an owner-occupier may be considered for rehousing on medical grounds, or if there are mortgage repayment problems. Service tenancies may be created, and dwellings are allocated to teachers, firemen and council workmen.

Priorities between the groups described in Table 7.3 are as follows:

(a) Clearance rehousing.

(b) Medical category 'A'.

(c) Transfer and waiting list applicants.

Since general need applicants are only eligible for flats or maisonettes, transfers have priority for the letting of houses. There are no fixed proportions of lettings assigned to the groups.

[1] *Local Housing Statistics—England and Wales.* H.M.S.O.

Practice—Allocations

On the basis of the survey sample, 2175 allocations were made in the year 1972–73. Of these, 36% went to applicants from the waiting list, 40% to transfer applicants, 6% to mutual exchanges, 16% to clearance households and 2% to other lettings, service tenancies, etc. The total number of new lettings (waiting list, clearance and other lettings) exceeded lettings to existing tenants (transfers and exchanges) by a small margin. The ratio of 'new' to 'transfer' lettings was 1 to 0·87. General needs applicants took 67% of the new lettings.

The type of property being allocated to each lettings group is shown in Table 7.4. Differences in terms of dwelling size allocated to each group can be accounted for in terms of household size, though there is a general tendency towards generosity in space standards, particularly among waiting list allocations. Forty-three per cent of allocations were at a density lower than a simple bedroom standard[1] (49% among general needs allocations). House type allocated shows less relationship to household structure—waiting list applicants were considerably less likely to be allocated a house than were transfers, but exactly the same proportion of households in the two groups included children aged 5 or under. Only 3% of waiting list applicants were allocated a dwelling on an 'attractive' estate, compared to one third of both clearance and transfer tenants.

Table 7.4. Types of Dwelling Allocated, Warley: 1972–73

House type:	Waiting list and other cases	Transfers and mutual exchanges	Clearance	Total
Sample number	163	201	68	432
	%	%	%	%
Bungalow	—	2	4	2
1 bed. flat	13	16	18	16
2 bed. flat/maisonette	46	12	21	26
2 bed. house	2	7	6	5
3 bed. flat/maisonette	25	1	3	11
3 bed. house	13	58	46	39
4 bed. house	1	3	1	2

Source: Local authority records.

Of course, allocations can only be made as vacancies arise, or are created by transfers. The turnover rates for different house types show wide variations (Table 7.5). About 18% of the vacancies arising during the year were the result of new building. At least 6% of vacancies were due to the death of the previous tenant.

[1] See Appendix IV for definition.

Table 7.5. Turnover Rates and House Type, Warley: 1972-73

House type:	Number in stock 1971	Number among allocations Sample × 5	Allocations as % stock
	Number	Number	% as index
Bungalow	267	40	15
1 bed. flat	1969	335	17
2 bed. flat/maisonette	4573	560	12
2 bed. house	2312	105	5
3 bed. flat/maisonette	1578	225	14
3 bed. house	13,720	840	6
4 bed. house	521	45	9

Source: I.M.T.A. *Housing Statistics (England and Wales) Part 1* and local authority records.

Practice—the Waiting List

As indicated in Table 7.3 a Live List and a Suspense List are maintained in Warley. Both these and the Total List are compared with the Successful List, that is waiting list applicants who were allocated a dwelling during the survey year.

Table 7.6 shows the household characteristics of applicants. Allocations are heavily selective of families with young children, while small elderly households are relatively unlikely to be successful. The similar average age of Live and Suspense List applicants conceals differences—Live List applicants are mostly young or elderly, Suspense List applicants are predominantly middle-aged.

Table 7.6. Household Characteristics—Waiting List, Warley: 1973

Household type:	Live List	Suspense List	All Lists	Successful Lis
Sample number	102	310	412	138
	%	%	%	%
Single person	10	7	8	8
Small adult	31	25	26	28
Small family	17	32	28	38
Large family	12	9	10	13
Large adult	4	12	10	7
Small elderly	27	16	18	7
Average household size (persons)	2·35	2·73	2·64	2·76
Households with children aged 5 or under	22%	22%	22%	41%
Average age of applicant (years)	42	43	43	35

Source: Local authority records.

The great majority of applicants were born in Great Britain—92% in all. Four per cent of applicants were born in the West Indies and 1% in India. Allocations also show 92% British born, with 3% West Indian and 2% born in India.

Indices of housing need are shown in Table 7.7. The Successful List shows higher proportions in many of the need categories. Underoccupation and lack of amenities provide marked exceptions to this—as does medical priority, though here the lack of distinction between degree of priority may be responsible. It is interesting that a date order priority scheme can apparently be highly selective of certain elements of housing need.

Table 7.7.   Indices of Housing Need—Waiting List, Warley: 1973

% of sample who are:	Live List	Suspense List	All Lists	Successful List
Lodging with family	17	27	25	59
Lodging—other	12	7	8	14
Without own living room	38	25	26	62
Sharing with 5 or more persons	8	3	4	17
Living at a density of more than 2 persons per bedroom	16	13	14	36
Living at a density of 0·3 persons per bedroom or less	13	4	6	1
Claiming medical priority	5	3	4	1
Without use of bath	23	21	21	8
Lone parent families	10	12	11	17
Registering within 1 year of marriage	35	24	27	39
Registering when baby expected	7	5	6	14
On list before 1971	26	67	57	17

Source: Local authority records.

All these indices of need are reflected in the main reason given for making an application (Table 7.8). Applicants giving poor conditions or house too big for their reason are not favoured. The prevalence of 'insurance' reasons is by definition, a feature of the Suspense List.

Table 7.8.   Reason for Application—Waiting List, Warley: 1973

Reason:	Live List	Suspense List	All Lists	Successful List
Sample number	86	238	324	128
	%	%	%	%
Seeking independence	14	9	10	36
Engaged/want to start family	12	3	6	2
Occupancy—				
Too little space	23	8	12	27
Too much space	7	3	4	2
Housing—				
Conditions	20	19	19	9
Location—				
Near work/relatives	4	5	5	1
Poor area/noise, etc.	4	1	2	2
Ill health	7	4	5	3
Insurance/tied accommodation	5	36	28	7
Other	4	12	9	11

Source: Local authority records.

Just under a third (30%) of applicants on the Live List had already received at least one offer of a tenancy (four per cent had had more than two offers which indicates the policy set out in Table 7.3 is not always rigidly applied). Over a third (38%) of those allocated a tenancy had previously received and refused at least one offer.

Practice—Transfers

A single transfer list is maintained for all eligible applicants. In terms of household characteristics, transfer applicants are not totally dissimilar to waiting list applicants in Warley (Table 7.9). Average age is greater because there are less young persons, not because there are markedly more elderly on the list. Households are generally larger, and contain more children. Transfer allocations are selective of households with children, and do not favour small elderly households (though many more elderly households are successful among transfers than among waiting list applicants).

Table 7.9. Household Characteristics—Transfer List, Warley: 1973

Household type:	Transfer List	Successful List
Sample number	380	169
	%	%
Single person	6	3
Small adult	15	8
Small family	31	40
Large family	14	15
Large adult	10	14
Small elderly	25	20
Average household size (persons)	2·96	3·24
Households with children aged 5 or under	31	41
Average age of applicant (years)	44	44

Source: Local authority records.

In terms of the indices of housing need in Table 7.10, transfer applicants appear markedly less crowded than waiting list applicants. Underoccupancy is similar in the two groups, and medical claims more frequent among transfers. Allocations are selective only of overcrowding. A concern with space and occupancy is evident in the reasons for application given (Table 7.11), and also with quality in the area, which is apparently less likely to be a successful reason for transfer.

Table 7.10. Indices of Housing Need—Transfer List, Warley: 1973

% of sample who are:	Transfer List	Successful List
Living at a density of more than 2 persons per bedroom	7	11
Living at a density of 0·3 persons per bedroom or less	8	5
Claiming medical priority	20	12
On list before 1971	23	41

Source: Local authority records.

Table 7.11.   Reason for Application—Transfer List, Warley: 1973

Reason:	Transfer List	Successful List
Sample number	374	166
	%	%
Occupancy—		
Too little space	9	15
Too much space	13	10
Housing—		
House type	26	25
Conditions	4	2
Location—		
Near work/relatives	11	14
Poor area/noise/neighbours	13	5
Ill health	20	27
Other	4	2

Source: Local authority records.

A number of offers had already been made to transfer applicants. Just a quarter of those on the list had received and refused at least one offer, and only 61% of those allocated a tenancy accepted the first offer made to them.

Transfer applications indicate a demand for more small accommodation. The net result of granting all transfer applications would be the release of 38 two- and 18 three-bedroomed houses. An additional 54 one-bedroomed and 3 four-bedroomed units would be required (all figures relate to the sample, and should be multiplied by 10 to give an idea of the requirements).

Practice—Clearance Rehousing

A variety of households are involved in clearance rehousing in Warley (Table 7.12). A third had lived in the houses affected for five years or less, and 46% for over twenty years. Evidently a young population is moving in amongst a pre-dominantly elderly residual group.

Table 7.12.   Household Characteristics—Clearance, Warley: 1972–73

Household type:	Clearance rehousing
Sample number	62
	%
Single person	8
Small adult	10
Small family	32
Large family	11
Large adult	13
Small elderly	26
Average household size (persons)	2·94
Households with children aged 5 or under	26%
Average age of applicant (years)	49

Source: Local authority records.

Just over a fifth of the clearance properties were in owner-occupation. Only 3% had a bathroom.

IMPROVEMENT GRANTS

Policies

The condition of much of the older housing in Warley is seen as one of the Borough's principal housing problems. Over 14,000 households were without exclusive use of all amenities at the 1971 Census. Improvement grants represent one part of the local authority effort to tackle the problems.

The present clearance programme should be complete in 1975–6; something over 800 houses remain to be dealt with. However, clearance is expected to continue beyond that date. The Council is also pursuing an energetic General Improvement Area programme, intended to deal with nearly 7000 houses. Three GIAs have already been designated, two in private sector and one in public sector housing areas. Response in the private sector has been mixed. A programme of council house modernization is also under way. It is intended to improve 1200 to 1300 houses a year in a scheme of 7500 properties. This may be seen as the beginning of a continuing programme.

Improvement grants to private house owners form part of this overall renewal strategy. Generally applicants are encouraged to make use of discretionary grants and to achieve as high a standard as possible. At the same time however, it is borne in mind that, if things are made too difficult for an applicant, no improvement at all may result. No written statement of allowable works for discretionary grants is available but the following indications are relevant:

(a) Grants are available for any house built before 1961. It is intended that a house, when improved, should reach the 12 point standard and have a life of 30 years.

(b) Any work required to achieve this is allowed. This can mean that a grant may be given for kitchen extension work (to bring the floor space to 75 square feet) alone, where the property otherwise meets the 12 point standard.

(c) In some areas of the town only standard grants will be given since the 30 year life cannot be assured. The Council is keen to give grants in these areas to achieve better living conditions in the short term.

Given that 'life' requirements can be satisfied, grants will be given on property covered by a Closing Order or included in the provisional unfit list, but such cases are rare. In this direct sense, improvement and clearance are rarely alternatives.

Practice—Improvement Grants

Discretionary grants were much the more important during the survey period, making up 62% of all those approved. Table 7.13 shows the type of work involved in the grant applications. The great majority include the installation of basic amenities. (See Appendix IV for definition of works used.)

Table 7.13. Improvement Grants and Work, Warley: 1972-73

Work involved:	Standard grant	Discretionary grant	All grants
Sample number	72	118	190
	%	%	%
Installation of missing amenities	43	14	25
Provision of bathroom	57	4	24
Provision of bathroom and kitchen	—	60	37
Kitchen extension	—	17	11
Conversion to flats	—	4	3

Source: Local authority records.

Over 90% of the grants approved were for less than £500—over a third were for less than £200. Table 7.14 shows the average amount of grant approved under various headings.

7.14. Average Grant Approved, Warley: 1972-73

Type of Grant:	Warley £
Standard grant	178
Discretionary grant	355
All grants	288
For kitchen extension	230
For bathroom installation with or without kitchen improvement	349

Source: Local authority records.

In 43% of the discretionary grants, repairs accounted for more than 20% of the approved expenditure. However, in 27% of all cases, no repairs element was included.

Some considerable time can elapse between a grant application being made, and approval being given. In only 20% of cases was official approval notified to the applicant within 6 weeks of the application being submitted. About a third of all applications took 15 weeks or over to approve.

In Warley nearly two-thirds of the grants approved went to property built before 1919. Since this figure relates only to discretionary grants (the information on age is not required for standard grants), the overall proportion of older houses receiving grant will be still higher. Seventy per cent of all grants went to terraced houses.

Owner-occupiers seem rather more likely to improve their houses than private landlords. Just under two-thirds of the houses receiving grants were owner-occupied, a further 23% were tenanted, whilst 13% were vacant at the time of application. Forty-nine per cent of the bathroom grants were to owner-occupiers (and 18% on vacant properties). In comparison, owner-occupiers made up only 46% of the private sector households lacking amenities at the 1971 Census. Fifty-seven per cent of the houses receiving grants were owned outright, while

21% had a building society or bank loan. Nearly a quarter had an outstanding local authority mortgage.

COUNCIL HOUSE SALES AND COUNCIL MORTGAGES

Policy—Council House Sales

Council tenants in Warley are no longer able to buy their houses. However, a scheme was in operation between 1966 and March 1973, and over 1500 houses were sold. Houses only, as opposed to bungalows or flats, were available for sale. No limit was set to the numbers to be sold. Any existing tenant of a pre- or post-war house was eligible to purchase his house. No minimum length of tenancy was required.

Houses were normally sold subject to a standard 5 year pre-emption clause in which case the purchase price was full market value less a 20% discount. Alternatively the purchaser could choose to pay full market value, with no pre-emption clause. The minimum price was set by the original cost price of the house and garage (where appropriate). All sales were freehold.

Policy—Council Mortgage Lending

Warley Council operates schemes for lending money for the acquisition, conversion, alteration, repair or improvement of houses in the Borough area, using Housing Act powers. Some of the regulations for mortgage lending are set out in Table 7.15. All loans are made entirely at the discretion of the Council, and lending policies are seen as being complementary rather than competitive to the services offered by building societies.

Practice—Mortgage Details

During 1972, 132 loans for private house purchase were made in Warley; 1911 loans were outstanding at December 1972. At the same date 1022 loans for countil house purchase were outstanding.

Table 7.16 shows that council advances are, on average, considerably smaller than those made by the building society. The average size of deposit (that is, the difference between the weighted average price and advance[1]), is shown for each group. Council house purchasers had to, or chose to, provide much smaller deposits. The average advance, in fact, represented 94% of average price. Comparable figures for council loans for private houses, and building society loans were 80% and 77% respectively.

[1] See Appendix III for method.

Table 7.15.　Regulations for Mortgage Lending, Warley: 1973

Regulation:	Private Sector Houses	Former Council Houses (when sold)
Property and purchasers	The property or purchaser must fall within one of the categories of DoE Circular 22/71. The property or purchaser must be situated within Warley. The property valuation must not exceed £7000	Any tenant acquiring his council house. Elderly purchasers may require a guarantor
Amount of advance	Advances are usually limited to 95% of valuation or purchase price, whichever is the less. New dwellings, or a sitting tenant may receive an advance 100% of valuation. Loans are not usually made where purchase price exceeds valuation by more than 10% An advance will not be made where repayments together with rates, water charges, ground rent and any hire purchase commitments would exceed 25% of applicant's gross average income. The earnings of the wife (up to age 40) are not normally considered in calculating income	Limited to 99% of purchase price. Income requirements as for private houses
Period of the loan	Maximum period 30 years. Period is limited at the discretion of the Finance Committee to the difference between the age of the house and 80 years. In certain cases where the age of the property exceeds 70 years, the maximum period may be 10 years, dependent on the observations of the valuer. Repayment should normally be complete by normal retirement age When the property is leasehold, the period of the advance is not to exceed the unexpired period of the lease reduced to the next 10 years below, and divided by 2. (35 years lease—30÷2 = 15) The income and repayments requirements may limit the terms of the loan	As for private houses. Younger relatives may be accepted as guarantors in the case of an elderly purchaser
Interest rates and repayment	A fixed interest rate is payable at a level ¼% above the Council's external borrowing rate for a comparable period at the date on which the loan is approved Repayment is on an annuity or instalment basis at the request of the borrower	As for private houses
Other conditions	Where repair costs (estimated by the valuer) exceed £50, the amount is withheld from the advance pending completion of repairs. Where the cost of repairs is less than £50, the borrower is required as a condition of the mortgage, to carry out the repairs within 3 months of receiving the advance. Where repair costs exceed 10% of the valuation, all repairs must be complete before the advance is made. Each applicant is required to give an undertaking that the dwelling will be used as such for himself, his wife and his children. Unless the Council dispense with this condition, the borrower must reside in the house for 3 years from the date of the advance	

Table 7.16.   Size of Mortgage Advance and Balance, Warley and Building Society

	Council advance		
	Private house	Council house	Building Society [2]
Advance:	(1966–73)	(1972–73)	(1972)
Sample number	85	83	1536
	%	%	%
Under £2000	42	2	2
£2000–£2995	50	46	7
£3000–£3995	8	43	15
£4000–£4995	—	7	27
£5000 and over	—	—	50
Average advance	£2080	£3020	£4520
Weighted [1] average advance (1972 prices)	£1870	£2700	£4520
Weighted [1] average balance (1972 prices)	£470	£160	£1290

Source: Nationwide Building Society (Midland Region) and local authority records.

[1] See Appendix III for method.

[2] Building Society figures here and in all other tables in this section relate to the Midland Region.

In just under a quarter (23%) of private house loans, the advance exceeded 90% of valuation. In a further quarter of cases, the advance was between 81% and 90% of valuation. This means that very nearly half of all private house loans equalled 80% of valuation or less. The pricing policy for sold council houses makes comparisons impossible—however, only 16% of council house purchasers received an advance which represented 90% of *price* or less. In about 90% of cases, the loan granted for private house purchase was that requested, and the figure rises to 99% for council houses.

The average period of council loans for private houses was 13 years, and for council houses was 22 years. The building society average is 23 years. There is an obvious difference between the two types of council loan; in the case of private houses only 19% of loans were for 20 years or longer, while over half of those for council houses were for either 25 or 30 years.

Council loans for private house purchase resulted in average annual repayments for the borrower of £270. The equivalent council house figure is £330 (both in 1972 prices) and the building society was £430. Table 7.17 shows what this means in terms of the proportion of income committed to repayments. In view of the difference in amounts of loans concerned, the difference between private and council house buyers is relatively slight when applicant's income is considered. The term of the loan has great influence here. However, the impact of total household income in reducing the proportion of income committed amongst council house buyers is particularly marked.

Table 7.17. Mortgage Repayments and Income, Warley and Building Society

Repayments as % income:	Applicant's income			Household income	
	Private houses (1966–73)	Council houses (1972–73)	Building Society (1972)	Private houses (1966–73)	Council houses (1972–73)
Sample number	85	81	1536	84	82
	%	%	%	%	%
Less than 10%	8	1	—	14	6
10–17%	54	52	—	55	77
18–25%	29	39	—	23	16
Over 25%	9	7	—	7	1
Average percentage	16	17	22	—	—

Source: Nationwide Building Society (Midland Region) and local authority records.

Practice—Households Buying Private Houses

Full information is available on the households buying private houses with council advances. Council purchasers seem very similar to building society borrowers in terms of age. Household size is rather larger than found among applicants for council tenancies (Table 7.6), and families seem further advanced in their development cycle. However, there are few elderly households among house buyers.

Table 7.18. Household Characteristics—Private House Buyers, Warley and Building Society

Household type:	Warley Council loan (1966–73)	Midland Region Building Society (1972)	Great Britain All owner-occupiers with an outstanding mortgage (1971)
Sample number	85	—	3199
	%	—	%
Single person	9	—	3
Small adult	27	—	17
Small and large family	61	—	58
Large adult	1	—	17
Small elderly	1	—	6
Average household size (persons)	3·46	—	—
Households with children aged 5 or under	52%	—	—
Age:			
Sample number	85	1536	—
	%	%	—
30 and under	61	63	—
31–45	28	28	—
46–60	11	8	—
Over 60	—	★	—
Average age (years)	31	30	—

Source: Nationwide Building Society (Midland Region) *General Household Survey—Introductory Report* and local authority records.

On the basis of applicant's names, it seems that at least 35% of mortgages in Warley went to immigrants (Asian). West Indian purchasers would not, of course, be distinguished in this way. The great majority of borrowers (60%) were in skilled manual occupations, with a further 21% in semi- or unskilled employment. Only 18% of borrowers, then, were in professional, intermediate or non-manual jobs.

Applicant's total income is shown in Table 7.19. The differential between average incomes of council and building society borrowers is considerably smaller than the differential between house prices financed by the two sources. Council average incomes are 83% as high as building society incomes, but prices only 40% as high. Average earnings for a full time male employee in Great Britain 1972 was £1870[1]—rather above the Warley borrower's average. The relationship between incomes and repayments has already been described.

Table 7.19. Borrower's Income—Private House Buyers, Warley and Building Society

Annual income:	Council loans (1966–73)	Weekly income:	Building Society (1972)
Sample number	85	Sample number	1536
	%		%
£1000 and under	2	£20 and under	3
£1005–£1500	35	£21–£30	28
£1505–£2000	47	£31–£40	36
£2005–£3000	15	£41–£60	27
Over £3000	—	Over £60	6
Average income	£1620	Average income	£1980
Weighted average (1972 prices)	£1640	Weighted average (1972 prices)	£1980

Source: Nationwide Building Society (Midland Region) and local authority records.

Practice—Households Buying Council Houses

Former tenants borrowing to buy their council house were appreciably older than those buying a private house, but no so old, on average, as all council tenants in Great Britain. The lack of small elderly households, despite the number of applicants aged over 60, indicates that these elderly purchasers may be living with younger relatives who can act as guarantor. The group generally seems further advanced in the family cycle than in the case of private house purchasers. There are more large adult households and fewer children aged 5 or under (but more aged 16 or under).

[1] *Department of Employment Gazette* Vol. LXXXI No. 12, Dec. 1973, Table 128.

Table 7.20. Household Characteristics—Council House Buyers, Warley and Great Britain

Household type:	Warley Council house buyer (1972–73)	Great Britain All council tenants (1971)
Sample number	83	3683
	%	%
Single person	1	4
Small adult	10	11
Small and large family	74	35
Large adult	15	21
Small elderly	—	28
Average household size (persons)	4·25	—
Households with children aged 5 or under	39%	—

Age:		Age:	
Sample number	83	Sample number	3688
	%		%
30 and under	18	Under 30	9
31–45	51	30–44	25
46–60	21	45–59	33
Over 60	10	60 and over	34
Average (years)	42		—

Source: *General Household Survey—Introductory Report* and local authority records.

Just a tenth of the purchasers had been council tenants for over 20 years, over half (52%) for over 10 years, and only 13% had been tenants for 5 years or less.

The social class figures show an even greater emphasis on skilled manual and on semi- or unskilled occupations than amongst private house buyers. The respective proportions are 68% and 18%. Four per cent of council house purchasers were retired.

Applicant's income was on average higher than among private house buyers. The average controlled to 1972 levels was £1910 compared to only £1640 for the private purchasers. This is above the national average income of £1870. Larger, older families also allow more scope for additional earners to supplement household income. The extent to which this affects the impact of repayments has already been quoted. (Table 7.17.)

Practice—Private Houses Bought with Council Loans

The price of private houses bought with a council loan in Warley is considerably lower than that found among either the building society sample, or the houses for sale with estate agents in Warley in 1973 (Table 7.21). The lower average price paid by those with council loans reflects the size and house type of dwellings purchased shown in Table 7.22.

Table 7.21. Price of Houses—Private Sector, Warley and Building Society

Price:	Warley		Midland Region
	Purchased with council loan	For sale with estate agents	Purchased with Building Society loan
	(1966–73)	(1973)	(1972)
Sample number	85	56	1536
	%	%	%
Under £2000	14	—	1
£2000–£2995	63	3	6
£3000–£3995	20	4	11
£4000–£4995	3	13	23
£5000 and over	—	80	59
Average price	£2550	£7770	£5810
Weighted average (1972 prices)	£2340	£6010	£5810

Source: Nationwide Building Society (Midland Region), estage agents survey and local authority records.

Table 7.22. Size and Type of Dwelling—Private Sector, Warley and Building Society

House size:	Warley		Midland Region
	Purchased with council loan	For sale with estate agents	Purchased with Building Society loan
	(1966–73)	(1973)	(1972)
Sample number	84	56	1536
	%	%	%
2 bedrooms	46	23	20
3 bedrooms	48	70	70
4 bedrooms or more	6	7	9
House type:			
Terraced	95	36	18
Semi-detached	5	55	40
Detached and other	—	9	42

Source: Nationwide Building Society (Midland Region), estage agents survey and local authority records.

House quality is less easy to judge. Eighty-eight per cent of the houses bought with a council loan were built before 1919, and a further 11% before 1939. Only one post-war house was included in the sample. Only 26% of the houses bought had a front and back garden, 11% had a garage, but 99% had a hot water supply. At the extreme, 75% of all houses bought required some repairs as a condition of the loan, and 80% had a rateable value of £50 or less (before the 1973 revaluation). Building society figures are not available for comparison, but it would seem the local authority is lending on older, poorer quality dwellings.

Practice—Council Houses Sold

When sales were discontinued in Warley, about 1500 houses had been sold—representing about 6% of the total stock, but 9% of the stock of *houses*. In the size and age comparisons which follow (Table 7.23), the 'total' figures refer to houses rather than the stock including flats and maisonettes. Two-bedroomed houses and those built in the post-war period seem slightly more popular, but there is very little difference in the figures. Over half (53%) of the houses sold were on 'attractive' estates, compared to only 5% of dwellings allocated to waiting list applicants. However, 64% of transfer allocations were to 'attractive' areas.

Table 7.23.   Size and Age of Council Houses Sold, Warley

	Houses sold	Total stock of houses
Size:	(1972–73)	(1971)
Sample number	65	16,553
	%	%
2 bedrooms	9	14
3 bedrooms	89	83
4 bedrooms or more	2	3
Age:		
Sample number	77	16,553
	%	%
Pre-war	57	59
Post-war	43	41

Source: *I.M.T.A. Housing Statistics (England and Wales) Part 1* and local authority records.

The weighted average purchase price of council houses sold was £2860 (compared to £2340 for private houses). The great majority (71%) cost between £3000 and £4000 (recent sales means the weighted average is below the true average—see Appendix III). The council houses sold were likely to be in much better structural condition than the private houses. Rateable values were certainly higher—only 5% had a rateable value of £50 or less. In these circumstances more than a £500 difference in average purchase price for council and private houses bought with a council loan might have been expected.

WARLEY—SUMMARY

The picture of Warley which emerges is interesting. The authority has slightly above average numbers of elderly households in its population. The housing stock is distinguished by a relatively large council sector (in which there is an above average proportion of flats and maisonettes), and a private sector in which many households lack basic amenities. Performance of housing policies in relation to the older age groups, and the older housing stock can be checked.

Warley operates a date order allocation scheme for the waiting list and transfer applicants. Yet certain groups are consistently favoured. Small families with young children, and households in overcrowded conditions (lodgers on the waiting list) are rehoused more rapidly. Conversely small elderly households, single persons and small adult households are not favoured. In short, those requiring small accommodation are 'discriminated against' and can expect to wait longer for rehousing. All the evidence from waiting list and transfer surveys speaks of a shortage of one-bedroomed accommodation in Warley which is dictating the allocation procedures and favouring one type of household relative to another.

Because the small elderly households on the waiting list tend to live in houses lacking amenities, households in this type of housing need are not being greatly helped by council house provision. However, the improvement grant system in Warley is aimed squarely at the older housing stock and the provision of basic amenities. Private landlords are contributing to the improvement process to some extent, though rather less than the size of the problem in the private rented sector suggests would be desirable. Improvement expenditure in Warley tends to be modest in each scheme, but this could well be in line with the present wishes and abilities of residents. The success of the improvement programme in dealing with older houses may be explained in this way. However, improvement to moderate standards, while improving conditions in the short term, implies a need for further upgrading in the future in a gradual and incremental process.

The older housing stock is also the main field of action for council mortgage lending. Property being lent on could well be considered marginal by building societies, and the council's financial policy complements the improvement and renewal strand. Purchasers, however, tend to be young families, scarcely different from the younger households on the council house waiting list (apart from the much higher proportion of immigrants among borrowers). The elderly are not helped in this way.

There is little evidence that the decision to discontinue selling council houses has prevented the Council from meeting objectively defined housing *needs* (though it may have thwarted some housing *desires*). The income of council house purchasers was generally above the national average, and certainly above that of buyers with council mortgages in the private sector. The price of houses sold with the pre-emption clause seems very favourable in terms of age and quality of house involved.

However, in some ways, the issue over council sales is peripheral to the main problems in Warley, since the sub-standard housing stock is unaffected, and the decision has no impact on the release of small accommodation. In the long term, the retention of houses in the rented stock might release resources for the building of smaller units by reducing the requirement for additional family-sized dwellings.

Housing policies in Warley seem complementary in their dealings with the older stock. Shortage of small accommodation prevents registered needs being fully met at present.

8. Wolverhampton C.B.

BACKGROUND

Wolverhampton is a county borough with a 1971 Census population of 269,112. Population has been slowly increasing since 1961, by 0·29% per annum—as net outward migration has been lower than natural increase by births and deaths. The age structure in Table 8.1 is seen to be very similar to the West Midland regional average.

Table 8.1. Age Structure of Population, Wolverhampton and Region: 1971

Age:	Wolverhampton	West Midland Region
	%	%
0–14	26	25
15–19	7	7
20–29	13	15
30–44	18	18
45–59	19	19
60 and over	16	17

Source: 1971 Census.

The proportion of persons born in New Commonwealth countries in Wolverhampton was 7·5% in 1971. Over half of these were born in India, and a further third in the West Indies.

There were 87,240 private households in 1971, giving an average household size of 3·05 persons, which is rather larger than the regional average (2·98 persons). The household and dwelling size structures are shown in Table 8.2. Wolverhampton is found to be remarkably similar to the regional average in both respects.The proportion of small elderly households is also very near the regional figure. The match of households to dwellings results in 2·5% of households living at a density of more than 1½ persons per room, and 31% at a density of less than ½ person per room. The proportion in overcrowded conditions is slightly above, and in 'underoccupation' slightly below the regional average.

Table 8.2. Household and Dwelling Size, Wolverhampton and Region: 1971

Household size:	Wolverhampton	West Midland Region	House size:	Wolverhampton	West Midland Region
	%	%		%	%
1 person	16	16	1–3 rooms	13	11
2 persons	30	31	4 rooms	20	21
3–4 persons	38	38	5 rooms	35	36
5–6 persons	12	13	6 rooms	27	25
7 persons and over	4	2	7 rooms and		
1 and 2 person households in which one or both members are of retiring age as % of all households	23	24	over	6	7

Source: 1971 Census.

Relatively more households are council tenants in Wolverhampton than in the Region, and less are owner-occupiers. Wolverhampton figures are 45% council tenants and 42% owner-occupiers. The regional figures are 34% and 50% respectively. The private rented sector is, therefore, slightly smaller locally than regionally.

Just over four-fifths (81%) of households in Wolverhampton had exclusive use of the Census amenities—fixed bath, hot water and an inside WC (Region 84%). The situation is particularly serious in the private rented sector, where nearly half the households lacked one or more of the amenities.

House building completions averaged nearly 1300 a year between 1968 and 1972.[1] The public sector accounted for over half the houses built. During the same period an average of about 350 houses a year were demolished or closed. The net gain to the housing stock, has, therefore, been about 900 houses a year.

Wolverhampton appears, then, as a town with a population and dwelling structure very similar to the West Midland Region. The housing stock contains above average numbers of council houses.

COUNCIL HOUSE ALLOCATIONS

Policies

Demand for council housing in Wolverhampton exceeds supply. Since the Council see their role as providing for those in greatest need the eligibility and priority rulings outlined in Table 8.3 have evolved. Transfer and clearance groups are also included in the Table.

Special cases are dealt with outside the normal waiting list system. These include key council employees appointed with accommodation provided, other service tenancies, owner-occupiers selling their houses to the Council, and former tenants who give up their tenancy to live with relatives but find they would like a house of their own again. Also included are homeless families (house allocated to the Social Services Department), potentially homeless elderly people, and any other cases approved by the Housing Committee outside the points scheme.

Groups are housed in the following order of priority:

(a) Special cases and clearance rehousing.

(b) Transfers.

(c) Waiting List.

Some flexibility is possible within this. If, for example, the natural workings of the system means that all the vacancies on a popular estate would go to transfers or clearance rehousing, it is possible to decide that a fixed percentage of all vacancies there will be reserved for general needs applicants.

[1] *Local Housing Statistics—England and Wales.* H.M.S.O.

Table 8.3. Eligibility and Priority Regulations, Wolverhampton: 1973

	General Needs Applicants	Transfer Applicants	Clearance Rehousing
Eligibility rules for application:	Anyone living in Wolverhampton who intend to settle in the Borough on discharge. Elderly persons who have lived in Wolverhampton for over 20 years, and have since moved away, but wish to return	Any council tenant	Not applicable
Eligibility for consideration:	Those registered on the waiting list who do not wish their application to be deferred. There are certain exceptions: (a) Tenants of self-contained accommodation will only be offered a dwelling if one or more of the following apply: (i) There is overcrowding (ii) There is substantial underoccupation and the applicant is of pensionable age (iii) The applicants live with one or more families in a house intended for one family (iv) Points have been awarded on medical grounds (v) Points have been awarded for having no living room (vi) Points have been awarded under the Service tenancy heading (b) Owner-occupiers will only be considered on grounds of severe ill health or social need (c) An allocation will not be made to an applicant if his house is to be cleared in the next year	The applicant must have been the tenant of his house for at least 12 months, and must have a satisfactory report in relation to rent payment, and house and garden maintenance	A tenancy is offered to any owner or tenant resident in a clearance area at the date of the confirmation of the Order. 'Lodgers' are usually rehoused with the main family. The attempt is made to avoid giving two tenancies for one house
Method of determining priority:	Applicants are divided into 8 groups according to bedrooms and accommodation required. Priorities are determined within these groups by means of a points scheme. Points are awarded for: (a) Overcrowding in the whole house (b) Overcrowding in the applicant's accommodation (c) Lack of a living room for the applicant's exclusive use (d) Lack of sex separation in sleeping arrangements	No formal system, each application is judged on its merits. Medical and other needs are considered. In the case of equality of claim, the waiting period is considered	Not specified

(e) Family living apart due to lack of accommodation

(f) Illness—points awarded by M.O.H.

(g) Lack of self-contained accommodation

(h) Living with one or more families in a house intended for one family only

(i) Service tenants, where the employer terminates employment or the tenancy, or the applicant resigns his employment

(j) Waiting time

Applicants are graded at a house visit, and the grading determines what type and age of property the applicant will be eligible for. Points levels are set for each accommodation group for different estates and areas reflecting supply and demand. In detail the allocation system takes account both of total points level, and the date at which the critical points limit was reached

Practice—Allocations

On the basis of the survey sample, it is estimated that about 3400 allocations were made during the year 1972–73. Of these, 37% went to applicants from the waiting list, 49% to transfers, 7% to mutual exchanges, 3% to clearance rehousing and 3% to other cases, including service tenancies. Lettings to existing tenants (transfers and exchanges) exceeded new lettings (waiting list, clearance etc.). The ratio of 'new' to 'existing' lettings was 1 to 1·27. General needs applicants took 84% of the new lettings.

The type of property being allocated to each letting group is shown in Table 8.4. Differences in terms of dwelling size allocated can be accounted for by differences in household size in the different groups. However, waiting list applicants seem slightly less likely to be allocated a house (rather than a flat or maisonette) than transfer applicants, despite the fact that waiting list households are more likely to include children aged 5 or under. Waiting list applicants are also relatively more likely to be allocated a dwelling on an 'unattractive' estate—37% compared to 16% of successful transfer applicants—and less likely to get a new dwelling.

Table 8.4.   Type of Dwelling Allocated, Wolverhampton: 1972-73

House type:	Waiting list and other cases	Transfers and mutual exchanges	Total[1]
Sample number	274	380	676
	%	%	%
Bungalow	★	2	2
1 bed. flat	15	13	14
2 bed. flat/maisonette	29	23	25
2 bed. house	15	7	11
3 bed. flat/maisonette	19	13	15
3 bed. house	21	39	31
4 bed. house	2	4	3

Source: Local authority records.

[1] Note that clearance rehousing has been omitted in detail because of inadequate sample numbers. Clearance lettings are included in the total column.

Of course, allocations can only be made as vacancies arise, or are created by transfers. The turnover rates for different house types are shown in Table 8.5. Fifteen per cent of the vacancies were due to new building, and this inflates turnover rates for two- and three-bedroomed flats and maisonettes. Even so, turnover in flats seems high. At least 7% of vacancies were due to the death of the previous tenant, and 47% were the result of transfers. Over 40% of transfer applicants were allocated a dwelling also released by transfer. Transfers were relatively more likely to release houses than flats or maisonettes. The whole transfer system is very well developed.

Table 8.5. Turnover Rates and House Type, Wolverhampton: 1972-73

House type:	Number in Stock 1971 Number	Number among allocations Sample × 5 Number	Allocations as % stock % as index
Bungalow	542	60	11
1 bed. flat	5090	460	9
2 bed. flat/maisonette	5179	835	16
2 bed. house	5050	360	7
3 bed. flat/maisonette	1355	495	37
3 bed. house	19157	1060	6
4/6 bed. house	1360	110	8

Source: *I.M.T.A. Housing Statistics (England and Wales) Part 1* and local authority records.

Practice—the Waiting List

In Wolverhampton a Deferred List is maintained of applicants who are not in immediate need of rehousing. Because the policy relating to the eligibility of owner-occupiers changed during the survey period, several applicants are included on the Live List in the tables which follow who are no longer strictly eligible for rehousing. Applicants on the Live List and the Deferred List are compared with the Successful List, that is applicants who were allocated a house during the survey year.

Table 8.6 shows the household characteristics of applicants. Allocations are selective of small families with young household heads, and including young children. Single persons and small adult and small elderly households are relatively less likely to be successful. The similarity of average age between Live and Deferred List applicants conceals differences. Deferred List applicants are predominantly middle-aged, while the Live List includes more young and elderly persons.

Table 8.6. Household Characteristics—Waiting List, Wolverhampton: 1973

Household type:	Live List	Deferred List	All Lists	Successful List
Sample number	448	182	630	230
	%	%	%	%
Single person	19	8	16	6
Small adult	23	26	24	15
Small family	23	26	24	58
Large family	7	8	7	7
Large adult	6	17	8	4
Small elderly	22	14	20	10
Average household size (persons)	2·26	2·72	2·39	2·89
Households with children aged 5 or under	23%	20%	22%	56%
Average age of applicant (years)	42	44	42	34

Source: Local authority records.

Four-fifths of Live List applicants were born in Great Britain. Eleven per cent were born in the West Indies and a further 3% in India. The proportions found among allocations are broadly similar.

Indices of housing need are shown in Table 8.7. The Successful List shows higher percentages in all need categories with the exception of underoccupying households. Note that information on availability of amenities is not available, nor can the details be gathered indirectly since applicants are not asked to give a reason for applying.

Table 8.7.   Indices of Housing Need—Waiting List, Wolverhampton: 1973

% of sample who are:	Live List	Deferred List	All Lists	Successful List
Lodging with parent	31	16	26	51
Lodging—other	20	7	16	18
Without own living room	53	21	44	73
Sharing with 5 or more other persons	13	2	10	15
Living at a density of more than 2 persons per bedroom	22	9	18	52
Living at a density of 0·3 persons per bedroom or less	8	5	6	2
Claiming medical priority	19	8	15	22
Lone parent families	11	14	12	12
Registering within 1 year of marriage	25	20	24	45
Registering when baby expected	10	5	9	24
On list before 1971	18	59	31	17

Source: Local authority records.

In all, 20% of applicants on the Live List had received at least one offer of accommodation. No less than 42% of those among the Successful List sample had refused at least one offer before accepting the tenancy they were finally allocated.

Practice—Transfers

Transfer applicants are rather older on average, and further advanced in the family development cycle than waiting list applicants. There were many fewer single persons and small adult families on the transfer list, and more large family and large adult households. Successful transfer applicants are less markedly different from those remaining on the list than is the case with general needs applicants. Younger applicants and families with children are favoured by the allocation process, apparently at the expense of the elderly.

Table 8.8   Household Characteristics—Transfer List, Wolverhampton: 1973

Household type:	Transfer List	Successful List
Sample number	355	321
	%	%
Single person	3	3
Small adult	9	10
Small family	28	33
Large family	19	21
Large adult	18	16
Small elderly	24	17
Average household size (persons)	3·28	3·44
Households with children aged 5 or under	30%	40%
Average age of applicant (years)	48	45

Source: Local authority records.

Indices of housing need for transfers are shown in Table 8.9. In no case is the need so extreme as amongst waiting list applicants. Allocations relieve over-crowding in particular. Concern with occupancy is also evident in the reasons for application (Table 8.10). The desire for a more modern house or a change of area are apparently less likely to prove successful as a reason for transfer.

Table 8.9.   Indices of Housing Need—Transfer List, Wolverhampton: 1973

% of sample who are:	Transfer List	Successful List
Living at a density of more than 2 persons per bedroom	6	12
Living at a density of 0·3 persons per bedroom or less	5	5
Claiming medical priority	10	12
On list before 1971	24	24

Source: Local authority records.

Table 8.10.   Reason for Application—Transfer List, Wolverhampton: 1973

Reason:	Transfer List	Successful List
Sample number	361	320
	%	%
Occupancy—		
Too little space	10	16
Too much space	14	17
Housing—		
House type	12	13
Conditions	9	4
Location—		
Near work/relatives	19	13
Poor area/noise/neighbours	16	15
Ill health	15	12
Other	5	9

Source: Local authority records.

Many applicants on the transfer list had already refused offers of accommodation —26% in all. Twenty-six per cent of those allocated a tenancy had previously refused an offer as well.

Current transfer applications reflect a need for one-bedroomed accommodation. The net result of granting all applications would be to release 47 three-bedroomed units, and would need 49 one-bedroomed dwellings. Two- and four-bedroomed needs and supply very nearly balance. (all figures relate to the sample, and should be multiplied by 10 to give an idea of total requirements). Bungalows and houses are being requested, and maisonettes would be released. The number of flats released and sought is similar, though sizes may be different.

Practice—Clearance Rehousing

The rehousing requirements of the clearance programme were particularly small in Wolverhampton during the survey year. Obviously a more extensive programme will have implications for the housing opportunities of waiting list applicants, since the two groups compete for vacancies.

Sample numbers for those involved in clearance rehousing are inadequate for full analysis (23 cases only). In general terms it is possible to say something however. Nearly two thirds of those affected were either large adult or small elderly households. Correspondingly, the average age of applicant was 55 years, and there were very few children involved. Over a third of households had lived in the house affected for over 20 years, and less than a quarter had moved in during the previous 5 years. Just over a tenth of those rehoused were owner-occupiers. Three quarters of clearance households were allocated either a bungalow or a house.

●

IMPROVEMENT GRANTS

Policies

Over 16,000 households lacked one or more of the three standard amenities at Census 1971 in Wolverhampton. Clearance and improvement are seen as joint approaches to the problem. Over 3500 houses are programmed for clearance between 1971 and 1981. It is acknowledged that more properties will become unfit, and that clearance is a continuing process. Wolverhampton also has two General Improvement Areas, one composed of local authority houses, and the other of mixed owner-occupied, private rented and council acquired properties. Council house modernization will proceed on GIA lines with both houses and environment being improved, and over 5000 houses should be dealt with 1971–81.

Improvement grants to private owners, of course, aid renewal in GIAs and elsewhere. Very full details of allowable works for discretionary grants are available to members of the public. Very generally the following applies:

(a) A discretionary grant will be given to bring a property to the 12 point standard where at least a 15 year life is assured.

(b) A discretionary grant for conversion to flats will be given where a 30 year life is assured. Flats provided should be Parker Morris standards for a 2 person household. Conversion of a two storey dwelling to flats will not be approved for grant purposes if, in the opinion of the Council, the existing dwelling forms a satisfactory and not over large unit of accommodation.

(c) Approval of a discretionary grant for conversion of a non-residential property to a dwelling will depend on the Council being satisfied that the building is sound and capable of conversion without fundamental reconstruction.

(d) Grants may be approved for schemes which only involve the improvement or extension of a small kitchen (normally in property built before October 3rd 1961). This type of improvement is felt to be valuable in updating the stock and deferring obsolescence.

(e) Applications which only involve the provision of central heating will not be approved. Central heating to Parker Morris standards will be approved in a full improvement scheme.

(f) Grants will not be given for the provision of an additional bedroom.

(g) The Housing Development Committee will itself decide applications for grants in property owned by a private landlord but which is untenanted.

While applicants are urged to make full use of discretionary grants with repair elements, standard grants are given where this is not possible or where the property has an expected life of about 10 years.

Practice—Improvement Grants

Discretionary grants were very much the more important during the survey period, making up 91% of all applications. Table 8.11 shows the type of work involved (see Appendix IV for definition). Under half the grants approved involved standard amenity provision.

Table 8.11. Improvement Grants and Work, Wolverhampton: 1972–73

Work involved:	Standard grant	Discretionary grant	All grants
Sample number	18	189	207
	%	%	%
Installation of missing amenities	50	2	6
Provision of bathroom	50	4	8
Provision of bathroom and kitchen	—	36	30
Kitchen extension	—	46	42
General improvement	—	12	11
Conversion to flat	—	3	3

Source: Local authority records.

Nearly three-quarters of the grants were for less than £500. Only 5% were at maximum grant level. Table 8.12 shows the average amount of grant approved under various headings.

Table 8.12.   Average Grant Approved, Wolverhampton: 1972-73

Type of grant:	Wolverhampton
	£
Standard grant	160
Discretionary grant	420
All grants	400
For kitchen extension	285
For bathroom installation with or without kitchen improvement	531

Source: Local authority records.

Nearly a third (32%) of discretionary grants included a repairs element representing over 30% of approved costs. In only 13% of cases was there no repairs element.

Grant applications were handled quite rapidly by the local authority. In 57% of grants, approval was given within 4 weeks of application, and in only 8% of cases did approval take 15 weeks or longer.

Information on the age of property being improved is not reliable. However, about 40% of grants were approved for terraced houses. Owner-occupiers are more likely than private landlords to make improvements. Seventy per cent of the applicants were owner-occupiers, and 23% landlords. The remaining 8% of houses were vacant at the time of application. Just over half (53%) of 'bathroom' grants went to owner-occupiers (10% vacant). In comparison owner-occupiers made up only 39% of the private sector households lacking amenities at the 1971 Census. Forty-four per cent of houses receiving grant had no outstanding mortgage. Just over half (55%) were mortgaged to a bank or building society. Just 1% had an outstanding council mortgage.

COUNCIL HOUSE SALES AND COUNCIL MORTGAGES

Policy—Council House Sales

Council houses are no longer sold in Wolverhampton, but a scheme was in operation until 1972. The scheme applied to all council houses on pre- or post-war estates, including maisonettes and flats in approved cases, and to houses acquired by the Council under Part V of the Housing Act 1957. Dwellings specifically excluded were old persons' bungalows, flats over shops, temporary bungalows, houses in high density developments, houses let on service tenancies and other houses which, in the opinion of the Housing Committee, should not be sold. An overall limit of $12\frac{1}{2}\%$ of the houses on any estate was set.

Sitting tenants could buy the houses they occupied, and applicants on the housing waiting list could buy a house offered to them when qualified for accommodation. Tenants with more than 5 years continuous tenancy of any council

Table 8.13. Regulations for Mortgage Lending, Wolverhampton: 1973

Regulation:	Private Sector Houses	Former Council Houses (where sold)
Property and purchasers	Any existing property or house under construction in Wolverhampton. The property or purchaser must fall within one of the categories listed in DoE Circular 22/71, or there must be special circumstances to justify a loan being given. Advances will not be made on property with a value of over £5000. A leasehold property must have an unexpired term of lease of 60 years at the date of the advance. No advance will be made to persons under 18 years of age, or to joint owners	Any tenant acquiring his council house
Amount of advance	The amount advanced does not usually exceed 90% of valuation. A 90% loan is more usual on post-war property. The percentage loan is lower on older property depending on the valuer's report The applicant must be able to satisfy the Corporation that he can undertake the financial obligations of the mortgage, and can find out of his own resources the difference between purchase price and advance. Full wife's earnings are not usually taken into account in calculating income	100% loans (less a £5 minimum deposit) were allowed Income requirements as for private houses
Period of the loan	Advances are normally repayable over 10, 15, 20, or 25 years at the choice of the applicant and with reference to the age and condition of the property, in suitable cases a 30-year period may be considered	30-year maximum repayment period. In the case of an elderly purchaser a guarantee may be required
Interest rates and repayments	The interest rate is fixed at $\frac{1}{4}\%$ above the rate which, at the time the terms of the advance are settled, has been fixed by the Treasury in respect of non-quota loans to local authorities by the Public Works Loan Board Repayments may be made either by the instalment or annuity methods	As for private houses
Other conditions	Normally the house purchased must be for the sole occupation of the borrower and his family, and it may be a condition of the loan that the purchaser must live therein for 3 years after the loan is made	

house immediately prior to purchase had the choice of accepting a reduction in the market price related to length of tenancy, subject to their acceptance of a 5 year pre-emption clause. The tenancy discount allowed a reduction of 10% of market price for tenants of 5 years standing, increasing by 1% for each further completed year's tenancy to a maximum of 20% (15 years). Tenants not qualifying for this discount, or not wishing to accept the pre-emption clause bought at full vacant possession market value. No house could be sold at a price less than the all-in cost of providing it. Sales were either freehold or leasehold (99 year lease).

Policy—Council Mortgage Lending

Wolverhampton Council will advance money for house purchase, alteration or improvement. Mortgages for house purchase are made under Small Dwellings Acquisition Act powers. The scheme is restricted, and seen as purely complementary to the service offered by building societies. Advances were also made for council house purchase. Some of the regulations are set out in Table 8.13.

Practice—Mortgage Details

As is explained more fully in Appendix I, the sample of private house mortgages in Wolverhampton was unsatisfactory, since loans made over a very long period of time were included. In the following text and tables relationships are quoted, while the average figures relate only to loans made over the last 10 years. It would be unwise to place too much reliance on these figures. The advances for purchase of council houses were much more recent, and the analysis more satisfactory.

Table 8.14 shows that council advances are, on average, much smaller than those made by the building society. The deposit (that is, the difference between weighted average price and advance[1]) is shown for each group. Council house purchasers had to, or chose to, provide rather lower average deposits. The average advance, in fact, represented 89% of the average price. Comparable figures for council loans for private houses, and building society loans were 73% and 77% respectively.

Only 4% of council loans for private houses represented over 90% of valuation. In a further 23% of cases the advance was between 81% and 90% of valuation. This means that over two-thirds of all private house loans equalled 80% of valuation or less. The pricing policy of council houses makes direct comparisons impossible, however, only one-third of purchasers received a loan representing 90% of price or less. Nearly three-quarters of the advances made for private house purchase were for the amount requested, as were all the council house loans.

The average period of loan granted for private house purchase was 20 years, and 18 years for council houses. The building society average is 23 years. About 15% of the council loans for private houses had terms of 30 years and a further 15% were for 10 years or less.

[1] See Appendix III for methods and terms.

Table 8.14. Size of Mortgage Advance and Balance, Wolverhampton and Building Society

	Council advances		
Advance:	Private house	Council house	Building Society[1]
	(1966–73)	(1971–73)	(1972)
Sample number	19	70	1536
	%	%	%
Under £2000	—	14	2
£2000–£2995	—	59	7
£3000–£3995	—	20	15
£4000–£4995	—	7	27
£5000 and over	—	—	50
Average advance	£1260	£2690	£4520
Weighted average advance (1972 prices)	£1420	£2620	£4520
Weighted average balance 1972 prices	£530	£320	£1290

Source: Nationwide Building Society (Midland Region) and local authority records.

[1] Building Society figures here and in all other tables in this section relate to the Midland Region.

Council loans made for private house purchase over the last 10 years resulted in average annual repayments for the borrower of £240. The equivalent council house figure was £340 (both 1972 levels), and for the building society was £430. Table 8.15 shows what this means in terms of the proportion of income committed to repayments. In terms of applicant's income alone council house buyers seemed willing to spend a higher proportion of income on repayments. However, the difference between the two groups is much reduced where total household income is considered. The impact of additional earners on family budgeting is particularly striking among council house purchasers.

Table 8.15. Mortgage Repayments and Income, Wolverhampton and Building Society

	Applicant's income			Household income	
Repayments as % income:	Private houses	Council houses	Building Society	Private houses	Council houses
	(1)	(1971–73)	(1972)	(1)	(1971–73)
Sample number	89	63	1536	89	63
	%	%	%	%	%
Less than 10%	19	3	—	24	6
10–17%	57	50	—	58	77
18–25%	24	33	—	17	16
Over 25%	1	14	—	—	1
Average percentage	13	18	22	—	—

Source: Nationwide Building Society (Midland Region) and local authority records.

[1] Note that the figures in the body of the table refer to all loans made (1955–73). The average percentage figure refers only to the most recent loans (1966–73).

Practice—Households Buying Private Houses

Full information is available on households buying a house with local authority loan. Purchasers with a council loan are slightly older on average than are building society borrowers. In comparison with applicants for a council house the borrowers include fewer very young or elderly persons.

Table 8.16. Household Characteristics—Private House Buyers, Wolverhampton and Building Society

Household type:	Wolverhampton Council loan (1955–73)	Midland Region Building Society (1972)	Great Britain All owner-occupiers with outstanding mortgage (1971)
Sample number	93	1536	3199
	%	%	%
Single person	—	—	3
Small adult	23	—	17
Small and large family	75	—	58
Large adult	3	—	17
Small elderly	—	—	6
Average household size (persons)	3·58	—	—
Age:			
30 and under	32	63	—
31–45	60	28	—
46–60	8	8	—
Over 60	—	★	—
Average age (years)	34	30	—

Source: Nationwide Building Society (Midland Region); *General Household Survey – Introductory Report* and local authority records.

Just two-thirds of borrowers from the Council were British born. Twenty-two per cent were born in the West Indies, and 12% in India or Pakistan. These figures are much higher than found among applicants for council houses.

The largest single occupational group among council borrowers were skilled manual workers (41%). A further 28% were in semi- or unskilled jobs. Thirty-one per cent were in professional, intermediate or skilled non-manual employment. The average income of recent borrowers (1972 level) was £1840. This compares to a building society average of £1980. Although the local authority average is below the building society, the difference is very much less than that observed between house prices. Thus average incomes were 93% as high as building society incomes, but house prices only 34% as high. The relationship between income and repayments has been shown in Table 8.15.

Practice—Households Buying Council Houses

Former tenants borrowing to buy their council houses were appreciably older than those buying a private house, but not so old, on average, as all council tenants in Great Britain. This group seems further advanced in the family cycle. In particular there are many more large adult households.

Table 8.17. Household Characteristics—Council House Buyers, Wolverhampton and Great Britain

Household type:	Wolverhampton Council house buyers (1971–73)	Great Britain All council tenants (1971)
Sample number	69	3688
	%	%
Single person	2	4
Small adult	12	11
Small and large family	56	35
Large adult	27	21
Small elderly	2	28
Average household size (persons)	3·87	
Age:		Age:
30 and under	6	Under 30 9
31–45	52	30–44 25
46–60	33	45–59 33
Over 60	9	60 and over 34
Average age (years)	45	—

Source: *General Household Survey—Introductory Report* and local authority records.

A quarter of those buying their house had been council tenants for over 20 years. Only 4% had been a tenant for 5 years or less.

The occupational structure figures show a greater emphasis on skilled manual employment than among private house buyers. Fifty-seven per cent were in skilled manual occupations, and 13% in semi- or unskilled jobs. Twenty-nine per cent were professional, intermediate or skilled non-manual workers and 2% were retired.

Applicant's income was on average slightly higher than among private house buyers with a council loan. The average, controlled to 1972 levels, was £1880, compared to £1840 for private buyers. Larger older families also allow more scope for additional earners to supplement household income (see Table 8.15).

Practice—Private Houses Bought with Council Loans

The average price of houses bought with a council loan in the last 10 years is considerably below that of either the building society or a sample of houses for sale with estate agents in Wolverhampton. The average price of houses for the different groups are as follows:

> Private houses bought with council loan £1950.
> Houses bought with building society loan £5810.
> Houses for sale with estate agents £6340.

All the figures have been weighted to 1972 price levels.

The lower average price levels are reflected to some extent in the type and size details in Table 8.18.

Table 8.18. Size and Type of Dwelling—Private Sector, Wolverhampton and Building Society

	Wolverhampton		Midland Region
House size:	Purchased with council loan	For sale with estate agents	Purchased with Building Society loan
	(1955–73)	(1973)	(1972)
Sample number	79	68	1536
	%	%	%
2 bedrooms	25	11	20
3 bedrooms	70	83	70
4 bedrooms or over	5	6	9
House type:			
Terraced	61	11	18
Semi-detached	33	63	40
Detached and other	6	26	42

Source: Nationwide Building Society (Midland Region), estate agents survey and local authority records.

Just over 60% of the houses bought with a council loan were built before 1919, and a further 17% before 1945. Eight per cent of the loans were for new houses under construction. Four-fifths of the houses had a garden, and 40% a garage. Just a fifth of the houses bought required some repairs as a condition of the loan. Rateable value figures are not reliable because of the time span covered. Older houses are therefore favoured by local authority lending.

Practice—Council Houses Sold

When sales were discontinued, about 800 houses had been sold—representing about 2% of the total council stock, and only 3% of the stock of houses. In the size and age comparisons which follow, the 'total' figures relate to houses only, and exclude flats, maisonettes and bungalows. In terms of size, the composition of houses sold and total stock is identical. Post-war houses are more popular. Over half (57%) of the houses sold were on estates classed as 'attractive'. This compares with 29% and 51% among dwellings allocated to waiting list and transfer applicants respectively.

Table 8.19. Size and Age of Council Houses Sold, Wolverhampton

Size:	Houses sold (1971–73)	Total stock of houses (1971)
Sample number	66	25567
	%	%
2 bedrooms	20	20
3 bedrooms	75	75
4 bedrooms or more	5	5
Age:		
Sample number	68	25567
	%	%
Pre-war	15	48
Post-war	86	52

Source: *I.M.T.A. Housing Statistics (England and Wales) Part 1* and local authority records.

The weighted average purchase price of council houses sold was £2940 (nearly £1000 above that of private houses bought with council loan). Two-thirds cost between £2000 and £3000.

WOLVERHAMPTON—SUMMARY

In population and household terms Wolverhampton is very similar to the West Midland Regional average. There are relatively more council houses in the total stock, and within the public sector above average numbers of flats and maisonettes.

The overall council lettings policy gives emphasis to transfers in a way which allows many lettings to be made from a single vacancy. The small demand for clearance rehousing allowed scope for rehousing from the waiting list. Both waiting list and transfer allocations show similar features. In both cases families with children are favoured, while single person, small adult and particularly small elderly households have to wait longer to be rehoused. Both systems tend to favour relief of overcrowding at the expense of the relief of underoccupation. The full effectiveness of transfers as a means of releasing family dwellings for waiting list applicants is reduced by a shortage of one-bedroomed accommodation. The present transfer list reflects an unsatisfied demand for small units, and a surplus of three-bedroomed houses. A greater use of small accommodation to relieve underoccupancy on the transfer list, would imply, of course, more difficulties in housing elderly waiting list applicants.

Lack of standard amenities is not considered as an element of housing need in the points scheme. Improvement grant approvals have increased very rapidly in recent years, but rather less than half are for works involving the installation of standard amenities. However a larger amount of expenditure is approved for each 'bathroom' grant than for kitchen extension work. Overall, average grant expenditure in Wolverhampton seems modest. Private landlords, while contributing to the improvement process, are not improving their property at the same rate as owner-occupiers.

Local authority lending for house purchase is mostly concentrated on cheaper old houses, which might be regarded as marginal, in a commercial sense. However, lending by the Council is very modest, and few households benefit in this way. Those who have been helped by council mortgages differ slightly from persons being allocated a council house—they include fewer very young and elderly persons, and more immigrant households. Average incomes among borrowers are near the national average.

Average incomes were slightly higher among persons buying their council house, and there were more likely to be extra earners to supplement family income. In this respect the decision to stop selling council houses cannot be seen as necessarily denying an opportunity to become an owner-occupier. Tenants who bought their house with a council advance were likely to be middle-aged, and have a skilled manual job; they were also likely to be tenants of some years standing. The refusal to sell council houses may be preventing the satisfaction of housing *desires* rather than housing *needs*.

9. Halesowen M.B.

BACKGROUND

Halesowen is a municipal borough with a 1971 Census population of nearly 54,000. Population has grown since 1961 at a rate of 1·49% per annum as a result of natural increase and net inward migration. The population age structure, though broadly similar to the regional average includes relatively fewer children and more people aged between 30 and 60. (Table 9.1).

Table 9.1. Age Structure of Population, Halesowen and Region: 1971

Age:	Halesowen	West Midland Region
	%	%
0–14	22	25
15–19	6	7
20–29	15	15
30–44	20	18
45–59	20	19
60 and over	17	17

Source: 1971 Census.

Halesowen has a very small proportion (1·1%) of people born in New Commonwealth countries.

There were 18,765 private households in Halesowen in 1971, giving an average household size of 2·85 persons, which is rather lower than the regional figure of 2·98.

The household and dwelling size structures are shown in Table 9.2. Halesowen has relatively more medium sized households (2–4 persons) and medium/large houses (5–6 rooms). This results in fewer households being at a density of more than $1\frac{1}{2}$ persons per room, and more living at a density of less than $\frac{1}{2}$ person per room than in the Region as a whole. The figures are 0·5% and 36% respectively. (Regional figures are 1·6% and 34%.)

Table 9.2. Household and Dwelling Size, Halesowen and Region: 1971

Household size:	Halesowen	West Midland Region	Dwelling size:	Halesowen	West Midland Region
	%	%		%	%
1 person	14	16	1–3 rooms	6	11
2 persons	33	31	4 rooms	20	21
3–4 persons	42	38	5 rooms	37	36
5–6 persons	9	13	6 rooms	32	25
7 persons and over	1	2	7 rooms and over	4	7
1 or 2 person households in which one or both members are over retiring age as % all households	23	24			

Source: 1971 Census.

Table 9.3. Eligibility and Priority Regulations, Halesowen: 1973

	General Needs Applicants	Transfer Applicants	Clearance Rehousing
Eligibility rules for application	Any person aged 18 years or over provided that: (a) The applicant or, in the case of a married male applicant, his wife has resided in the Borough for the whole of the preceding 12 months; or (b) The applicant or, in the case of a married male applicant, his wife, has lived the greater part of his or her life in the Borough; or (c) The applicant, being the family breadwinner, has worked in the Borough during the whole of the preceding twelve months An applicant may be eligible for inclusion if the Council is satisfied that there are special reasons why these qualifications should be waived. Engaged couples are accepted on the list if one of the parties is eligible in the normal way There is, in addition, a restricted list. For inclusion, it is only necessary that: (a) The applicant (or wife) live in the Borough; or (b) The applicant (or wife) was born or has lived the greater part of his (her) life in the Borough; or (c) The applicant (or wife) works in the Borough Applicants on this list are eligible only for the tenancy of dwellings designated as 'restricted waiting list dwellings' Applicants must also establish a prima facie need for housing. This can be defined as lack of separate accommodation, overcrowding, poor conditions, ill health, etc. In the case of elderly owner-occupiers, financial need is acceptable	Any council tenant who can prove to be: (a) Living in overcrowded conditions or (b) Underoccupying his accommodation or (c) Suffering from ill health attributed to his accommodation; or (d) Living in a flat for 5 years or longer	Not applicable

Eligibility for consideration	All registered applicants	A tenant must have a 3-month clear rent record before an allocation will be made	All persons in residence at the time the Order is confirmed. Lodgers are rehoused as a matter of course, and there is no objection to rehousing more than one family from a house
Method of ordering priority	Registered applicants are grouped according to accommodation needed and location requested. Within these groupings a date order system operates — Priority can be given to medical cases. The M.O.H. may 'support' or 'strongly support' a case	No formal system. The Housing Manager has discretion to use transfers to make the best use of any vacancy occuring in the stock	Not specified

The owner-occupied sector is relatively large in Halesowen. Sixty two per cent of households were owner-occupiers in 1971 compared with 50% in the Region. Twenty-nine per cent of households locally were council tenants (Region 34%). The private rented sector is also relatively small in Halesowen.

Provision of standard amenities in Halesowen is good. Eighty-eight per cent of households enjoyed exclusive use of bath, hot water and inside WC in 1971 (Region 84%). Even in the private rented sector over half the households had exclusive use of amenities.

House building completions averaged over 400 a year between 1968 and 1972.[1] The private sector accounted for about two-thirds of the total. During the same period an average of just under 50 houses a year were demolished or closed. The net gain has therefore been about 350 houses a year, representing almost a 2% growth in the total stock each year.

Halesowen emerges as a growing conurbation fringe town with a high degree of owner-occupation, and a relatively high quality housing stock. The population does not include the numbers of young children often associated with population growth.

COUNCIL HOUSE ALLOCATIONS

Policies

There is no policy acceptance in Halesowen that anyone who wants a council house should be able to have one. Need has to be established for consideration for general needs or transfer rehousing, as seen in Table 9.3.

Special cases may be considered for rehousing outside the normal scheme. New council staff may be offered accommodation, though key workers are not housed. Owner-occupiers may be rehoused if they will allow their house to be let to a nominated tenant. The Housing Manager has powers to rehouse homeless families, or those evicted from private accommodation.

Priorities between lettings groups are not always clearly defined. In general terms the following order applies:

(a) 'Strongly recommended' medical case.

(b) Clearance rehousing.

(c) Transfers in the allocation of houses and bungalows.

(d) General needs and transfers in the letting of flats and maisonettes.

No fixed proportions of lettings are assigned to any group.

Practice—Allocations

On the basis of the survey sample, 496 allocations were made during the year 1972–73. Of these, 47% went to applicants from the waiting list, 29% to

[1] *Local Housing Statistics England and Wales.* H.M.S.O.

transfer applicants, 7% to mutual exchanges, 10% to clearance rehousing and the remaining 6% to special cases, service tenancies, etc. The total number of 'new' lettings (to waiting list applicants, clearance and other cases) exceeded lettings to existing tenants (transfers and mutual exchanges). The ratio of new to existing lettings was 1 to 0·57. General needs applicants took 73% of the new lettings.

The type of property being allocated to the different groups is shown in Table 9.4. The differences in dwelling type and size correspond to the households being housed in the different categories—for example, there were many more small elderly households among transfers, and more children, hence the link with old persons' dwellings and houses.

Table 9.4.   Type of Dwelling Allocated, Halesowen: 1972-73

House type:	Waiting list and other cases	Transfers and mutual exchanges	Total[1]
Sample number	66	45	124
	%	%	%
Old persons flatlet or bungalow	19	40	26
1 bed. flat	26	9	19
2 bed. flat/maisonette	33	11	23
2 bed. house	—	7	4
3 bed. flat/maisonette	17	14	14
3 bed. house	5	20	14
4 bed. house	—	—	—

Source: Local authority records.

[1] Note that clearance cases are included in this, but not in the body of the table.

Of course, allocations can only be made as vacancies arise, or are created by transfer. The turnover rates of different house types are shown in Table 9.5. Old persons' dwellings and bungalows have been excluded since new building inflated the apparent turnover rates greatly. In fact, 22% of all vacancies were created by new building, almost entirely for old persons. This has had a distorting effect on all allocations during the survey year, and emphasizes the problems involved in taking a single year for survey purposes, particularly in a small authority. Flats and maisonettes show higher turnover rates than do houses.

Table 9.5.   Turnover Rates and House Type, Halesowen: 1972-73

House type:	Number in stock 1971	Number among allocations (Sample × 4)	Allocations as % stock
	Number	Number	% as index
1 bed. flat	388	96	25
2 bed. flat	711	112	16
2 bed. house	301	20	7
3 bed. flat/maisonette	392	68	17
3 bed. house	2,288	72	3

Source: *I.M.T.A. Housing Statistics (England and Wales) Part 1* and local authority records.

Practice—the Waiting List

Applicants on the Restricted List in Halesowen were not distinguished in the survey, so a single Waiting List is compared with the Successful List, that is, waiting list applicants who were allocated a dwelling during the survey year.

Table 9.6 shows the household characteristics of applicants. Allocations are heavily selective of elderly households, and single persons. In direct contrast to the findings in other authorities families with children were not favoured. This is clearly the result of the pattern of allocations due to new building. Apparently houses released by households transferring to the small new units were not adequate to meet waiting list needs. The average age of the Successful List is reduced by a number of very young applicants being allocated a house.

Table 9.6. Household Characteristics—Waiting List, Halesowen: 1973

Household type:	Waiting List	Successful List
Sample number	114	58
	%	%
Single person	8	16
Small adult	42	38
Small family	28	19
Large family	4	2
Large adult	7	3
Small elderly	11	22
Average household size (persons)	2·43	1·99
Households with children aged 5 or under	22%	18%
Average age of applicant (years)	36	38

Source: Local authority records.

Indices of housing need are shown in Table 9.7. The Successful List shows higher proportions in most of the need categories in both overcrowded conditions and in underoccupation. It is interesting that a date order priority scheme can apparently be selective of elements of housing need—even in an atypical year.

Table 9.7. Indices of Housing Need—Waiting List, Halesowen: 1973

% of sample who are:	Waiting List	Successful List
Lodging with family	54	55
Lodging—other	4	9
Without own living room	49	64
Sharing with 5 or more persons	3	12
Living at density of more than 2 persons per bedroom	17	31
Living at density of 0·3 persons per bedroom or less	3	7
Claiming medical priority	2	16
Lone parent families	7	3
Registering within 1 year of marriage	42	46
On list before 1971	36	14

Source: Local authority records.

Applicants in Halesowen are not asked to give a reason for making an application.

A fifth of the applicants on the waiting list had received and refused at least one offer of accommodation. Only 7% of those actually allocated a house from the waiting list in the survey year had previously refused an offer.

Practice—Transfers

A single transfer list is maintained for all eligible applicants. In terms of household characteristics, transfer applicants in Halesowen are rather further advanced in the family development cycle than waiting list applicants—there are more large family and large adult households. Allocations are very heavily biased towards small elderly households by the dwellings available. However, relatively more allocations were made to families with children than amongst waiting list allocations.

Table 9.8.   Household Characteristics—Transfer List, Halesowen: 1973

Household type:	Transfer List	Successful List
Sample number	113	36
	%	%
Single person	1	6
Small adult	5	3
Small family	36	14
Large family	13	17
Large adult	23	8
Small elderly	21	53
Average household size (persons)	3·43	2·47
Households with children aged 5 or under	35%	20%
Average age of applicant (years)	46	55

Source: Local authority records.

Examination of the indices of housing need in Table 9.9 shows, not surprisingly, that transfer allocations in the survey year were particularly aimed at the relief of underoccupation, and helping those with ill health. The reasons for application in Table 9.10 support this, though it is interesting that underoccupation *as such* may not always be seen as the prime reason for a move.

Table 9.9.   Indices of Housing Need—Transfer List, Halesowen: 1973

% of sample who are:	Transfer List	Successful List
Living at a density of more than 2 persons per bedroom	11	—
Living at a density of 0·3 persons per bedroom or less	—	14
Claiming medical priority	26	44
On list before 1971	42	37

Source: Local authority records.

Table 9.10.   Reason for Application—Transfer List, Halesowen: 1973

Reason:	Transfer List	Successful List
Sample number	111	32
	%	%
Occupancy:		
Too little space	16	3
Too much space	14	6
Housing:		
House type	16	6
Conditions	3	—
Location:		
Near work,relatives	9	6
Poor area,noise,neighbours	8	19
Ill health	30	47
Other	4	13

Source: Local authority records.

Offers had already been made to 17% of applicants on the transfer list. Seventeen per cent of successful applicants had also previously turned down at least one offer of accommodation.

The net result of granting all current transfer requests would be the release of 22 two-bedroomed units (mainly flats), and an increase in demand for 11 one-bedroomed, 9 three-, and 2 four-bedroomed dwellings (the figures relate to sample numbers, and should be multiplied by 4 to give an idea of total requirements). The continuing shortfall of small accommodation gives an impression of the backlog of demand which must have existed prior to the new building programme of the survey year.

Practice—Clearance Rehousing

Only 13 families were included in the sample for clearance rehousing—too few for analysis in detail. Over half were either large adult or small elderly households. Relatively few were families containing children. Fifteen per cent were owner-occupiers. Evidence on length of residence in the effected property is not available. Over two-thirds of the clearance households were allocated a house or old person's dwelling.

IMPROVEMENT GRANTS

Policies

Older housing is not regarded as a major problem in Halesowen. In all, a little over 2300 households lacked exclusive use of one or more amenity at the 1971 Census. Clearance and improvement are seen as being complementary, and to some extent, alternatives.

A possible clearance programme of nearly 700 houses to be dealt with by 1980 has been drawn up. However, many of the dwellings included are felt to be capable of (and warranting) improvement rather than demolition. Halesowen has been enthusiastic in its adoption of General Improvement Area powers, and two areas have been designated, with a third planned. One of the designated areas consists mainly of council houses, and is part of a programme for modernizing all the 1660 inter-war council houses in the Borough.

Within this framework, improvement has been left to private owners in a voluntary system encouraged by improvement grants. No written statement of allowable works is available to the public. In general the local policy for grants is liberal. Any work falling within the provision of the 12 point standard is eligible for discretionary grant, including providing kitchen extensions only, or general improvements for renewing wiring or damp proof course. Applicants are encouraged to undertake work to bring the house to as high a standard as possible.

Practice—Improvement Grants

Discretionary grants were very much the more important during the survey period—78% of the total. Table 9.11 shows the type of work the grant was made for. It is interesting to see the number of grants given for work which does not include the provision of standard amenities. Over half the discretionary grants approved fall into this category. (See Appendix IV for definitions of work.)

Table 9.11.   Improvement Grants and Work, Halesowen: 1972-73

Work involved:	Standard grant	Discretionary grant	All grants
Sample number	23	81	104
	%	%	%
Installation missing amenities	65	—	14
Provision of bathroom	35	7	14
Provision of bathroom and kitchen	—	26	20
Kitchen extension	—	48	38
General improvement, DPC, etc.	—	14	11
Conversion to flats	—	5	4

Source: Local authority records.

About two thirds of all grants approved were for less than £500. Table 9.12 shows the average amount of grant approved in different categories.

Table 9.12.   Average Grant Approved, Halesowen: 1972-73

Type of Grant:	Halesowen
	£
Standard grant	120
Discretionary grant	555
All grants	460
For kitchen extension	390
For bathroom installation with or without kitchen improvement	715

Source: Local authority records.

Discretionary grants, of course, include an allowance for repairs expenditure. In fact, in only 36% of cases did the repairs element of approved costs exceed 20% of total approved costs. In one-tenth of all cases no repairs element was included.

The local authority seems able to cope quite quickly with grant applications. Over a quarter were approved within a month of submission, and over four-fifths within two months. No grant took as much as 15 weeks to approve.

Only 40% of all grants were approved for property built before 1919. In contrast, 50% were for houses built during the 1930s. (These figures relate to discretionary grants only since information on age is only available here; the inclusion of standard grants would presumably alter the balance in favour of older property.) Forty-two per cent of all grants went to terraced houses—the proportion for discretionary grants only is very similar. Three-quarters of the grant applicants were owner-occupiers. However the situation in relation to the private rented sector is much more favourable if 'bathroom' grants alone are considered. Forty-three per cent of these went to private landlords. However, 53% of the private sector households lacking amenities in the 1971 Census were tenants. Nearly half, 48%, of owners making improvements had no outstanding mortgage on their property, while another 47% had a loan from a building society or bank. Only 5% had a local authority mortgage.

COUNCIL HOUSE SALES AND COUNCIL MORTGAGES

Policy—Council House Sales

A scheme whereby council tenants can buy their house is at present in force. The scheme is limited to tenants of at least one year (not necessarily in the house to be bought) and to houses only, as compared to flats or bungalows. No ceiling figure has been set for the proportion of total stock which may be sold.

The normal purchase price is vacant possession market value less a discount of 20% when a standard 5 year pre-emption clause is introduced. If a pre-emption clause is not accepted by the purchaser, the price is set at full market value. The minimum price in any case is set by original construction costs. All sales are freehold.

Policy—Council Mortgage Lending

Halesowen Council will advance money for the acquisition, alteration, conversion or improvement of houses in the Borough, under Housing Act powers. Some of the regulations for mortgage advances are set out in Table 9.13. Lending policies are seen to be complementary to the services offered by building societies.

Practice—Mortgage Details

Over 100 loans for private house purchase or improvement had been completed by May 1973. In addition most of the 300 council houses sold had been bought with the aid of council loans.

Table 9.13. Regulations for Mortgage Lending, Halesowen: 1972–73

Regulations:	Private Sector Houses	Former Council Houses
Property and purchasers	Property or purchaser must fall within one of the categories listed in DoE Circular 22/71. Any existing, or new house, or house to be built in Halesowen is eligible. The market value must not exceed £10,000. The dwelling must be in all respects fit for human habitation	Any tenant acquiring his council house
Amount of advance	The Council will normally advance up to 95% of valuation set by the Borough Surveyor. In special cases, considered on their merits, an advance of 100% of valuation may be made. The amount may be adjusted to ensure the applicant can meet his mortgage repayments. As a rule of thumb it is assumed that monthly repayments shall not exceed gross weekly earnings. Earnings are defined as basic income, plus regular overtime payments and half the wife's income where applicable	The entire purchase price less £5 may be advanced Income requirements apply as for private houses
Period of the loan	The advance shall be repaid over a period selected by the applicant not exceeding 30 years. In the case of older property the period of loan may be reduced to take account of the condition of the property and its estimated future life. Repayments on a leasehold property must be complete at least 10 years before the lease expires	As for private houses
Interest rates and repayments	The interest rate is fixed at ¼% above the Public Works Loan Board rate for loans to local authorities at the time the advance is made	As for private houses
Other conditions	The Council may withhold payment of a portion of the advance until essential repairs required as a condition of the loan have been carried out Loans are normally made only for houses for the borrower's own occupation	

Table 9.14 shows that the size of advances made by the Council are, on average, much less than made by the building society. The average size of deposit (that is the difference between weighted average price and advance[1]) is shown for each group. Council house purchasers had to, and chose to provide a very much smaller deposit. The average advances, in fact, represented 94% of purchase price. Comparable figures for council loans for private houses and building society loans were 76% and 77% respectively.

Table 9.14.   Size of Mortgage Advance and Balance, Halesowen and Building Society

Advance:	Council advances		Building Society[1]
	Private houses	Council houses	
	(1967–72)	(1971–73)	(1972)
Sample number	67	72	1536
	%	%	%
Under £2000	63	3	2
£2000–£2995	24	32	7
£3000–£3995	10	57	15
£4000–£4995	2	8	27
£5000 and over	—	—	50
Average advance	£2000	£3180	£4520
Weighted average advance (1972 prices)	£2170	£3150	£4520
Weighted average balance 1972 prices	£700	£200	£1290

Source: Nationwide Building Society (Midland Region) and local authority records.

[1] Building Society figures here and in all other tables in this section relate to the Midland Region.

In over half (53%) of loans for private house purchase, the amount advanced represented over 90% of valuation. In a further quarter of loans the advance was between 81% and 90% of valuation. In only a quarter of cases did the advance represent 80% of valuation or less. The pricing policy for sold council houses makes direct comparison less relevant, but only 19% of council house buyers received an advance which equalled 90% of *price* or less. In about 90% of cases the loan granted was that sought.

The average period of council loan for both private and council houses was nearly 20 years, while the building society average is 23 years. About 16% of council loans for the purchase of a private house were for 30 years, and only 4% were for 10 years or less.

Council loans for private house purchase resulted in average annual repayments for the borrower of £280. The equivalent council house figure was £390 (both 1972 prices) and the building society was £430. Table 9.15 shows what this means in the proportion of income committed to repayments. In terms of applicant's income only, former council tenants seem willing to spend a higher

[1] See Appendix III for method and definitions.

proportion of income on repayments. However, the difference between the groups is very much reduced when total household income is considered.

Table 9.15. Mortgage Repayments and Income, Halesowen and Building Society

	Applicant's income			Household income	
Repayments as % income:	Private house (1967–72)	Council house (1971–73)	Building Society (1972)	Private house (1967–72)	Council house (1971–73)
Sample number	61	72	1536	61	72
	%	%	%	%	%
Less than 10%	11	1	—	11	2
10–17%	54	27	—	56	50
18–25%	33	61	—	31	46
Over 25%	2	11	—	2	3
Average percentage	15	19	22	—	—

Source: Nationwide Building Society (Midland Region) and local authority records.

Practice—Households Buying Private Houses

Full household details are available for persons buying private houses with council loans. Council borrowers are rather older than building society borrowers. Household size is appreciably larger than the average for applicants for a council house, and there are many more families with children. Housing aid of this type

Table 9.16. Household Characteristics—Private House Buyers, Halesowen and Building Society

Household type:	Halesowen Council loan (1967–72)	Midland Region Building Society (1972)	Great Britain All owner-occupiers with outstanding mortgages (1971)
Sample number	70	—	3199
	%		%
Single person	10	—	3
Small adult	26	—	17
Small and large family	60	—	58
Large adult	3	—	17
Small elderly	1	—	6
Average household size (persons)	3·67	—	—
Households with children aged 5 or under	50%	—	—
Age:			
Sample number	68	1536	—
	%	%	
30 and under	34	63	—
31–45	54	28	—
46–60	10	8	—
Over 60	2	★	—
Average age (years)	36	30	—

Source: Nationwide Building Society (Midland Region); *General Household Survey—Introductory Report* and local authority records.

seems to be requested at a rather later point in the family development cycle. However, the small elderly households found among waiting list applicants are not found in the mortgage sample.

On the basis of applicant's name, over half the loans (51%) in Halesowen were given to families of Asian origin.

The majority of borrowers (60%) were in skilled manual occupations. A further 36% were in semi- or unskilled jobs. Only 5% of borrowers, then, were in professional intermediate or skilled non-manual employment.

Applicant's total income is shown in Table 9.17. The differential between the average income of council and building society borrowers is considerably smaller than the differential between house prices financed by the two sources. Council average incomes are 94% as high as building society incomes, but prices only 49% as high. Average earnings for a full time male employee in Great Britain in 1972 were £1872.[1] The relationship between income and repayments has already been described (Table 9.15).

Table 9.17. Borrower's Income—Private House Buyers, Halesowen and Building Society

Annual income:	Council loans (1967–72)	Weekly income:	Building Society (1972)
Sample number	71	Sample number	1536
	%		%
£1000 and under	7	£20 and under	3
£1005–£1500	61	£21–£30	28
£1505–£2000	25	£31–£40	36
£2005–£3000	6	£41–£60	27
Over £3000	1	Over £60	6
Average income	£1460	Average income	£1980
Weighted average (1972 prices)	£1860	Weighted average (1972 prices)	£1980

Source: Nationwide Building Society (Midland Region) and local authority records.

Practice—Households Buying Council Houses

Former tenants borrowing to buy their council house were appreciably older, on average, than those buying a private house. The greater average age is due to larger numbers of middle-aged purchasers, and not to any greater numbers of the elderly. Average household size is lower than among the private purchasers, and there are fewer children aged 5 or under in the families.

Over a fifth (21%) of persons buying their council house had been tenants for over 20 years, and 61% had been tenants for over 10 years. Only 23% had been tenants for 5 years or less.

[1] *Department of Employment Gazette.* Vol. LXXXI No. 12, Dec. 1973. Table 128.

Table 9.18. Household Characteristics—Council House Buyers, Halesowen and Great Britain

Household type:	Halesowen Council house buyer (1971–73)	Great Britain All council tenants (1971)
Sample number	72	3683
	%	%
Single person	4	4
Small adult	31	11
Small and large family	62	35
Large adult	1	21
Small elderly	1	28
Average household size (persons)	3·19	—
Households with children aged 5 years or under	21%	—

Age:			Age:	
Sample number	72		Sample number	3683
	%			%
30 and under	8		Under 30	9
31–45	40		30–44	25
46–60	50		45–59	33
Over 60	1		60 and over	34
Average age (years)	45			—

Source: *General Household Survey—Introductory Report* and local authority records.

The social class structure of council house buyers is similar to that of the private house purchasers, though there are relatively fewer in semi- or unskilled occupations. The figures are: skilled manual 59%, semi- or unskilled 23%, professional, intermediate or skilled non-manual 17%, and retired 1%. Applicant's income was on average higher than among private house buyers. The average controlled to 1972 prices was £2060, compared to only £1860 for the private purchasers. This is a higher figure then for all building society borrowers. Larger, older families also seem to have more scope for additional household earnings—the difference between applicant's and household income is greater for buyers of council houses than of private houses, as seen in Table 9.15.

Practice—Private Houses Bought with Council Loans

The average price of house bought with a council loan in Halesowen is very much lower than that of houses for sale with estate agents in the town in spring 1973 or that of houses in the building society sample. (Table 9.19).

Only details of size are available for the council loan group of houses. However, in conjunction with the age details shown later, it seems fair to assume that relatively many more terraced houses are receiving council finance.

Table 9.19. Price of House—Private Sector, Halesowen and Building Society

Price:	Halesowen		Midland Region
	Purchased with council loan	For sale with estate agents	Purchased with Building Society loan
	(1967–73)	(1973)	(1972)
Sample number	71	49	1536
	%	%	%
Under £2000	27	—	1
£2000–£2995	55	—	6
£3000–£3995	10	—	11
£4000–£4995	5	2	23
£5000 and over	2	98	59
Average price	£2510	£9600	£5810
Weighted average price (1972 prices)	£2870	£7430	£5810

Source: Nationwide Building Society (Midland Region), estate agents survey and local authority records.

Table 9.20. Size of Dwelling—Private Sector, Halesowen and Building Society

House size:	Halesowen		Midland Region
	Purchased with council loan	For sale with estate agents	Purchased with Building Society loan
	(1967–73)	(1973)	(1972)
Sample number	66	49	1536
	%	%	%
2 bedrooms	38	6	20
3 bedrooms	56	80	70
4 bedrooms or more	6	14	9

Source: Nationwide Building Society (Midland Region), estate agents survey and local authority records.

Ninety-four per cent of the houses bought with a council loan were built before 1919—the remainder were either being built or were completed in the 1960s. Repairs were required as a condition of the loan in 35% of cases. The limited evidence suggests that local authority finance is being channelled to the older, poorer quality housing stock.

Practice—Council Houses Sold

By May 1973, 302 council house sales had been completed in Halesowen. This figure represents about 6% of the total local authority stock, but 11% of the stock of *houses*. In the size and age comparison in Table 9.21, the 'total' stock figures relate to houses only, that is, excluding flats and bungalows. There is very little difference between the size structures shown, while post-war houses seem slightly more popular.

Table 9.21.   Size and Age of Council Houses Sold, Halesowen

Size	Council houses sold (1971–73)	Total stock of houses (1971)
Sample number	71	2728
	%	%
2 bedrooms	13	11
3 bedrooms	83	84
4 bedrooms	4	5
Age:		
Sample number	70	2728
	%	%
Pre-war	27	37
Post-war	73	63

Source: *I.M.T.A. Housing Statistics (England and Wales) Part 1* and local authority records.

The weighted average purchase price of council houses sold was £3350—about £500 above the average of private houses bought with council aid. In view of the likely difference in size, age and quality of the two, a greater price differential might have been expected.

HALESOWEN—SUMMARY

Halesowen has been shown as a town which has been gaining in population, and housing stock in recent years. The population is essentially young and middle-aged adult, without large numbers of elderly persons and children. The housing stock is of relatively high quality, and the public sector is smaller than the regional average.

There is evidence of continuing demand for council houses. During the survey year a highly specialized new building programme distorted the pattern of allocations, favouring small elderly households rather than families with children. The transfer system is not very well-developed—transfers and exchanges made up only about a third of all lettings. A similar pattern of households being re-housed is found among transfer and general needs lists.

Both general needs and transfer allocations were selective of those in housing need, achieved through a date order allocation system. The exception to this was the relief of overcrowding among transfer applicants. In fact the current transfer list generates a need for one-, three- and four-bedroomed accommodation, with an accompanying release of two-bedroomed units.

Improvement grants to private owners have proved popular, and the numbers given have grown rapidly since 1970. However, less than half the grants are going to houses built before 1919, or for improvement schemes involving the installation of standard amenities. Private landlords are not making use of grants to the extent which the problems in the rented sector suggests would be desirable. Since improvement is given an important role in the future renewal strategy in Halesowen, it is important to realize that, while grants are being used to update the stock generally, they may not be tackling the core problem as rapidly as is required.

Council mortgages are used mainly to buy old property, and are serving a valuable function in maintaining a market within the older stock. Purchasers helped by the Council include large numbers of Asian immigrants, and persons in semi- or unskilled occupations (the latter point is relative only, skilled manual workers make up the largest single group). Households are large, and family commitments must be considerable. Although incomes are not unduly low, it is likely that purchasers would find it difficult to buy if finance was not available for old cheap houses.

By comparison, persons buying council houses make up a much more affluent group. Applicants' average incomes are higher (above the building society average) and extra earners often boost household income. Other means of achieving owner-occupation would seem open to many of the purchasers. Sales have also accounted for over a tenth of the council stock of houses, while demand is continuing from transfer and waiting list applicants for family-sized accommodation. While it would be unrealistic to think of council house sales reducing vacancies in the short term, long term considerations might be rather different. It is arguable that a council house sales policy at present is at variance with other strands of council housing strategy.

10. Stafford M.B.

BACKGROUND

Stafford is a municipal borough with a 1971 Census population of 55,000. This figure represents a growth in population by about 1·4% a year between 1961 and 1971—the result of natural increase and net inward migration. The age structure in Table 10.1 shows Stafford to be very similar to the West Midlands Region as a whole. There are slightly fewer elderly persons locally than regionally.

Table 10.1. Age Structure of Population, Stafford and Region: 1971

Age:	Stafford	West Midland Region
	%	%
0–14	26	25
15–19	7	7
20–29	16	15
30–44	18	18
45–59	18	19
60 and over	16	17

Source: 1971 Census.

Stafford has a relatively low proportion of its population born in New Commonwealth countries—2·0% compared to 2·8% in the Region.

There were just 17,250 private households in Stafford in 1971, giving an average household size of 3·01 (Region 2·98). The household and dwelling size structures are shown in Table 10.2. While household size is very similar to the Region, there are appreciably more large houses in Stafford. This corresponds to occupancy, since relatively fewer households in Stafford live at a density of more than $1\frac{1}{2}$ persons per room (0·8% compared to 1·6% in the Region). However, under-occupation, that is households living at a density of less than $\frac{1}{2}$ person per room, is very similar to the Region (33% compared to 34% of households). There are relatively few small elderly households in Stafford.

Table 10.2. Household and Dwelling Size, Stafford and Region: 1971

Household size:	Stafford	West Midland Region	Dwelling size:	Stafford	West Midland Region
	%	%		%	%
1 person	15	16	1–3 rooms	8	11
2 persons	30	31	4 rooms	17	21
3–4 persons	39	38	5 rooms	31	36
5–6 persons	13	13	6 rooms	37	25
7 persons and over	3	2	7 rooms and over	8	7
1 and 2 person households in which one or both members are of retiring age as % all households	22	24			

Source: 1971 Census.

Stafford is also very similar to the Region in terms of tenure. Thirty-three per cent of households were council tenants and 50% owner-occupiers in 1971. The remaining 17% of households rented their accommodation from a private landlord.

The standard of basic amenity provision in Stafford is high. Eighty-eight per cent of households had exclusive use of fixed bath, hot water and inside WC at the Census (Region 84%). Even in the private rented sector about two-thirds of households had exclusive use of these amenities.

New house completions averaged 378 a year in Stafford between 1968 and 1972.[1] The public sector accounted for just 18% of these. During the same period, about 50 houses a year were demolished or closed. Public sector completions more than offset this dwelling loss.

Stafford emerges as a growing town, with a population rather more youthful than the regional average. Amenity provision in the housing stock is good, and dwelling size is relatively generous. Council houses make up about a third of all dwellings.

COUNCIL HOUSE ALLOCATIONS

Policies

There is felt to be a shortage of council dwellings in Stafford, so eligibility and priority rules are applied. However, in terms of official Council policy, the Housing Manager has complete discretion to decide who shall be eligible for housing, and what priority shall be given to different applicants. The regulations set out in Table 10.3 are, therefore, rules followed in everyday practice rather than formally approved procedures. The emphasis within the entire system is on flexibility, and the ability to accommodate needs as they arise.

Within this system special cases cannot arise as such. Homeless families, or persons forced to leave tied accommodation through no fault of their own may be rehoused as necessary.

Priorities between groups are as follows:

(a) Clearance rehousing.

(b) Medical priority cases.

(c) Overcrowding cases.

(d) Others—either waiting list or transfer applicants not falling into (b) or (c).

In practice transfer applicants may receive some priority if making the transfer will release accommodation needed for clearance or some other more urgent need. Flexibility is urged.

[1] *Local Housing Statistics. England and Wales.* H.M.S.O.

Table 10.3. Eligibility and Priority Regulations, Stafford: 1973

	General Needs Applicants	Transfer Applicants	Clearance Rehousing
Eligibility for application	Anyone living within a 10-mile radius of Stafford town centre	Any council tenant	Not applicable
Eligibility for consideration	The following will be considered: (a) Waiting list applicants (b) Key workers with employers' certificate (c) Incoming local authority staff (d) Regular members of HM Forces who have absolute priority for rehousing if they have 9 years' service on discharge Dwellings are also allocated to the Hospital Management Board, Fire Service, after-care organizations and local firms	All those on the list Applicants not falling into the priority categories below will be charged a £6·00 administration fee when rehoused An allocation will not be made unless the tenant has a clear rent record for 6 months prior to the offer being made	Clearance procedures under 'individual unfits' Household rehoused as soon as possible after Order made. Persons moving in after the Order is made, or living in lodging houses affected will be rehoused if children are affected
Method of determining priority	Applicants are divided: (a) Old age pensioners—including those within 2 years of retirement (b) Lodgers and persons without a house of their own (c) Householders, either tenants or owners of self-contained accommodation (d) Applicants for multi-storey flats. (Single persons and engaged couples may be rehoused more rapidly in this way) Priority system is flexible, points are given to householders for lack of amenities. Medical recommendation can give priority There is no overall formal priority system	Preference is given to the following groups: (a) Those wishing to transfer to a house from a flat after a minimum period of 12 months (b) Those suffering from ill health (c) Those with too few or too many bedrooms (d) Those having financial reasons for requesting a transfer (e) Any transfer desirable for housing management reasons Applicants are grouped according to the type and size of accommodation wanted. Date of commencement of tenancy at the present dwelling may be used for ordering priority. Again there is no overall formal priority system	Not applicable

Practice—Allocations

On the basis of the survey sample, 760 allocations were made during the year 1972–73. Of these, 56% went to waiting list applicants, 27% to transfers, 14% to mutual exchanges, 1% to clearance rehousing, and 3% to other cases, including service tenancies. Thus, lettings to new tenants via the waiting list and clearance exceeded the number going to existing tenants (transfers and exchanges). The ratio of 'new' to 'existing' lettings was 1 to 0·68. General needs applicants took 94% of the new lettings.

The type of property being allocated to each lettings group is shown in Table 10.4. While size differences correspond roughly with household size, waiting list applicants were rather less likely than transfers to be allocated a house. Just the same proportion of waiting list and transfer households included children aged 5 or under. However transfer families did include *more* young children. Waiting list applicants were also less likely to be allocated a dwelling on an 'attractive' or 'very attractive' estate. Twenty-four per cent of transfers were allocated a dwelling on a good estate in these terms, compared with only 17% of waiting list applicants.

Table 10.4.   Type of Dwelling Allocated, Stafford: 1972–73

House type:	Waiting list and other cases	Transfers and mutual exchange	Total[1]
Sample number	111	77	189
	%	%	%
Bungalow	—	4	2
1 bed. flat	14	14	14
2 bed. flat/maisonette	48	14	34
2 bed. house	4	9	6
3 bed. flat/maisonette	1	1	1
3 bed. house	31	56	41
4 bed. house	2	1	2

Source: Local authority records.

[1] The total includes the single clearance case in the sample.

Of course, allocations can only be made as vacancies arise or are created by transfer. The turnover rate for different house types show wide variations (Table 10.5). The vacancy rate among one-bedroomed flats was inflated by new building during the survey year. New building accounted for 6% of all vacancies, transfers for 27%, mutual exchanges 13%, deaths 11%, tenants leaving Stafford 17%, and the remainder arose when tenants moved to other accommodation in Stafford itself. Three-quarters of the vacancies arising because of transfer were allocated to waiting list applicants.

Table 10.5.   Turnover Rates and House Type, Stafford: 1972-73

House type:	Number in stock 1971	Number among allocations Sample × 4	Allocations as stock
	Number	Number	% as index
Bungalow	144	12	8
1 bed. flat	459	108	22
2 bed. flat/maisonette	732	256	35
2 bed. house	384	48	13
3 bed. flat/maisonette	10	8	80
3 bed. house	3345	312	9
4 bed. house	161	12	7

Source: *I.M.T.A. Housing Statistics (England and Wales) Part 1* and local authority records.

Practice—the Waiting List

A single waiting list is maintained in Stafford (no distinction was made for survey purposes between the general list and the multi-storey flat list). Applicants are compared with those allocated a house from the waiting list in the survey year—i.e. the Successful List.

Table 10.6 shows the household characteristics of applicants. The remarkable feature is the degree of similarity between applicants and allocations. Small families with children are very slightly favoured at the expense of small elderly households.

Table 10.6. Household Characteristics—Waiting List, Stafford: 1973

Household type:	Waiting List	Successful List
Sample number	165	101
	%	%
Single person	9	9
Small adult	24	19
Small family	31	39
Large family	12	14
Large adult	5	5
Small elderly	20	15
Average household size (persons)	2·73	2·78
Households with children aged 5 or under	29%	36%
Average age of applicant (years)	41	38

Source: Local authority records.

Usual indices of housing need are shown in Table 10.7. The Successful List shows higher proportions in almost all of the need categories. The exception is medical priority, which may be misleading since no measure of seriousness of need was recorded in this survey. The flexible allocation system seems well able to take account of a wide variety of housing needs. Applicants are not asked to give a reason for making the application, so the objective and subjective measures of need cannot be compared.

Table 10.7. Indices of Housing Need—Waiting List, Stafford: 1973

% of sample who are:	Waiting List	Successful List
Lodging with family	19	28
Lodging—other	9	14
Without own living room	31	40
Sharing with 5 or more persons	3	7
Living at a density of more than 2 persons per bedroom	17	25
Living at a density of 0·3 persons per bedroom or less	5	7
Claiming medical priority	7	5
Without use of a bath	15	20
Lone parent families	8	17
Registering within 1 year of marriage	24	30
On list before 1971	21	23

Source: Local authority records.

Less than 5% of those on the Waiting List had already been made an offer of accommodation. Thirteen per cent of those allocated a house had previously received and refused at least one offer.

Practice—Transfers

A single transfer list is maintained in Stafford. In terms of household characteristics transfer applicants are seen to be more predominantly middle-aged than waiting list applicants. There are fewer young and elderly applicants. More households include young children. Allocations during the survey year were selective of elderly households, but this cannot be simply accounted for by the new building programme, since several of the new dwellings were let to waiting list applicants. Families with children were also favoured by the allocation process (children under 17 rather than 5 or under).

Table 10.8. Household Characteristics—Transfer List, Stafford: 1973

Household type:	Transfer List	Successful List
Sample number	110	51
	%	%
Single person	2	4
Small adult	9	8
Small family	36	29
Large family	17	20
Large adult	26	10
Small elderly	11	29
Average household size (persons)	3·40	3·02
Households with children aged 5 or under	37%	36%
Average age of applicant (years)	43	47

Source: Local authority records.

The indices of need shown in Table 10.9 suggest need in terms of occupancy is less extreme in absolute terms among transfers than waiting list applicants. Transfer allocations were particularly aimed at the relief of underoccupation.

Table 10.9.   Indices of Housing Need—Transfer List, Stafford: 1973

% of sample who are:	Transfer List	Successful List
Living at a density of more than 2 persons per bedroom	4	—
Living at a density of 0·3 persons per bedroom or less	3	14
Claiming medical priority	11	20
On list before 1971	26	36

Source: Local authority records.

The concern with underoccupancy is also seen in the main reasons given for transfer applications in Table 10.10. A desire to change area or neighbours seems to have relatively low priority as a transfer reason.

Table 10.10.   Reason for Application—Transfer List, Stafford: 1973

Reason:	Transfer List	Successful List
Sample number	107	46
	%	%
Occupancy—		
Too little space	10	15
Too much space	13	28
Housing—		
House type	15	13
Conditions	8	9
Location—		
Near work/relations	10	9
Poor area/noise/neighbours	16	9
Ill health	15	11
Other	13	6

Source: Local authority records.

Only 3% of transfer applicants had already received and refused an offer of accommodation. Only 2% of successful applicants had previously refused an offer.

The net result of granting all transfer applications in terms of dwelling size alone would be very small. Only 4 one- and 1 four-bedroomed units are needed, and 5 three-bedroomed dwellings would be released. (The figures relate to the sample and should be multiplied by 4 to give an idea of total requirements.) Demands in terms of house type is more marked with a desire to move from flats and maisonettes to houses and bungalows.

Practice—Clearance Rehousing

Only one household was rehoused through clearance during the survey year. Those involved were a small elderly household, who were rehoused in a two-bedroomed flat. It is impossible to say how typical of clearance needs in Stafford this was.

IMPROVEMENT GRANTS

Policies

About 2000 households in Stafford lacked one or more of the basic amenities at the Census 1971. Improvement is now seen as the major means by which the deterioration of the stock can be interrupted, while clearance is thought appropriate for fewer properties. About 310 houses may be represented as unfit in the next 8 years (to 1980), and an additional 100 houses have been identified which may require clearance thereafter.

Stafford has one designated General Improvement Area, intended as part of a wider programme of area improvement based on a partnership between the public and the local authority. The record so far in the GIA has not been encouraging since problems have beset the environmental improvements, and very few grant applications have been received.

There are just over 1000 council houses in Stafford built during the inter-war period. About half have already been modernized and the remainder will be dealt with at the rate of about 80 a year.

Against this background, improvement grants are given to private owners. It is hoped that about 2100 houses can be improved to the 12 point standard, and about 650 to the standard grant level in the next 8–10 years.

An applicant is urged to make use of a discretionary grant where possible. The underlying aims of the system are:

(a) To save houses from clearance.

(b) To update otherwise sound houses, and

(c) To produce extra accommodation units.

In accordance with this, improvement is encouraged to the 12 point standard, with a view to giving property a 30 year life. Social arguments may however temper the purely physical, and a reduced life may be acceptable. The updating aim leads to approval of kitchen extension applications in more modern houses (to Parker Morris standards). Conversions to flats are approved, but not the addition of an extra bedroom as the sole piece of work. Standard grants aim to give the house a 15 year life.

Practice—Improvement Grants

Slightly more standard than discretionary grants were given in Stafford during the survey period—53% of the applications were for standard grants. Table 10.11 shows the type of work involved in the grant applications. While four-fifths were for works including the installation of basic amenities, general improvement and conversion to flats constitute a sizeable minority. (See Appendix IV for a definition of the works involved.)

Table 10.11. Improvement Grants and Work, Stafford: 1972-73

Work involved:	Standard grant	Discretionary grant	All grants
Sample number	62	52	114
	%	%	%
Installation of missing amenities	27	4	17
Provision of bathroom	73	44	60
Provision of bathroom and kitchen	—	6	3
Kitchen extension	—	6	3
General improvement	—	25	11
Conversion to flats	—	15	7

Source: Local authority records.

Over three-quarters of the grant applications were for less than £500. Only 6% were at maximum grant level. Table 10.12 shows the average amount of grant under different headings.

Table 10.12. Average Grant Approved, Stafford: 1972-73

Type of grant:	Stafford
	£
Standard grant	152
Discretionary grant	486
All grants	304
For bathroom installation with or without kitchen improvement	312

Source: Local authority records.

Nearly half the discretionary grants included no repairs allowance, and a further 22% had an element of 10% or less. In only 12% of cases did the repairs allowance exceed 40% of total approved costs.

A considerable amount of time can elapse between the submission of grant application and the formal notification of approval by the authority. This is due to the procedure followed in Stafford whereby a statement of required repairs is sent to owners when the application is received. In some cases, long-protracted discussion can go on, and in others the application may lapse in face of the requirements. It may therefore be misleading to say that a third of applications took over 13 weeks for approval. A further third were approved within 6 weeks.

Over three-quarters (77%) of the discretionary grant applications were for the improvement of houses built before 1919. The addition of standard grants would doubtless increase this figure. Four-fifths of all grants went to terraced property.

Owner-occupiers seem more likely to improve their houses than private landlords. Just under two-thirds (60%) of the applicants were owner-occupiers, and 29% landlords. Eleven per cent of the houses were empty at the time the application was made. Sixty-two per cent of the 'bathroom' grants were made to owner-occupiers. In comparison, owner-occupiers made up only 36% of the private sector households lacking one or more amenities at the Census 1971.

Fifty-seven per cent of the applicants owned their houses outright, while 21% had a building society or a bank loan. Twenty-two per cent had an outstanding council mortgage.

COUNCIL HOUSE SALES AND COUNCIL MORTGAGES

Policy—Council House Sales

Council tenants are no longer able to buy their houses in Stafford. Before the policy was discontinued, over 200 houses had been sold. The scheme as operated excluded flats and maisonettes, old person's dwellings, bungalows and four-bedroomed houses, and any dwelling held on a service tenancy. Sales were restricted to tenants who had lived for at least 2 years in the house they intended to buy.

The sale price was either current vacant possession market value as determined by an independent valuer, or this price less a discount of 15% for the introduction of a standard 5 year pre-emption clause. In any case the minimum price level was set by the total cost of providing the house that was incurred by the Council. All sales were freehold.

Policy—Council Mortgage Lending

Stafford Council will advance money for the purchase or improvement of property under Housing Act powers. The Council aims to serve as a 'lender of last resort' and as such to complement the building societies. Some of the regulations for mortgage lending are set out in Table 10.13.

Practice—Mortgage Details

During the year 1972–73, 73 loans for private house purchase or improvement were made in Stafford. During the same period 92 loans for the purchase of council houses were made.

Table 10.14 shows that council advances are, on average, considerably smaller than those made by the building society. The average deposit (that is, the difference between weighted average price and advance)[1] is also shown. Council house purchasers had to, or chose to provide much smaller deposits. The average advance, in fact, represented 94% of average price. Comparable figures for council loans for private houses, and building society loans were 82% and 77% of price respectively.

Just a quarter of loans represented over 90% of valuation (private houses). In a further 49% of cases the loan was for 81% to 90% of valuation. Just over a quarter of the loans, then, represented 80% or less of valuation. The pricing policy for council houses sold makes direct comparison misleading. However, only 13% of council house purchasers received a loan representing 90% of price

---

[1] See Appendix III for methods and definitions.

Table 10.13. Regulations for Mortgage Lending, Stafford: 1973

Regulation:	Private Sector Houses	Former Council Houses (when sold)
Property and purchaser	Either the property or purchaser must fall into one of the categories listed in DoE Circular 22/71. Houses (existing or to be built) within the new District Council area will be considered. No upper price limit is set A leasehold property must have 60 years of unexpired lease at the time the advance is made	Any tenant acquiring his council house
Amount of advance	The total advance will not normally exceed 95% of valuation, or purchase price, whichever is the lower. A 100% advance may be made if the Council consider special circumstances exist The amount is also governed by the term of the loan and applicant's gross annual salary, through the following rules: 5-year loan—1½ times income 10 ,, 2 ,, 15 ,, 2¼ ,, 20 ,, 2½ ,, 25 ,, 2¾ ,, Applicant's income for this purpose usually excludes overtime earnings (which may be included with Committee approval) and wife's earnings. (£500 of wife's annual earnings may be included if she is aged over 40)	Purchase price less a £5 minimum deposit Income rules as for private house
Period of the loan	The maximum repayment period is 25 years, and this may be reduced at the applicant's request, or on the advice of the valuer, CPHI, Planning Officer or Borough Surveyor, having in mind the possible future life of the property	Maximum repayment period is 30 years
Interest rates and repayments	The interest rate is fixed at ¼% above that of the Public Works Loan Board for local authority borrowing at the date the advance is made Repayments are by the annuity or instalments method	As for private houses
Other conditions	Normally the borrower must personally reside in the house bought	

Table 10.14.   Size of Mortgage Advance and Balance, Stafford and Building Society

	Council advances		
Advance:	Private house	Council house	Building Society[1]
	(1971–73)	(1971–73)	(1972)
Sample number	89	100	1536
	%	%	%
Under £2000	30	—	2
£2000–£2995	31	51	7
£3000–£3995	26	49	15
£4000–£4995	9	—	27
£5000 and over	4	—	50
Average advance	£2630	£2960	£4520
Weighted average advance (1972 prices)	£2270	£2690	£4520
Weighted average balance (1972 prices)	£500	£150	£1290

Source: Nationwide Building Society (Midland Region) and local authority records.

[1] Building Society figures here and in all other tables in this section relate to the Midland Region.

or less. In three-quarters of cases the loan given for private house purchase was that requested. The figure rises to 98% for council houses.

The average period of council loans for private houses was 18 years, and for council houses 22 years. The building society average is 23 years. There is a considerable difference between the two types of council loan—in the case of private houses, only 25% of loans were for 25 years or longer, while nearly half those for council houses were for 25 or 30 years.

Council loans for private house purchase resulted in average repayments for the borrower of £310. The equivalent council house figure is £320 (both in 1972 prices) and the building society £430. Table 10.15 shows what this means in terms of the proportion of income committed to repayments. In view of the close similarity in repayments between council house and private house loans

Table 10.15.   Mortgage Repayments and Income, Stafford and Building Society

Repayments as % income:	Applicant's income			Household income	
	Private house	Council house	Building Society	Private house	Council house
	(1971–73)	(1971–73)	(1972)	(1971–73)	(1971–73)
Sample number	86	99	1536	86	99
	%	%	%	%	%
Less than 10%	5	1	—	5	1
10–17%	30	54	—	31	57
18–25%	44	43	—	47	40
Over 25%	21	1	—	17	1
Average percentage	20	17	22	—	—

Source: Nationwide Building Society (Midland Region) and local authority records.

the differences in income proportion are high. Information on household income may not be complete since this is rarely taken into account in Stafford. Lack of information may be responsible for the slight differences between repayments as a percentage of applicant's and household income, rather than the absence of additional earners.

Practice—Households Buying Private Houses

Information is only available on the age of applicants for a council loan. The average age is seen to be below that of building society borrowers, and also below the average for council house applicants.

Table 10.16. Household Characteristics—Private House Buyers, Stafford and Building Society

Age:	Council loan (1971–73)	Building Society (1972)
Sample number	89	1536
	%	%
30 and under	67	63
31–45	25	28
46–60	8	8
Over 60	1	★
Average age (years)	29	30

Source: Nationwide Building Society (Midland Region) and local authority records.

On the basis of name of borrower, it can be estimated that about 12% of loans in Stafford went to persons of Asian origin.

The majority of borrowers (53%) were in skilled manual occupations. A further 17% had semi- or unskilled jobs. Thirty per cent fell within professional, intermediate or skilled non-manual social class groups. One applicant was retired.

Applicant's total income is shown in Table 10.17. Although average levels are below the building society average, the differential is less in terms of income than in terms of house price financed by the two sources. Council average incomes were 78% as high as building society incomes, but prices only 48% as high. Average earnings for a full-time male employee in Great Britain in 1972 were £1870[1]—quite considerably above the Stafford borrower's income level. The relationship between income and repayments was shown in Table 10.1⁵

Practice—Households Buying Council Houses

Former tenants buying their council houses were appreciably older than households buying private houses with council aid. Just 40% of the borrowers are over 45 years of age—a higher proportion than is found on the council house waiting list, but lower than found on the transfer list.

[1] *Department of Employment Gazette*. Vol. LXXXI No. 12, Dec. 1973. Table 128.

Table 10.17.   Borrower's Income—Private House Buyers, Stafford and Building Society

Annual income:	Council loan (1971–73)	Weekly income	Building Society (1972)
Sample number	87	Sample number	1536
	%		%
£1000 and under	9	£20 and under	3
£1005–1500	39	£21–£30	28
£1505–£2000	35	£31–£40	36
£2005–£3000	16	£41–£60	27
Over £3000	1	Over £60	6
Average income	£1600	Average income	£1980
Weighted average (1972 prices)	£1550	Weighted average (1972 prices)	£1980

Source: Nationwide Building Society (Midland Region) and local authority records.

Table 10.18.   Household Characteristics—Council House Buyers, Stafford and Great Britain

Age:	Stafford Council house loan (1971–73)	Age:	Great Britain All council tenants (1971)
Sample number	98	Sample number	3688
	%		%
30 and under	6	Under 30	9
31–45	54	30–44	25
46–60	39	45–59	33
Over 60	1	60 and over	34
Average age (years)	42		—

Source: *General Household Survey—Introductory Report* and local authority records.

Twenty-three per cent of buyers had been council tenants for more than 20 years—about two-thirds for more than 10 years. Only 13% had been tenants for 5 years or less.

The emphasis on skilled manual occupations is slightly less than among private house buyers (47%). There are relatively more in semi-skilled or unskilled groups (22%) and similar proportions in professional, intermediate and skilled non-manual jobs.

Applicant's income was on average higher than among private house buyers. The average controlled to 1972 levels was £1890, compared to only £1550 for the private purchasers. This figure is above the national average of £1870.[1]

Practice—Private House Bought with Council Loans

The prices of houses bought with council loans are considerably lower, on average, than those found in the building society. The levels are also very

[1] *Department of Employment Gazette* op. cit.

much below those of houses for sale with estate agents in Stafford in 1973. (Table 10.19.) The lower average price among the council group is reflected in the size and type details given in Table 10.20.

Table 10.19.   Price of House—Private Sector, Stafford and Building Society

	Staff“Stafford”		Midland Region
Price:	Purchased with council loan	For sale with estate agents	Purchased with Building Society loan
	(1971–73)	(1973)	(1972)
Sample number	88	66	1536
	%	%	%
Under £2000	24	—	1
£2000–£2995	22	—	6
£3000–£3995	27	2	11
£4000–£4995	16	2	23
£5000 and over	11	97	59
Average price (1972 prices)	£3250	£10,240	£5810
Weighted average (1972 prices)	£2770	£7930	£5810

Source: Nationwide Building Society (Midland Region), estate agents survey and local authority records.

Table 10.20.   Size and Type of Dwelling—Private Sector, Stafford and Building Society

	Stafford		Midland Region
House size:	Purchased with council loan	For sale with estate agents	Purchased with Building Society loan
	(1971–73)	(1973)	(1972)
Sample number	88	66	1536
	%	%	%
2 bedrooms	38	18	20
3 bedrooms	61	70	70
4 bedrooms or over	1	12	9
House type:			
Terraced	85	5	18
Semi-detached	15	52	40
Detached and other	—	44	42

Source: Nationwide Building Society (Midland Region), estate agent sample and local authority records.

Eighty-six per cent of the houses bought with a council loan were built before 1919, and another 13% before 1939. Only one post-war house was included in the sample. Just over 40% of the houses had a garden and 20% had a garage. Two-thirds required some repairs as a condition of the loan, and over a third (36%) had a rateable value of £50 or less (before the 1973 revaluation). Older, poorer quality houses seem to be bought with council mortgages.

Practice—Council Houses Sold

When sales were discontinued in Stafford, about 200 houses had been sold. This figure represents about 4% of the total council stock, and 5% of the *houses*. In the size and age comparisons which follow in Table 10.21, the 'total' figures relate to houses only, and exclude flats, maisonettes and bungalows. Three-bedroomed houses and those built post war seem the most popular for purchase. Two-thirds of the houses sold were on estates classed as 'attractive' or 'very attractive'. This compares to 24% and 17% of allocations to transfer and general needs applicants on such estates.

Table 10.21. Size and Age of Council House Sold, Stafford

Size:	Houses sold (1971–73)	Total stock of houses (1971)
Sample number	100	3890
	%	%
2 bedrooms	8	10
3 bedrooms	91	86
4 bedrooms	1	4
Age:		
Pre-war	16	28
Post-war	84	72

Source: *I.M.T.A. Housing Statistics (England and Wales) Part 1* and local authority records.

The weighted average purchase price of council houses sold was £2860 (compared to £2770 for private houses). Virtually all cost between £2000 and £4000. Council houses were much more modern than private houses bought with a council loan, and likely to be in better structural condition. Rateable values were certainly higher—only 2% had a value of £50 or less. Seventeen per cent had a garage and 11% central heating. In these circumstances more than a £90 difference in average purchase price of council and private houses might have been expected.

STAFFORD—SUMMARY

Stafford has a growing population which is relatively youthful in that there are lower proportions of elderly persons than in the West Midland Region. The housing stock is of good quality in terms of amenity provision. The tenure structure is similar to the regional average.

There is a very flexible system for all council house allocations which seems able to be selective of most elements of housing need. Small families and households with children were particularly favoured by waiting list allocations, while greater numbers of households in both overcrowded conditions and in under-occupation were found among allocations than on the waiting list as a whole. Transfer allocations in the survey year seem to have been aimed particularly at the relief of under-occupancy—and thus to have favoured small elderly households.

While householders lacking basic amenities are rehoused by the council, the improvement grant system is aimed particularly at the older housing stock. Clear aims for the grant system exist, and actual performance corresponds well. The majority of grants are given for installation of amenities in older terraced houses. It was stated that social arguments might temper the purely physical in not demanding too high standards of improvement. In the survey sample the number of standard grants, and the relatively modest amount spent on each grant scheme suggest this may be working in practice. Improvement in Stafford may have to be seen as the first step in an incremental process with expenditure growing as aspirations rise and income permits. Private landlords at present do not seem to be contributing fully to improvement through the grant system.

Mortgage lending by the council is almost exclusively aimed at the older housing stock. Cheap, older houses are being mortgaged, and loans are being used by young households, often with relatively low incomes. Repayments make up a considerable proportion of income in many cases. In this sense both property and purchaser could be regarded as marginal in a commercial sense, and the council is truly acting as a 'lender of last resort'.

Incomes of council house purchasers are considerably higher, while prices were very little above the level of private houses bought. Borrowers were generally older than those buying private houses, and often well-established council tenants. In objective terms it would seem these purchasers might be able to buy houses in the private sector (with the proviso that age could create financial problems in some cases). The decision to discontinue selling council houses may have had the effect of thwarting the satisfaction of housing *desires* rather than of housing *needs*. In the situation of continuing demand for council houses, together with a small stock in absolute terms, the decision to stop selling is understandable, though sales may have little effect on the number of vacancies arising in the short term. In the longer term vacancies would be lost.

The different strands of housing policy in Stafford seem to complement each other. Council housing is providing homes for young families, while the improvement grant and mortgage policies are aimed at the older housing stock. Flexibility was frequently mentioned in relation to policies, and this appears to have been achieved in a way which might be difficult in a larger town.

11. Ludlow R.D.

BACKGROUND

Ludlow Rural District covers a wide area of southern Shropshire including the towns of Ludlow, Church Stretton, Craven Arms and Cleobury Mortimer, as well as many smaller villages. Unless otherwise stated, 'Ludlow' as used in this Chapter denotes the Rural District, and not the town of Ludlow alone. The Census population of the Rural District in 1971 was 23,522. Population had grown between 1961 and 1971 at a rate of 0·29% a year as a result of natural increase and net inward migration. The age structure details presented in Table 11.1 show the district to include above average proportions of elderly persons and relatively fewer children and young adults than in the West Midland Region as a whole.

Table 11.1. Age Structure of Population, Ludlow and Region: 1971

Age:	Ludlow R.D. %	West Midland Region %
0–14	22	25
15–19	7	7
20–29	12	15
30–44	17	18
45–59	19	19
60 and over	23	17

Source: 1971 Census.

There were just over 8000 private households in Ludlow, giving an average household size of 2·83 persons—a figure lower than the regional average of 2·98. Thirty-one per cent of all households in the area were 'small elderly households' —that is one or two person households in which one or both members are of retiring age. This is well above the regional average of 24%.

The housing stock in Ludlow is distinguished in terms of size by the high proportion of dwellings having 7 or more rooms. Sixteen per cent of all dwellings were of such a size locally, compared to only 7% regionally. Not surprisingly, occupancy levels in Ludlow were correspondingly lower than in the Region. In the Rural District 0·7% of households were living at a density of more than $1\frac{1}{2}$ persons per room, and 41% at a density of less than $\frac{1}{2}$ person per room. The regional figures are 1·6% and 34% respectively.

Council housing makes up a smaller proportion of the housing stock in Ludlow than in the Region. Just a fifth of households locally were council tenants (34% Region), and 52% were owner-occupiers (50% Region). The privately rented sector is much more important in Ludlow, since over a quarter of households were renting their accommodation unfurnished from a private landlord. The number of private tenant households exceeds the number of council tenant households.

Only 79% of households had exclusive use of all amenities—fixed bath, hot water and inside WC at the 1971 Census (Region 84%). Conditions in these terms were rather worse among the private tenants—for example, only 62% of tenant households had use of all amenities compared to 84% of owner-occupiers.

New house completions have averaged about 140 a year between 1968 and 1972.[1] The public sector accounts for under a quarter of all completions. During the same period about 50 houses a year were demolished or closed. (Local authority building did not offset the loss from demolition.)

Significant features to emerge include the number of elderly persons in the population, the relatively poor standard of amenity provision in the housing stock, the relatively small public sector, and the relatively large proportion of privately rented accommodation, some at least, likely to be available on tied tenancy arrangements.

COUNCIL HOUSE ALLOCATIONS

Policies

As demand for council housing outstrips supply, rules of eligibility and priority are applied in determining allocation policies. Some of the regulations are set out in Table 11.2.

Special cases may be reported to Committee outside the points scheme for general needs applicants, with the aim of speeding rehousing. Most usually these will be persons under Court eviction notices, deserted wives, or families in damaged houses. Owner-occupiers or persons under Notice to Quit are dealt with through usual points procedures.

There is no formal statement of policy relating to the relative priority for allocations between different groups. In practice, clearance rehousing needs are very small, leaving the order of priority between transfers and general needs applicants for any specific letting. By implication transfers may have prior claim since the transfer system is used to make efficient use of the housing stock.

During the year 1972–73, 118 allocations were made. Of these 48% went to applicants from the waiting list, 40% to transfer applicants, 11% to mutual exchanges and 1% to clearance rehousing. Thus, there were more lettings made to existing tenants than to 'new' tenants (from the waiting list or clearance re-housing). In Ludlow the ratio of 'new' to 'transfer' lettings was 1 to 1·03. General needs applicants took 98% of the new lettings.

The type of property allocated to each lettings group is shown in Table 11.3. Differences in terms of dwelling size seem to correspond well with observed differences in household size between the waiting list and transfer groups. How-ever, families on the waiting list seem less likely to be allocated a house (rather than a flat) than families on the transfer list. Families including children aged 16 or under made up 41% of waiting list allocations, while only 34% of the dwellings let to waiting list applicants were houses. Comparable figures for the transfer list are families, 49% and houses 76%.

[1] *Local Housing Statistics England and Wales.* H.M.S.O.

Table 11.2. Eligibility and Priority Regulations, Ludlow: 1973

	General Needs Applicants	Transfer Applicants	Clearance Rehousing
Eligibility rules for application	Anyone living or working in the Rural District is eligible to apply	Any council tenant	Not applicable
Eligibility for consideration	All on the Waiting List	All on the Waiting List	No apparent restrictions on persons rehoused. Rehousing usually dealt with through transfer system as Council buys properties in advance of clearance
Method of ordering priority	Applicants are grouped within the 7 geographical areas in which they would like a house, and further sub-divided by the size of dwelling required Within these groupings priorities are determined by a points scheme: (a) For general needs applicants points are awarded for: (i) Overcrowding in terms of bedroom accommodation (ii) Statutory overcrowding of the whole dwelling (iii) Sharing a living room (iv) Sharing a kitchen (v) Unsuitable accommodation—in terms of conditions, situation, etc. (vi) Length of time the applicant has lived in a flat (vii) Ill health or physical disability (on the recommendation of the M.O.H. (viii) Discretionary points awarded by the Tenancies Committee as they think fit (b) For old people's dwellings points are awarded for: (i) Unsuitability of accommodation—distance from roads, proximity of neighbours, conditions, etc. (ii) Ill health—graded by the M.O.H. (iii) Lack of a separate house (iv) Age—points for each 2 years over pensionable age (v) Suitability of applicant (not defined) (vi) Discretionary points awarded by the Committee as they think fit The priority waiting list drawn up on these lines is approved by Committee and the Housing Manager makes lettings in accordance	No formal rules for determining priority among transfer requests. The Housing Manager uses delegated powers to use transfers as a means of making full and efficient use of the available stock and the voids arising Transfer applications may have medical support	Not applicable

Table 11.3. Type of Dwelling Allocated, Ludlow: 1972-73

House type:	Waiting list	Transfers and mutual exchanges	Total[1]
Sample number	57	60	118
	%	%	%
Bungalow	28	5	16
1 bed. flat	14	3	9
2 bed. flat/maisonette	19	7	13
2 bed. house	9	22	16
3 bed. flat/maisonette	5	8	7
3 bed. house	25	53	39
4 bed. house	—	1	1

Source: Local authority records.

[1] Note the Total figures include the single clearance case in the sample.

Allocations can only be made as vacancies arise, or are created by transfers. The turnover rates for different house types show wide variation (Table 11.4). Figures for bungalows have been omitted since the turnover was inflated by the new building programme during the survey year. New building accounted for 10% of all vacancies arising, and nearly all the new dwellings were let to waiting list applicants.

Table 11.4. Turnover Rates and Housing Type, Ludlow: 1972-73

House type:	Number in stock 1971	Number among allocation	Allocations as % stock
	Number	Number	% as index
1 bed. flat	67	10	15
2 bed. flat/maisonette	67	15	22
2 bed. house	174	19	11
3 bed. flat/maisonette	20	8	40
3 bed. house	943	46	5
4 bed. house	56	1	2

Source: *I.M.T.A. Housing Statistics (England and Wales) Part 1* and local authority records.

Practice—the Waiting List

For survey purposes, no distinction was made between applicants requiring family or old person's accommodation. Figures for a single total Waiting List are compared with the Successful List—that is the waiting list applicants who were allocated a house during the survey year.

Table 11.5 shows the household characteristics of applicants. The predominance of small elderly households is particularly striking. Allocations seem to have favoured both the elderly and young families with children. It is interesting that a fifth of Waiting List applicants were aged over 70, and no less than 26% of the Successful List were of this age.

Table 11.5. Household Characteristics—Waiting List, Ludlow: 1973

Household type:	Waiting List	Successful List
Sample number	207	57
	%	%
Single person	8	4
Small adult	15	11
Small family	27	32
Large family	4	9
Large adult	6	2
Small elderly	40	44
Average household size (persons)	2·19	2·42
Households with children aged 5 or under	24%	33%
Average age of applicant (years)	50	49

Source: Local authority records.

Indices of housing need are shown in Table 11.6. The Successful List shows larger proportions in all the need categories save underoccupation. This is interesting in light of the number of small elderly households who were rehoused, since this type of household is frequently found living at very low density in houses 'too big' for them.

Table 11.6. Indices of Housing Need—Waiting List, Ludlow: 1973

% of sample who are:	Waiting List	Successful List
Lodging with family	16	33
Lodging—other	2	4
Without own living room	20	39
Sharing with 5 or more persons	1	7
Living at a density of more than 2 persons per bedroom	12	28
Living at a density of 0·3 persons per bedroom or less	10	2
Claiming medical priority	30	40
Lone parent families	6	16
On list before 1971	27	28

Source: Local authority records.

Table 11.7 shows what a variety of reasons can exist for making an application for a council house. Medical reasons show as particularly important among those allocated a dwelling.

Only 5% of applicants on the waiting list had already received and refused an offer of accommodation. Five per cent of those on the Successful List had also received at least one offer prior to the one they accepted.

Table 11.7. Reason for Application—Waiting List, Ludlow: 1973

Reason:	Waiting List	Successful List
Sample number	179	51
	%	%
Seeking independence	17	8
Engaged/want to start family	2	4
Occupancy—		
Too little space	3	16
Too much space	5	6
Housing—		
Conditions	21	18
Location—		
Near work/relatives	6	6
Ill health	7	22
Under notice to quit/insurance	8	12
Tied accommodation/insurance	21	10
Other	10	—

Source: Local authority records.

Practice—Transfers

A single transfer list of eligible applicants is maintained. The transfer list includes rather fewer young and elderly applicants than are found on the waiting list. Transfer allocations (the Successful List) are remarkably similar to applicants remaining on the list, but include slightly fewer small elderly households.

Table 11.8. Household Characteristics—Transfer List, Ludlow: 1973

Household type:	Transfer List	Successful List
Sample number	149	47
	%	%
Single person	1	—
Small adult	13	17
Small family	31	34
Large family	15	15
Large adult	15	15
Small elderly	25	19
Average household size (persons)	3·12	3·28
Households with children aged 5 or under	31%	26%
Average age of applicant (years)	47	46

Source: Local authority records.

The indices in Table 11.9 show housing need in terms of occupancy to be rather less among transfer than waiting list applicants. Medical claims are rather similar. Transfer allocations seem to have been aimed particularly at the relief of over-crowding, and this is supported by the main reason for application given in Table 11.10. Applicants wanting a house, and those wishing to leave a 'poor area' are often successful.

Table 11.9.   Indices of Housing Need—Transfer List, Ludlow: 1973

% of sample who are:	Transfer List	Successful List
Living at a density of more than 2 persons per bedroom	5	9
Living at a density of 0·3 persons per bedroom or less	2	—
Claiming medical priority	36	32
On list before 1971	27	40

Source: Local authority records.

Table 11.10.   Reason for Application—Transfer List, Ludlow: 1973

Reason:	Transfer List	Successful List
Sample number	120	34
	%	%
Occupancy—		
Too little space	17	29
Too much space	16	12
Housing—		
House type	12	15
Conditions	2	3
Location—		
Near work/relatives	13	6
Poor area/noise/neighbours	10	12
Ill health	20	15
Other	10	8

Source: Local authority records.

Eight per cent of applicants on the transfer list had already refused an offer, while 9% of those allocated a dwelling had previously turned down an offer.

The full effect of granting all current transfer applications cannot be shown precisely since the required accommodation was not always known. In general terms, however, there would be a movement from three-bedroomed dwellings, and an increase in demand for one-bedroomed accommodation.

Practice—Clearance Rehousing

Only one family was rehoused through clearance in the survey year. A small elderly household was involved, and they were allocated a two-bedroomed house. There is, of course, no way of telling how typical this was of clearance needs generally.

IMPROVEMENT GRANTS

Policies

The housing stock of Ludlow Rural District includes many old properties— some of considerable architectural and historical merit. Over 1600 households at the 1971 Census lived in accommodation lacking exclusive use of one or more of the basic amenities.

At present, there is no clearance programme as such. In two areas of Ludlow (town) the Council are buying properties with a view to demolition and re-development at a future date. Elsewhere and in the rural areas, individual orders are used where such a course seems socially desirable. Such properties are often improved rather than demolished. There is no General Improvement Area in the district, and some doubt is expressed as to whether this would be appropriate in this particular area. Two Conservation Areas exist, one in Ludlow (town) and one in Cleobury Mortimer. Older council houses are being improved, and all those built during the inter-war period will soon have been dealt with.

Improvement grants are seen as the major tool whereby the older houses can be brought up to modern standards. There is no statement available to the public of works allowable for discretionary grant purposes. In general, grants will be given for works to bring dwellings to the 12 point standard, but not for extension work alone. Thus a grant would not be given for the provision of an additional bedroom or the extension of an existing kitchen. Grants are given for the conversion of a building into a dwelling house, or the conversion of a house into self-contained flats. In major schemes central heating is allowable to Parker Morris standards.

Houses known to be second homes are eligible only for standard grants, but it is not always easy to ensure that an improved house will be lived in permanently by the owner. This, of course, is the result of the district's position as an attractive rural area. In practice this also means that many of the schemes proposed amount to virtually complete rearrangement and rebuilding of the dwelling interior.

Practice—Improvement Grants

Discretionary grants were much more important in the survey period, making up 76% of all those approved. Table 11.11 shows the type of work involved in the grant applications. The majority include more than simple bathroom installation, and may in some cases amount to virtually new interiors. (See Appendix IV for the definition of work used.)

Table 11.11. Improvement Grants and Work: 1972-73

Work involved:	Standard grant	Discretionary grant	All grants
Sample number	39	126	165
	%	%	%
Installation of missing amenities	15	—	4
Provision of bathroom	85	17	33
Provision of bathroom and kitchen	—	40	31
General improvement	—	19	14
Conversion to flats	—	13	10
Conversion to dwelling	—	10	8

Source: Local authority records.

Two-thirds of the grants were for £500 or more, and 44% were for £1000 or over (the grant limits for conversion work are above £1000). Table 11.12 shows the average amount of grant approved under various headings.

Table 11.12. Average Grant Approved, Ludlow: 1972–73

Type of grant:	Ludlow R.D.
	£
Standard grant	280
Discretionary grant	850
All grants	715
For bathroom installation with or without kitchen improvement	700

Source: Local authority records.

Only one-tenth of discretionary grants included no repairs element, and 23% of all cases included a repairs allowance of more than 20% of approved costs. The majority, then, included a moderate allowance for repairs.

The time elapsing between submission of a grant application and official notification of approval was lengthy in many cases. Only 20% of grants were approved within 6 weeks, and in 40% of cases notification of approval took 15 weeks or longer.

Nearly two-thirds of the houses receiving a discretionary grant in Ludlow were built before 1880, and only 10% were built after 1919. Over half the dwellings were detached—ranging from a cottage to a manor house. About one-fifth were terraced houses.

Over a third (38%) of the houses being improved were in owner-occupation, and 15% were definitely tenanted. The remaining 41% were vacant at the time the application was made, and in many cases these were likely to be owner-occupied in future. On this evidence owner-occupiers seem much more likely to improve their property than do landlords. Owner-occupiers represented less than half the households lacking amenities at the 1971 Census. Seventy-one per cent of the properties receiving grants were owned outright. Just a quarter had an outstanding building society or bank loan. Only 4% of the houses were covered by an outstanding local authority mortgage.

COUNCIL HOUSE SALES AND COUNCIL MORTGAGES

Policy—Council House Sales

Council houses in Ludlow are sold to sitting tenants. Houses and family bungalows, as opposed to flats and old persons' bungalows, are sold. No limit has been set to the number which may be sold.

The usual purchase price is the District Valuer's estimate of full market value with vacant possession, less a discount, the amount of which depends on the length of tenancy of the purchaser. A tenant of less than 5 years standing receives no discount. At 5 years a 5% discount is allowed, and the amount rises by 1% for each completed year to a maximum of 20% for 20 years tenancy. A standard 5 year pre-emption clause is introduced when a discount is allowed. In any case the minimum price is set by the original cost of providing the house.

Table 11.13. Regulations for Mortgage Lending, Ludlow: 1973

Regulation:	Private Sector Houses	Former Council Houses
Property and purchaser	Purchasers who are unable to raise finance in other ways on the property they wish to buy within the Rural District. Preference is given to older property	Any tenant acquiring his council house
Amount of advance	Loans of 90–100% of valuation may be made or of purchase price, whichever is the lower. 100% loans are allowed if repayments would not prove excessive. The total amount lent is limited to £6000, or to 2½ times applicant's earnings. Wife's income is rarely taken into account in calculating earnings	100% loans are more common. Income rules as for private houses
Period of the loan	The repayment period is set with reference to the borrower's ability to make repayments and the state of the property. 30-year loans may be made, but under normal circumstances a 20-year repayment period is advised. This may be reduced on the advice of the Valuer as to the expected life of the property, or at the borrower's request	As for private houses
Interest rate	Interest rates are fixed at ¼% above the rate set by the Treasury for loans to local authorities from the Public Works Loan Board at the time the advance is made	As for private houses
Other conditions	Under certain circumstances an amount may be withheld from the advance until necessary repairs have been completed satisfactorily. When extensive repairs or alterations requiring planning permission are necessary, all permissions must be obtained before a loan is made	

Policy—Council Mortgage Lending

The provision of council loans for house purchase or improvements in Ludlow is seen against a wider background of providing a financial counselling service for potential applicants. Council mortgages are usually given where other sources of finance are unavailable, or would be disadvantageous to the borrower. One of the aims of lending is that of helping people to buy older property, thus maintaining the character of the area. Mortgages are made using Small Dwellings Acquisition Act powers. Some of the regulations governing loans for house purchase are set out in Table 11.13.

Practice—Mortgage Details

As is explained in Appendix I, only 2 council house loans were included in the survey sample. The remainder of this section refers only to loans made for the purchase of private houses.

Table 11.14 shows that council advances were, on average, much smaller than those made by the building society. The average deposit (that is, the difference between weighted average price and advance[1]) was also smaller. If the average loan is expressed as a percentage of the average price, the council loan represented 81% and building society loan 77% of price.

Table 11.14.   Size of Mortgage Advance and Balance, Ludlow and Building Society

Advance:	Council loan (1968–72)	Building Society[1] (1972)
Sample number	76	1536
	%	%
Under £2000	32	2
£2000–£2995	29	7
£3000–£3995	27	15
£4000–£4995	2	27
£5000 and over	11	50
Average advance	£2620	£4520
Weighted average advance (1972 prices)	£2830	£4520
Weighted average balance (1972 prices)	£670	£1290

Source: Nationwide Building Society (Midland Region) and local authority records.

[1] Building Society figures here and in all other tables in this section relate to the Midland Region.

In over half (55%) of the loans, the advance made represented over 90% of the valuation. In a further 28% of cases, the loan was between 81% and 90% valuation. Only a tenth of the advances were for 80% of valuation or less. The average period of council loan was 17 years compared to a building society average of 23 years. The bulk of council lending (61%) has a repayment period of 20 years.

[1] See Appendix III for method of calculation and definition.

Council advances resulted in average annual repayments for the borrower of
£390 (1972 levels). The building society figure was £430. The relatively slight
difference between the two, despite the difference in size of advance is, presumably,
partly accounted for by the shorter repayments period among council loans.
Table 7.15 shows what repayments mean in terms of proportion of income
committed. Repayments bulk large in family budgeting, since they represent
23% of applicant's income. The comparable figure for building society borrowers
is 22%.

Table 11.15. Mortgage Repayments and Income, Ludlow

Repayments as % income:	Applicant's income Council loan	Household income Council loan
Sample number	72	72
	%	%
Less than 10%	1	1
10–17%	27	32
18–25%	41	45
Over 25%	33	22

Source: Local authority records.

Table 11.16. Household Characteristics—Private House Buyers, Ludlow and Building Society

Household type:	Ludlow Council loan (1968–72)	Midland Region Building Society (1972)	Great Britain All owner-occupiers with outstanding mortgage (1971)
Sample number	75	—	3199
	%	—	%
Single person	1	—	3
Small adult	29	—	17
Small and large family	66	—	56
Large adult	3	—	17
Small elderly	—	—	6
Average household size (persons)	3·31	—	—
Households including children aged 5 and under	47%	—	—
Age:			
Sample number	73	1536	—
	%	%	%
30 and under	38	63	—
31–45	51	28	—
46–60	8	8	—
Over 60	2	★	—
Average age (years)	35	30	—

Source: Nationwide Building Society (Midland Region), *General Household Survey—Introductory Report,* local authority records.

Practice—Households Buying Private Houses

Those buying houses with a council loan emerge as rather older, on average, than those using a building society advance. The purchasers are also distinct from those applying for council houses in that they include many fewer elderly people, and more families with children.

Skilled manual workers made up the largest single social class group among borrowers (43%). A further 14% were semi-skilled or unskilled workers. Forty-three per cent of purchasers fell into the professional, intermediate and skilled non-manual workers group.

Average borrower's income in Ludlow was relatively low. The average applicant's income of £1660 is below the building society average, and well below the national average for full-time male earnings in 1972 of £1870.[1] However, the differential between council and building society borrowers is less in terms of income, than in terms of price of house bought. Council average incomes are 84% as high as building society incomes, but prices only 60% as high.

Table 11.17.   Borrower's Income—Private House Buyers, Ludlow and Building Society

Annual income:	Council loan (1968–72)	Weekly income:	Building Society (1972)
Sample number	75	Sample number	1536
	%		%
£1000 and under	21	£20 and under	3
£1005–£1500	47	£21–£30	28
£1505–£2000	16	£31–£40	36
£2005–£3000	15	£41–£60	27
Over £3000	1	Over £60	6
Average income	£1370	Average income	£1980
Weighted average (1972 prices)	£1660		£1980

Source: Nationwide Building Society (Midland Region) and local authority records.

Practice—Houses Bought with Council Loans

The average price of house bought with a council loan is considerably below the building society average. It is still further below the average found among a sample of houses for sale with estate agents in the Rural District in 1973. (Table 11.18.)

The big differences in price evident between houses in Ludlow bought with a council loan, and those for sale with estate agents are not accounted for by the size details shown in Table 11.19. House type seems to explain more of the difference.

[1] *Department of Employment Gazette*, Vol. LXXXI No. 12, Dec. 1973. Table 128.

Table 11.18. Price of Houses—Private Sector, Ludlow and Building Society

Price:	Ludlow R.D.		Midland Region
	Purchased with council loan	For sale with estate agents	Purchased with Building Society loan
	(1968–72)	(1973)	(1972)
Sample number	75	33	1536
	%	%	%
Under £2000	20	—	1
£2000–£2995	30	—	6
£3000–£3995	30	3	11
£4000–£4995	4	6	23
£5000 and over	15	91	59
Average price	£3220	£10,910	£5810
Weighted average (1972 prices)	£3500	£8440	£5810

Source: Nationwide Building Society (Midland Region), estate agents sample and local authority records.

Table 11.19. Size and Type of Dwelling—Private Sector, Ludlow and Building Society

House size:	Ludlow R.D.		Midland Region
	Purchased with council loan	For sale with estate agents	Purchased with Building Society loan
	(1968–72)	(1973)	(1972)
Sample number	61	33	1536
	%	%	%
1 bedroom	2	—	*
2 bedrooms	39	39	20
3 bedrooms	39	43	70
4 bedrooms or more	20	18	9
House type:			
Terraced	34	21	18
Semi-detached	29	12	40
Detached and other	37	67	42

Source: Nationwide Building Society (Midland Region), estate agents sample and local authority records.

House quality is less easy to judge as the information is less complete. The generalizations which follow are based on a reduced sample. Sixty-eight per cent of the houses bought with a council loan were built before 1919, and a further 13% before 1944. Thirteen per cent were either new or being built by the applicant. Over half the houses required some repairs as a condition of the loan. About three-quarters of the existing houses had a rateable value of £50 or less (before the 1973 revaluation). Local authority lending seems concentrated into older houses, possibly of a low quality.

LUDLOW—SUMMARY

The Census shows that Ludlow has above average numbers of elderly people, and small elderly households. The housing stock includes relatively more large houses, and many properties lacking basic amenities. The private rented sector is large, and probably includes many tied tenancies.

While the council sector is small, the lettings policy increases the total number of allocations which can be made, by use of a well-developed transfer system. Elderly households were particularly favoured by allocations from the waiting list, while transfer lettings tended to reduce overcrowding rather than under-occupation. Families with children were helped through both waiting list and transfer procedures. Despite the high numbers of allocations made during the survey year to small elderly households, the waiting list still represents considerable demand for small accommodation. The transfer list also suggests the need for more one-bedroomed units, the provision of which would allow the release of family sized houses.

Many of the improvement grants given seem not to be of direct benefit to existing local residents. Enormous sums of money are being spent on older properties in the rural district—in nearly a quarter of cases, the grant element constituted less than 20% of the total costs. Besides major improvement and conversion schemes, more moderate 'orthodox' improvement is taking place with grant aid, and some in tenanted properties. The danger in taking grant figures at face value is clear if improvement is seen as important in improving living conditions for residents rather than simply improving the housing stock.

Council mortgages are also aimed chiefly at the older housing stock. Here relatively cheap property is involved, and the purchasers have relatively low incomes. Mortgages repayments represent sizeable commitments in terms of applicant's and household income. At the same time many borrowers have families with young children, and family commitments are high. It is probable that those buying houses with council loans would not be able to become owner-occupiers if a source of finance for cheap, old property was not available. The continuation of lending, and the continuation of a supply of cheap property for purchase, have obvious implications for future demand for council housing.

Appendices

Appendix I Details of the Local Authority Survey Samples

Samples of local authority records were drawn for analysis purposes. The samples were as follows:

Waiting list for council houses

West Bromwich A 1 in 10 sample of all lists as at April 1973—

Live list	Number 153
Dormant list	Number 291
Application held in abeyance	Number 152

Warley A 1 in 10 sample of all lists as at June 1973—

Live list	Number 102
Dormant list	Number 310
Application apparently lapsed	Number 186

Wolverhampton A 1 in 10 sample of all lists as at September 1973—

Live list	Number 450
Deferred list	Number 182

Halesowen A 1 in 10 sample of the total list as at May 1973—

Total list	Number 115

Stafford A 1 in 9 sample of the total list as at October 1973—

Total list	Number 171

Ludlow A 1 in 2 sample of the total list as at October 1973—

Total list	Number 208

Transfer list:

West Bromwich A 1 in 10 sample of all lists as at April 1973—

Live list	Number 280
Dormant list	Number 156

Warley A 1 in 10 sample of the total list as at June 1973—

Total list	Number 436

Wolverhampton A 1 in 10 sample of the total list as at September 1973—

Total list	Number 363

Halesowen A 1 in 4 sample of the total list as at May 1973—

Total list	Number 114

Stafford A 1 in 3 sample of the total list as at October 1973—

Total list	Number 111

Ludlow All the transfer applicants as at October 1973—

Total list	Number 149

Council house allocations and voids:

West Bromwich   A 1 in 5 sample of weekly lettings sheets for the year April 1st 1972–March 31st 1973. All allocations from the selected weeks.
Allocations   Number 510

Warley   A 1 in 5 sample of weekly lettings sheets for the year 1972–73. All allocations from the selected weeks.
Allocations   Number 435

Wolverhampton   A 1 in 5 sample of weekly lettings sheets for the year 1972–73. All allocations from the selected weeks.
Allocations   Number 679

Halesowen   A 1 in 4 sample of weekly lettings sheets for the year 1972–73. All allocations from selected weeks.
Allocations   Number 124

Stafford   A 1 in 4 sample of weekly lettings sheets for the year 1972–73. All allocations from the selected weeks.
Allocations   Number 190

Ludlow   All allocations made in the year 1972–73.
Allocations   Number 118

Improvement grants:

West Bromwich   A 1 in 2 sample of all completed grants and a 1 in 3 sample of grants without completion certificate. Grants approved January 1972–April 1973.
Grants   Number 225

Warley   A 1 in 3 sample of grant approvals listed for Committee February 1972–March 1973.
Grants   Number 191

Wolverhampton   A 1 in 3 sample of grant applications reported to Committee January 1972–June 1973.
Grants   Number 207

Halesowen   A 1 in 2 sample of grant approvals between January 1972–June 1973.
Grants   Number 104

Stafford   All grant applications made between January 1972 and May 1973.
Grants   Number 116

Ludlow   All grant applications approved with the application dated January 1972 and May 1973.
Grants   Number 165

Council mortgages for purchase of private houses:

West Bromwich A sample of the most recent completed mortgages, 1968–73.
                                                                    Number 61

Warley   A sample of the most recent completed mortgages, 1966–73.
                                                                    Number 85

Wolverhampton A sample of the most recent completed mortgages, 1955–73.
                                                                    Number 100

Halesowen   A sample of the most recent completed mortgages, 1967–72.
                                                                    Number 71

Stafford   A sample of the most recent completed mortgages, 1971–73.
                                                                    Number 89

Ludlow   A sample of the most recent completed mortgages, 1968–72.
                                                                    Number 76

Council house sales:

West Bromwich (a) A 1 in 6 sample of recent sales from Housing Department
                   records, 1972–73   Number 100

              (b) A sample of the most recent completed advances for
                   council house purchase.   Number 50

Warley   A sample of the most recent completed advances for council
              house purchase, 1972–73.   Number 84

Wolverhampton A sample of the most recent completed advances for council
              house purchase, 1971–73.   Number 70

Halesowen   A sample of the most recent completed advances for council
              house purchase, 1971–73.   Number 72

Stafford   A sample of the most recent completed advances for council
              house purchase, 1971–73.   Number 100

Ludlow   Inadequate number of houses sold—no sample possible.

The following points must be made:

(a) The guiding principle in sample selection was that of achieving a minimum
    sample size of 100, or a 1 in 10 sample of all occurrences. This leads to
    sample proportions varying between 100% and 10%.

(b) Where samples were drawn for waiting list, transfer list, allocations and
    improvement grants, the method was to start at a random point, then
    select every tenth, fourth or other fifth as relevant. The mortgage samples
    were not, in fact, true samples in that they were a selection of all the most
    recent files working back from the present day. A proportional fraction

for the sample cannot be calculated. The method of selection means that the statistical validity of analysis is dubious for mortgages. Results should be regarded as indicative rather than precise.

(c) Mortgage samples were also unsatisfactory:

    (i) A full 100 cases were rarely achieved as it was not always possible to tell if the mortgage had been completed.

    (ii) The small total number of mortgages given by the authorities meant that, even to achieve the samples selected, loans made over a considerable period of time were included. This made necessary the weighting of prices and income described in Appendix III.

(d) Except in West Bromwich where a separate sample was drawn, the Survey figures for council house sales relate only to houses bought with council finance. Since on average 90% of sales were financed in this way, this is relatively unimportant.

Appendix II Examples of Recording Sheets

Samples of local authority housing files and records were selected in the way described in Appendix I. The actual material surveyed was most usually a personal file containing the relevant application forms, visit forms, letters, and details recorded by the local authority officers. The information was recorded for subsequent analysis on forms specially designed for each local authority. Examples of these forms follow.

The procedure was quite simple. Each piece of information required was considered as a variable and given codes. For example the classes and codes for number of children aged 5 and under was:

No Child	6
1 Child	1
2 Children	2
3 Children	3
4 Children	4
5 or more children	5
Not known	9

The appropriate code was then entered in the space on the recording sheet. Most items of information were coded in this way directly from the files. Spaces at the top of the sheet were designed to allow other pieces of information to be recorded for coding later. The whole process worked very well, and quickly. The recording sheets were then used directly for transfer of the data to punched cards for computer analysis.

WOLVERHAMPTON C.B. COUNCIL HOUSE ANALYSIS

Reg. No.

Address: Address:

Reason: Persons:

Area choice: Bedrooms:

Variable	Code	Column
Local Authority	5	1
		2
Identification		3
		4
		5
Type of List		6
Marriage		7
Place of Birth		8
Residence		9
Household Size		10
Children Under 16		11
Children Under 5		12
Household Type		13
Household Summary		14
Age		15
		16
Type of House		17
Tenure		18
Living Room		19
Bedrooms		20
Other Persons		21
		22
Medical Claim		23
Expectant Mother		24
Date		25
		26
Group		27
Total Points		28
		29
Type Wanted		30
Reason		31
		32
Offers—Applicant		33

Variable	Code	Column
Offers—Dwelling		34
Council House		35
Bedrooms Needed		36
Standard		37
		38
Rent Record		39
Type Allocated		40
		41
Rent Allocated		42
Period Void		43
		44
Origin of Letting		45
		46
Present Location		47
		48
Present Age		49
Present Grade		50
Choice Location		51
		52
Choice Age		53
Choice Grade		54
Allocated Location		55
		56
Allocated Age		57
Allocated Grade		58
Density Present		59
Occupancy Present		60
Density Choice		61
Occupancy Choice		62
Density Allocated		63
Occupancy Allocated		64
		65
		66

IMPROVEMENT GRANT ANALYSIS

Number:

Address:

Application Date: Nature of work:
Approval Date:
Completion Date:

Variable	Punch	Column	Variable	Punch	Column
Local Authority		1			20
		2	Cost of Repairs		21
Identification Number		3			22
		4	Repairs/Cost		23
Type of Grant		5			24
Nature of Work		6	Grant/Cost		25
		7			26
Approved Cost		8			27
		9	Total Cost		28
		10			29
Approved Grant		11	Date of Application		30
		12			31
Age of Property		13	Application—Approval		32
		14	Approval—Completion		33
Tenure		15	Application—Completion		34
Mortgage		16	Area		35
Cost of Improvement		17	House Type		36
		18	Moving In		37
		19			

LUDLOW MORTGAGE LOANS, ETC. ANALYSIS

Applicant's Name

Present Address:

Mortgage Address:

Date of application:
Date of approval:
Tenancy commenced:

Rent:	per
Repayments:	per
Basic wage:	per
Overtime:	per
Other income:	per
Occupation:	
Rate of Interest:	

Variables	Punch	Col.
Local Authority	6	1
Identification Number		2
		3
		4
Period Sought		5
Income Satisfactory		6
Period Granted		7
Group		8
		9
Category		10
		11
Price		12
		13
		14
Loan applied for		15
		16
		17
Valuation		18
		19
		20
Advance		21
		22
		23
Balance		24
		25
		26
Annual Repayments		27
		28
		29
Valuation/Price		30
		31
		32
Loan granted/ Loan sought		33
		34
		35
Loan/Price		36
		37

Variables	Punch	Col.
		38
Loan/Valuation		39
		40
Time Taken		41
Time commenced		42
		43
		44
Place of Birth		45
		46
		47
Rate of Interest		48
		49
		50
		51
		52
		53
Age		54
Socio-Econ. Group		55
Children 16 & under		56
Children 5 & under		57
Household type		58
Household size		59
Is app. pr. tenant		60
Part to be let		61
Freehold/Leasehold		62
Rateable Value		63
Repairs		64
Type		65
Garden		66
Garage		67
Hot Water		68
Central Heating		69
No. of bedrooms		70
Age of property		71
Mortgage held		72
Location		73
Attractive		74

Variables	Punch	Col.
Origin of tenure		75
Previous tenant		76
Density of Occup.		77
Occupancy		78

CARD 2

Variables	Punch	Col.
Local Authority	6	1
Identification Number		2
		3
		4
		5
Basic earnings		6
		7
		8
Overtime, etc.		9
		10
		11
Other income		12
		13
		14
Total earnings applicant		15
		16
		17
Household income		18
		19
Repayments/ Applicant		20
		21
Repayments/ Household		22
		23
Rent		24
		25
		26
		27
Repayments/Rent		28
		29

Appendix III Method of Calculating Weights for Prices and Incomes

Because the mortgage advances included in the samples described in Appendix I were made over a considerable period of time, some means had to be devised to bring price and income information to a common value to enable inter-authority comparisons to be made. This was done by means of the following weights:

(a) *Income*

Indices of weekly rates of wages for manual workers over time are available from the *Department of Employment Gazette*, Vol. LXXXI, No. 12, Dec. 1973, Table 130. These indices were related to 1972 income levels and transferred to a factor by which the average income figures for each year could be multiplied.

Year	D. of Emp. Gazette Index	Controlled to 1972	Weight used in calculation
1965	146·7	58·0	1·724
1966	153·5	60·7	1·647
1967	159·3	63·0	1·587
1968	169·9	67·2	1·488
1969	178·8	70·7	1·414
1970	196·7	77·8	1·285
1971	222·1	87·9	1·138
1972	252·8	100·0	1·000
1973	278·4	110·1	0·908

(b) *House Prices*

An exactly similar process was followed for calculating weights for house prices. This time the index used was that available in the *Nationwide Building Society Occasional Bulletin* No. 116, Table 1. This relates to prices of older existing dwellings.

Year	Nationwide Index	Controlled to 1st half 1972	Weight used in calculation
1965	100	69·4	1·441
1966	103	71·5	1·399
1967	107	74·3	1·346
1968	112	77·8	1·285
1969	116	80·6	1·241
1970	129	89·6	1·116
1st half 1971	140	97·2	1·029
2nd half 1971	142	98·6	1·014
1st half 1972	144	100·0	1·000
2nd half 1972	167	116·0	0·862
1st half 1973	186	129·2	0·774

The income weights were used with applicant's income and annual repayment data. The house price weights were used with price, valuation, advance and balance data.

Appendix IV Definitions used in the Surveys

The following conventions are used in the survey tabulations:

— denotes nil or zero

$\star$ denotes less than 0·5%

The sample numbers included in the tabulations may vary slightly from table to table because 'not known' or 'no information' cases are always excluded.

The definition of household type used in table and text is:

Single person — a single person aged under 60 years.

Small adult   — two persons aged 16–59.

Small family — one or two adults aged 16–59 and one or two children aged 0–15.

Large family — *either* three children aged 0–15 and any number of persons aged 16 or over, OR two children aged 0–15 and three or more persons aged 16 or over.

Large adult   — Three or more persons aged 16 or over, with or without one child aged 0–15.

Small elderly — *either* a single person aged 60 or over, *or* two persons both aged 60 or over, *or* two persons one of whom is aged 60 or over.

The term 'household' used in describing waiting list or mortgage applicants, relates to the persons applying to be housed together as a single unit. The term 'dwelling' applies to the accommodation in which the household lives, and may either be rooms or a self-contained flat or house.

A simple bedroom standard was used in assessing relative density of occupation of accommodation. This is as follows: 1 bedroom—1 or 2 persons

2 bedrooms—3 persons

3 bedrooms—4 or 5 persons

4 bedrooms—6 or 7 persons

A three-way distinction was made between households living at this standard, in conditions more crowded than the standard, or in conditions less crowded than the standard.

The definitions of the 'work' categories used in improvement grant analysis are:

Installation of missing amenities. This implies that the property already has most of the standard amenities, but the grant may be for the provision of a wash hand basin in an existing bathroom, or the provision of a WC in an existing bathroom.

Provision of bathroom. As the heading suggests, this involves the provision of a 3-piece bathroom for the first time.

Provision of bathroom and kitchen. When a back extension is built to provide a bathroom, the kitchen is also considerably modified in most cases. Such work would fall into this category. Conversion of a bedroom to a bathroom may also be accompanied by modification to an existing kitchen. Bathroom provision must be for the first time.

Kitchen extension. This category includes no basic amenity work. An existing kitchen is being extended.

General improvement. No basic amenities are provided for the first time in this class, though some replacement may take place. Most usually general improvement implies re-roofing, or installation of a damp proof course. In Ludlow it can mean virtual rebuilding of the house, but with no *new* provision of amenities.

Conversion to flats. Conversion of an existing dwelling to one or more self-contained flats.

Conversion to a dwelling. Conversion of a building other than a dwelling house is only found in Ludlow where barns and farm out-buildings are involved.

Grants are grouped in this way according to the major improvement element whether or not repairs were involved.

The Twelve-Point Standard is frequently referred to when discussing improvement. To meet this standard a dwelling must:

(i)   be in a good state of repair and substantially free from damp;

(ii) have each room properly lighted and ventilated;

(iii) have an adequate supply of wholesome water laid on inside the dwelling;

(iv) be provided with efficient and adequate means of supplying hot water for domestic purposes;

(v)   have an internal water-closet if practicable; otherwise a readily accessible outside water-closet;

(vi) have a fixed bath or shower in a bathroom;

(vii) be provided with a sink or sinks and with suitable arrangements for the disposal of waste water;

(viii) have a proper drainage system;

(ix) be provided in each room with adequate points for gas or electric lighting (where reasonably available);

(x)   be provided with adequate facilities for heating;

(xi) have satisfactory facilities for storing, preparing and cooking food;

(xii) have proper provision for the storage of fuel (where required).

Appendix V Statistical Methods used in Chapter 3

A *Correlation analysis with length of waiting and transfer list*

The Spearman rank coefficient of correlation was used to check the association between the length of the lists and other variables thought to have an influence.

The formula used is $R = 1 - \dfrac{6\Sigma d^2}{n^3 - n}$

where d = the difference in ranks and n = the number of cases ranked.

All the variables included in the analysis and the resulting coefficients of correlation are shown below.

General Needs List	Coefficient	Transfer List	Coefficient
Proportion of council houses in stock, 1971	+·743	Proportion of waiting list applicants allocated a flat, 1972–73	+·743
Growth in population, 1961–71	−·657	Proportion small elderly households, 1971	+·714
Average house price, 1973	−·571	Proportion of old houses in council stock, 1971	+·714
Total population, 1971	+·571	Proportion owner-occupation, 1971	−·657
Proportion of allocations going to clearance, 1972–73	+·543	Proportion of flats in council stock, 1971	+·600
Proportion of small elderly households, 1971	−·457	Proportion of transfers in allocations, 1972–73	+·571
Council house completions, 1968–72	+·457	Average house prices, 1973	−·543
Proportion of population aged 20–29, 1971	+·429	Proportion population 5–14, 1971	−·314
Restrictiveness of eligibility rules,[1] 1973	+·343	Birth rate, 1971	+·314
Proportion of houses and bungalows in council stock, 1971	−·314	Size of council stock, 1971	+·257
Private house completions, 1968–72	+·229	Length of waiting list, 1973	+·229
Proportion of households lacking standard amenities, 1971	−·114		

[1] The scaling of this variable is subjective, and derived from Table 2.1. The ranking from most to least restrictive is: Warley, West Bromwich, Halesowen, Wolverhampton, Ludlow and Stafford.

Because of the very small sample number involved, i.e. 6 authorities, none of these relationships is statistically significant at the 5% level.

B *Chi square analysis*

Chi square calculations were used to check the similarity and difference between:

(a) Waiting list and waiting list allocations for each authority.

(b) Transfer list and transfer allocations for each authority.

(c) Waiting list and allocations for every pair of authorities.

(d) Transfer list and transfer allocations for every pair of authorities.

The differences and similarities were measured in terms of the household type structure in each case.

The formula used is $\chi^2 = \Sigma \dfrac{(O-E)^2}{E}$

where O = the value in one population (observed)

and E = the value in the second population (estimated)

The results of the within authority analyses are as follows:

Authority	All waiting list and allocations Chi square	Live waiting list and allocations Chi square	Transfer list and allocations Chi square
West Bromwich	32·765	17·306	19·192
Warley	13·603	24·393	11·597
Wolverhampton	89·773	85·858	6·852
Halesowen	7·915	7·915	20·414
Stafford	3·140	3·140	12·438
Ludlow	6·185	6·185	1·555

The results of the between authority analyses are as follows:

All waiting lists

Pairs of authorities:	Chi Square
Ludlow–West Bromwich	89·833
Wolverhampton–West Bromwich	47·720
Wolverhampton–Ludlow	44·029
Ludlow–Halesowen	42·333
Ludlow–Warley	41·236
Ludlow–Stafford	24·294
Halesowen–Wolverhampton	21·884
Stafford–Halesowen	18·842
Stafford–West Bromwich	16·358
Warley–Wolverhampton	15·622
Halesowen–West Bromwich	14·705
Halesowen–Warley	14·634
Stafford–Wolverhampton	12·801
Warley–West Bromwich	12·219
Stafford–Warley	4·550

Waiting list allocations

Pairs of authorities:	Chi Square
Halesowen–West Bromwich	43·283
Ludlow–West Bromwich	42·859
Ludlow–Warley	39·330
Halesowen–Wolverhampton	39·256
Stafford–Warley	33·956
Ludlow–Wolverhampton	25·801
Warley–Halesowen	22·254
Ludlow–Halesowen	22·063
Warley–Wolverhampton	20·186
Stafford–Halesowen	18·300
Ludlow–Stafford	17·478
Stafford–West Bromwich	12·763
Warley–West Bromwich	12·254
Stafford–Wolverhampton	11·529
West Bromwich–Wolverhampton	5·670

Transfer list		Transfer allocations	
Pairs of authorities:	Chi Square	Pairs of authorities:	Chi Square
Stafford–Ludlow	41·797	Halesowen–Wolverhampton	28·039
West Bromwich–Warley	32·985	Halesowen–Warley	21·160
Stafford–Warley	28·762	Halesowen–West Bromwich	20·621
Halesowen–Warley	23·010	Halesowen–Ludlow	17·296
Warley–Wolverhampton	22·167	Stafford–West Bromwich	12·600
West Bromwich–Halesowen	15·121	West Bromwich–Warley	9·709
West Bromwich–Wolverhampton	12·106	Stafford–Halesowen	6·366
West Bromwich–Ludlow	11·566	West Bromwich–Wolverhampton	6·364
Stafford–Wolverhampton	11·526	West Bromwich–Ludlow	5·846
Stafford–West Bromwich	10·589	Stafford–Ludlow	5·570
Warley–Ludlow	10·076	Stafford–Wolverhampton	5·300
Halesowen–Ludlow	7·782	Warley–Ludlow	4·462
Halesowen–Wolverhampton	7·543	Wolverhampton–Ludlow	4·306
Stafford–Halesowen	5·883	Stafford–Warley	3·974
Wolverhampton–Ludlow	5·319	Warley–Wolverhampton	3·888

In every case a smaller number indicates a closer similarity between the household type structures being examined.

C *Standard error calculations of selectivity*

The standard error of differences in proportions was used as a measure of selectivity in allocation procedures.

The formula used in Standard error $= \sqrt{\dfrac{\pi_1(1-\pi_1)}{n_1} + \dfrac{\pi_2(1-\pi_2)}{n_2}}$

where π_1 is the proportion found in the first sample and n_1 is the sample size of the first sample.

and π_2 is the proportion found in the second sample and n_2 is the sample size of the second sample.

This can be illustrated using the example quoted in the text relating to Table 3.8. An extract of Table 3.8 is as follows:

Household Group:	Allocation p.a.	List in year 5
Sample number	20	100
	%	%
A	10	37
B	40	13
C	20	29
D	30	31

The standard error of difference in proportion for household group B is

$$\sqrt{\frac{40 \times 60}{20} + \frac{13 \times 87}{100}} = \sqrt{131 \cdot 31} = 11 \cdot 44$$

The standard error is thus 11·4, and since the observed differences between the two proportions is 27, the difference exceeds 2 standard errors. The difference is significant in a statistical sense.

Directly comparable calculations were made to produce Tables 3.9, 3.10 and 3.19.

Appendix VI Checklist of Major Pieces of Information Collected and Analysed

Information:	Waiting list	Transfer list	Improvement grants	Council mortgages
Date of application	★	★	★	★
Household size	★	★		★
Household type	★	★		★
Applicant's age	★	★		★
Children aged 5 or under	★	★		★
Children aged 16 or under	★	★		★
Lone parent household	★			
Birthplace	★			★
Length of tenancy (LA)		★		★
Tenure	★		★	
Amenity provision	★			
Number of bedrooms	★	★		★
House type		★	★	★
Living room present	★			
Density of occupation	★	★		
Medical claim	★	★		
Reason for application	★	★		
Offers made	★	★		
Size house wanted	★	★		
Type house wanted		★		
Type house allocated	★	★		
Origin of void allocated	★	★		
Grade of estate allocated	★	★		
Present grade of estate		★		★
Type of improvement work			★	
Amount of grant approved			★	
Repair allowance			★	
Time taken application to approval			★	★
Is house mortgaged?			★	
Age of dwelling			★	★
Is there a garden?				★
Is there a garage?				★
Is there central heating?				★
Rateable value				★
Any repairs required?				★
Size of advance				★
Price of house				★
Size of deposit				★
Valuation				★
Loan as % valuation				★
Loan as % price				★
Loan given as % loan requested				★
Period of loan				★
Annual repayments				★
Applicant's occupation				★
Applicant's income				★
Household income				★
Repayments as % applicant's income				★
Repayments as % household income				★

Related C.U.R.S. Publications

O.P. = Occasional Paper   R.M. = Research Memorandum   W.P. = Working Paper

Housing

O.P.1.   *The Development of a Housing Association: The Experience of the Hanover Housing Association, 1963–1967*, Unity Stack, 1968, 64pp. £0·50. An examination of problems which have arisen in the implementation of a housing association's programme which illustrates the difficulties facing the voluntary housing movement today.

O.P.8.   *East Kilbride Housing Survey: A Study of Housing in a New Town*, 77pp. ⎫ V. A. Karn,
O.P.9.   *Aycliffe Housing Survey: A Study of Housing in a New Town*, 68pp.   ⎪ 1970
O.P.10. *Stevenage Housing Survey: A Study of Housing in a New Town*, 73pp.   ⎬ £0·75
O.P.11. *Crawley Housing Survey: A Study of Housing in a New Town*, 73pp   ⎭ each

As part of the study of the ownership and management of housing in the new towns, commissioned by the Ministry of Housing and Local Government, social surveys were undertaken in 1966 in four new towns. These papers present the results of the surveys in greater detail than was possible in the general report, and deal particularly with the tenure preferences of people living in the new towns and the potential demand for owner occupation.

O.P.19. *Social Housing Policy in Belgium*, C. J. Watson, 1971, 46pp. £1·50. A detailed account of Belgium's housing policies in relation to owner-occupation, 'social housing' and slum clearance: the housing problem in Belgium is, in many ways, similar to that in Britain, but the policies adopted for dealing with it differ significantly.

O.P.20. *Measuring Housing Quality: A Study of Methods*, T. L. C. Duncan, 1971, 129pp. £2·00. An examination of the limitations of existing sources of information available to policy-makers on the physical quality of housing: examples of many recent appraisal methods are here brought together for the first time.

O.P.21. *Voluntary Housing in Scandinavia*, J. Greve, 1971, 102pp. £1·50. A study of the housing associations and cooperatives in Denmark, Norway and Sweden, together with a discussion of the relevance of their experience for Britain.

O.P.24. *Estimating Local Housing Needs: A Case Study and Discussion of Methods*, C. J. Watson, Pat Niner and Gillian R. Vale, with Barbara M. D. Smith, 1973, 132pp. £1·50. A study commissioned by the County Borough of Dudley. Population and potential household projections provide the basis for a comprehensive assessment of present and future housing needs and the policies and housing programme required. Special studies, based on departmental and other available records, consider local authority and owner occupied housing, house improvement and the employment situation in the County Borough. A monitoring system is proposed. The introductory discussion of methods describes the study technique and considers the relative advantages of carrying out a housing study using either existing data from local authority and other records, or data specially collected by means of social survey.

O.P.25. *Housing Standards and Costs: A Comparison of British Standards and Costs With Those in the U.S.A., Canada and Europe*, Valerie A. Karn, 1973, 78pp. £1·75. A study of space and equipment standards, particularly for new housing, based on National Government Publications and other official sources.

O.P.26. *Household Movement in West Central Scotland: A Study of Housing Chains and Filtering*, C. J. Watson, 1973, 67pp. £1·75. A study of the chains of moves and the process of filtering through the housing system, initiated by the building of a sample of new owner occupied and local authority dwellings in the Clydeside conurbation. The extent to which households are able to improve their housing situation by moving and the wider effects of the new house-building programme are considered.

O.P.28. *Household Movement and Housing Choice*, Alan Murie, 1974, 131pp. £2·25. This study is based on the West Yorkshire Movers Survey of 1969. It presents the results of this survey in a fuller form than currently available and consolidates evidence about the main patterns of household movement in the British housing system. A discussion and assessment of the significance of this evidence is presented.

R.M.7.   *Housing Associations: Three Surveys*, Dilys Page (Ed.), 1971, 118pp. £1·50. Studies of the voluntary housing movement. Two deal with the views and experience of housing associations and of the local authorities through which they operate; the third is a survey of co-ownership housing societies in the Midlands.

R.M.13.   *Winchester Housing Needs Study 1971–72*. A Report to the City Council, 1972, 52pp. £1·00. The study was commissioned to provide a basis for housing policy-formulation and to provide proposals for the monitoring of future needs, and investigates the totality of housing needs in the city and the ways in which these are being met by private and public agencies.

R.M.24.   *The Liverpool Improved Houses Study*, Janet Curry, 1973, 52pp. £0·75. An introductory study of the organisation, policy and procedure of a charitable housing association; its relationship with local authorities; and its function within the housing system.

R.M.25.   *Liverpool Estates Survey*, Barbara Weinberger, 1973, 84pp. £0·75. A household survey among a one in ten sample, was carried out in contrasting estates (i.e. a 'settled' estate and an estate with high social malaise indications), in order to try to establish the factors relating to satisfaction and dissatisfaction with living on the estate.

R.M.28.   *Housing Improvement Policies in England and Wales*, T. L. C. Duncan, 1973, 213pp. £2·00. This product of two years' research is a commentary on the 1969 Housing Act and the contribution made by General Improvement Areas to the solution of housing and environmental problems in the inner city. There is a comprehensive analysis of local authority action in this field, and three detailed case studies of projects at Coventry, Plymouth and Winchester. Suggestions for the future are explored.

R.M.30.   *Housing Tenure in Britain: A Review of Survey Evidence 1958–71*, Alan Murie, 1974, 96pp. £1·00. This study presents and reviews evidence from ten major housing surveys carried out during a period in which the tenure structure of British housing has changed considerably. It draws together evidence which is not available under one cover elsewhere. It presents evidence from a range of sources in a form which enables comparison and consideration of trends. The focus of the presentation is on tenure and the association between tenure, household characteristics, dwelling characteristics and patterns of household movement. In conclusion a discussion of consistent features, of trends and of the policy implications suggested by the review of survey evidence is offered.

R.M.32.   *No Place That's Home: A Report on Accommodation for Homeless Young People in Birmingham*, Valerie A. Karn, 1974, £1·00. This is a report on the accommodation situation of young working people in Birmingham. It concentrates upon the needs of the lowest paid and those who actually become homeless in the city. It concludes that the services provided to help young working people are strikingly worse than those provided for students, and that a more comprehensive approach to housing provision is needed in order to give them a better chance in the competitive housing market.

W.P.16.   *Research Directions in Urban Sociology: Neighbourhood Associations and Housing Opportunities*, C. T. Paris and R. Blackaby, 1973, 57pp. £0·50. The paper aims to develop a framework for carrying out empirical research in urban sociology. It attempts to present a short critical review of the development in the field. This is followed by some discussion of the work of J. Rex, R. E. Pahl, N. Dennis and J. G. Davies. The final section is devoted to methodology. The authors attempt a critique of conventional sociological research methods followed by an outline of a research/action project underway in Birmingham.

W.P.18.   *The Interpretation by the Birmingham Press of the Housing Finance Issue*, D. Alexander, R. Forrest, D. O'Sullivan and P. Young, 1973, 26pp. £0·50. Testing various hypotheses relating to selection and emphasis in news presentation, the paper examines the coverage by the local Birmingham Press of the main issues surrounding the Housing Finance Act, 1972. The presentation was found to be influenced, firstly by the operation of news value criteria determined by over-riding commercial goals, and secondly (and more speculatively), by underlying ideological considerations.

W.P.21. *Provision for the Homeless in a Comprehensive Housing Service: Proceedings of a Seminar,* Christine D. McKee (Ed.), 1974, 31pp. £0·50. This Working Paper records the proceedings of a Seminar which attempted to identify the problems of different homeless groups, to discuss present and future provision in the context of a comprehensive housing service, and consider the difficulties likely to be encountered in transferring responsibility for homelessness, formally to Housing Departments.

A full list of publications, including the informal Working Paper series, is available from the Publications Officer, Centre for Urban and Regional Studies, Selly Wick House, Selly Wick Road, Birmingham B29 7JF.

Orders should be placed with the officer but no money should be sent with the order as invoices are prepared and forwarded with the volumes ordered. There is a 10p handling charge for items in the U.K. and a charge of 25p per item abroad.